Praise for

LITTLE HEATHENS

"[Kalish's] terrifically soaring love for [her] childhood memories saturates this book with pure charm, while coaxing the reader into the most unexpected series of sensations: joy, affection, wonder and even envy. . . . Kalish has . . . unpacked her memories into a story that is . . . polished by real, rare happiness. It is a very good book, indeed. In fact, it is a veryveryverygoodbook."
—Elizabeth Gilbert, author of *Eat, Pray, Love*, in the *New York Times Book Review*

"A book about hardship, frugality and ingenuity [as well as] about the power of nature [and] the love of family . . . A delightful read."
—*San Jose Mercury News*

"When you finish Mildred Kalish's lovely memoir, you might not want to leave. We didn't. We wanted to pitch our tent in its pages and just stay there, lingering with her stories and the odd comfort they bring."
—*Arizona Republic*

"A wise, rich memoir . . . expressed with a clear sense of urgency."
—Marion Elizabeth Rodgers in the *Washington Times*

"This lovely book, so unaffected and so generous, opens the door to a past I knew as a child in Iowa, and I wept with joy and recognition as I read it. It deserves a distinguished place next to Hamlin Garland's *A Son of the Middle Border* but, with its deep humility, it would also fit, without a single word of protest, next to the *Betty Crocker Cookbook*."
—Ted Kooser, U.S. Poet Laureate, 2004–2006

"Now that cell phones are a way of life, you won't find a better way to participate in the Good Old Days. Whether you are of farm origins or not, *Little Heathens* is a bit of history begging to be borrowed. Like a neighborly cup of sugar, it will sweeten your modern-day life."
—MaryJane Butters, author of *MaryJane's Ideabook, Cookbook, Lifebook: For the Farmgirl in All of Us*

"Using this book alone, one could reconstruct, with glorious exactness, a lost time and place. Mildred Kalish has a novelist's eye for detail and a beautiful understanding of what the gestures of daily life mean. A lovely, wise, transporting memoir."
—Joan Silber, author of *Ideas of Heaven: A Ring of Stories*

1914.

LITTLE HEATHENS

*Hard Times and High Spirits
on an Iowa Farm
During the Great Depression*

MILDRED ARMSTRONG KALISH

LITTLE HEATHENS
A Bantam Book

PUBLISHING HISTORY
Bantam hardcover edition published June 2007
Bantam trade paperback edition / May 2008

Published by Bantam Dell
A Division of Random House, Inc.
New York, New York

Cover illustration by Ben Perini

Book design by Virginia Norey

"A Blessing" by James Wright from *Collected Poems* (Wesleyan University Press, 1971) © 1971 by James Wright and reprinted by permission of Wesleyan University Press.

Emily Dickinson material reprinted by permission of the publishers and the Trustees of Amherst College from THE POEMS OF EMILY DICKINSON, Thomas H. Johnson, ed., J193, Cambridge, Mass.: The Belknap Press of Harvard University Press, Copyright © 1951, 1955, 1979, 1983 by the President and Fellows of Harvard College.

Library of Congress Catalog Card Number: 2006032730

ISBN 978-0-553-38424-6

Printed in the United States of America
Published simultaneously in Canada

www.bantamdell.com

BVG   10 9

This book is for my three families—

To my birth family, who share the everlasting bonds of kinship.

To my husband's warm and loving family, who welcomed me to their bosom in total acceptance from the day I walked into their lives over sixty-two years ago.

And finally, to my immediate family, who give my life meaning.

Contents

Introduction

I. The Family
1. Foreground 11
2. Great-Grandpa Jonathan 23
3. Aunt Belle 30
4. Thanksgiving 40

II. Building Character
5. Oral Influences 51
6. Literary Influences 63
7. Religious Influences 69
8. Thrift 82
9. Medicine 92
10. Chores 104
11. Farm Food 117
12. An Especially Pleasant Chore ... 144
13. Water Windmill 148
14. Milking and Other Nightly Chores ... 151
15. Wash Day 156
16. Outhouses 162

III. Fall/Winter
17. Country School: Monroe Number 6 ... 169
18. Box Social 179
19. Gathering Nuts 182

20.	Gathering Wood	191
21.	Winter Is Icumen In, Lhude Sing Goddamm!	196
22.	Town School: Garrison	204

IV. Spring/Summer

23.	Leisure Time	213
24.	Gardening	224
25.	Spring in Yankee Grove	233
26.	May Baskets	243
27.	Birds	246
28.	Animal Tales	250
29.	Raccoons and Other Critters	259

Epilogue

30.	Me	269

LITTLE
HEATHENS

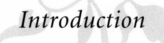

Introduction

Aunt Hazel, Aunt Wilma, Mama, and Shep

This is the story of a time, and a place, and a family. The time was the Depression years, the place a rural area of Iowa, the family—mine. To begin it I shall take you back, briefly, to my mother's people, the Urmys, all the way to my great-great-grandparents.

Susannah and Jacob Urmy had the distinction of being among the first pioneers to settle in the state of Iowa. After arriving in Monroe township in Benton County, Iowa, about halfway between Cedar Rapids and Waterloo, sometime around 1846, the year Iowa became a state, they built a log cabin to house themselves and their five children. Eventually they acquired farmland on which they built structures to hold their livestock, as well as a sprawling, no-nonsense, clapboard house that still stands—though in a sad state of disrepair—and is known as "the home place." They also bought a substantial part of the surrounding woodland which, in a nod to their past, they named Yankee Grove, for they themselves were Yankees, having come to Iowa in a covered wagon by way of Connecticut, Pennsylvania, Virginia, Kentucky, and Indiana.

Susannah and Jacob helped establish two churches; broke sod

three times in their lives, plowing virgin soil to prepare it for raising crops; and were almost totally self-sufficient. Like other pioneers, they did their own doctoring from home remedies. They raised, butchered, canned, and cured their own cows, hogs, and chickens. They hunted squirrels, rabbits, pheasants, and quail right there in Yankee Grove. They tanned their own leather in a hollowed-out hickory log. For the most part, they mended the harnesses for their horses and repaired their own shoes.

They made their own bread and sometimes ground their own flour of oats and wheat; they ground the corn to feed to their chickens and to make cornmeal mush for themselves. They made their own shirts, knitted their own sweaters, scarves, and socks, and sewed their own aprons, dresses, and night-wear. They patched together and tied their own wool quilts. Their industry and independence were nothing short of astonishing. Ralph Waldo Emerson could have learned a thing or two about self-reliance from my great-great-grandparents.

One of Susannah and Jacob's sons, Jonathan, married Harriet Turner, a pioneer he had met in Indiana. They settled on a farm near Yankee Grove. Family lore has it that Harriet was a descendant of the *Mayflower* Turners, but that has never been verified. Having each been born to parents who had the fortitude to cover half the continent in covered wagons, Jonathan and Harriet continued in the self-sufficient ways of the pioneer tradition which was their legacy. They produced twelve children. Arthur Urmy, my grandfather, was their first son. I came to know Grandpa Arthur very well, but Jonathan I met only once—on a very memorable occasion (which I describe later).

Like his parents and grandparents before him, Grandpa Arthur married a pioneer woman, Emma Fry, who was also the descendant of first settlers in Iowa. Both were still in their teens when they wed, and they immediately set up housekeeping on a farm in Monroe Township, about three miles from Garrison. They had eight children. Two boys and two girls died before the age of two; four daughters, including my mother, Merle, and my aunt Hazel, survived.

Emma Fry's family, like Grandpa's folks, had immigrated to Iowa around the 1850's, crossing the country from Pennsylvania by covered wagon. But by nature the Frys were just about the opposite of the Urmys. They looked at life as a jolly event. They could and did spend money on luxury items. It was Emma's family who provided the young couple with a dowry that included a double set of Haviland china, real silver, and fine bed and table linens. The Frys spent money on chocolate, cosmetics, entertainment, clothing, barbershop haircuts, and even moderate amounts of alcohol, all without consuming themselves with guilt. As a child, my assessment of them was that they were a very cheery bunch of relatives. However, it was the Urmys, not the Frys, who would set the tone of our family life.

Coming from a background firmly rooted in the New England Puritan tradition, the Urmys could easily have served as models for the source of H. L. Mencken's definition of Puritanism as "the haunting fear that someone, somewhere, may be happy." They were a somber lot, generally speaking. To them, life was a serious challenge and they brooked few frivolities. They read the Bible, prayed every day, and entertained themselves by critiquing the minister's Sunday sermons and quarreling over his interpretations of the Bible. One perpetual topic of debate was whether miracles were still happening, for God was real to them and His actions a source of constant interest and discussion. Anyone careless enough to lay a knife or a pair of scissors on my grand-parents' Bible could expect a hard knuckle rap on the head, for we were taught to respect God and His word above all else.

It was into this background that my mother, my two brothers, my baby sister, and I were precipitously thrust when I was lit-tle more than five years old. The year was around 1930. The Depression was imminent, as was the terrible weather that would become known as the Dirty Thirties. Hard times were going to be especially difficult for us in the decade that followed, for we were without a breadwinner, and would be completely dependent on the largesse of Grandma and Grandpa Urmy, two very strict and stern individuals. For us children, building character, developing a sense of responsibility, and above all, improving one's mind would become the essential focus of our lives.

One of my earliest and most vivid memories was when Grandma apparently decided that my puny twelve-month-old sister, Avis, should be weaned, and snatched the nursing baby from my mother's breast. The tiny infant wailed at the top of her lungs. "Let her cry!" Grandma declared. "You can't begin char-acter building too soon!"

A few years ago, a friend whose background is somewhat akin to mine reported that his father used to assemble him and his four brothers at the kitchen table every Saturday morning for "soup practice." In front of each brother was a bowl of cold water and a soup spoon. They were to practice eating the cold water as if it were a bowl of soup: no noise, no slurping, and no dribbling it down their chins. The children had to participate in this weekly activity so as not to disgrace the parents at mealtime when they had guests and were eating real soup. When I heard this story, I knew I had met a kindred soul.

Endure deprivation without complaining; mind your manners

at all times; do as your elders say. This was what the elders in our family expected of us and what the discipline and training they imposed were designed to elicit. In a very real way the value system that shaped my early days has also shaped my life.

In recent years, as my children and grandchildren have peppered me with questions about my childhood, I discovered, somewhat to my surprise, that I have come to view that time as a gift. Austere and challenging as it was, it built character, fed the intellect, and stirred the imagination.

In looking back, I realize that I have had the good fortune to have absorbed the events that transpired during my childhood years into my very being, as if no boundary exists between then and now, as if the past has not really passed. For some time, I have had the urge to share that treasure trove, lest it vanish. In the pages that follow I describe the effect of that decade on me as a young child, and introduce you to those altogether decent, tough, eccentric people whose bravery, endurance, dedication, and resourcefulness influenced me during all the years that followed. I tell of a time, a place, and a way of life long gone, nearly forgotten by the world, but still indelible in my memory. It is my hope to resurrect them, to make them live again.

So, partly in response to the basic human instinct to share feelings and experiences, and partly for the sheer joy and excitement of it all, I report on my early life. It was quite a romp.

PART ONE

The Family

John, Millie, and Jack

1

Foreground

My childhood came to a virtual halt when I was around five years old. That was when my grandfather banished my father from our lives forever for some transgression that was not to be disclosed to us children, though we overheard whispered references to bankruptcy, bootlegging, and jail time. His name was never again spoken in our presence; he just abruptly disappeared from our lives. The shame and disgrace that enveloped our family as a result of these events, along with the ensuing divorce, just about destroyed my mother. Is it possible today to make anyone understand the harsh judgment of such failures in the late 1920's? Throughout my entire life, whenever I was asked about my father, I always said that he was dead. When he actually died I never knew.

So it was that Grandma and Grandpa chose to make our family of five—Mama, my ten-year-old brother Jack, my eight-year-old brother John, my one-year-old sister Avis, and me—their responsibility. They decided to settle us on the smallest of Grandpa's four farms, which was located about three miles from the village of Garrison, where they had retired after a lifetime of farming. However, because the fierce blizzards and subzero temperatures of Iowa winters made it hazardous to walk to the one-room rural school we would be attending, it had been arranged that we would live with Grandma and Grandpa in Garrison and attend school there from January until the school year ended in mid-May. At that time our family would move out to the farm. Each year from then on, we went to school in the country from September until Christmas, then moved back to Garrison and finished the school year in town.

Our new life began when we arrived at Grandma and Grandpa's on a cold winter day in February. The house we moved into that day was a large, substantial structure. It was located about seven miles from Vinton, the seat of Benton County. Grandpa was born, raised, married, and buried all within an eight-mile radius of Garrison and Yankee Grove, the wooded area where his parents had settled as pioneers.

Though the house we shared boasted eight large rooms, suggesting that we had lots of space and privacy, in fact, all seven of us spent most of our waking hours confined to the living room

Grandma and Grandpa's house in Garrison

and the kitchen because they were the only rooms that were heated. The frigid upstairs bedrooms were rarely used except for sleeping. The conditions under which we lived were a perfect demonstration of the wisdom of Kahlil Gibran's observation: "Let there be spaces in your togetherness."

Grandpa and Grandma must have had some unspoken, perhaps even unrecognized, resentment at having toiled all their lives raising their own family, only to be confronted with the inescapable fact that now, retired at last, they had to do the whole thing all over again and raise their daughter's "spawn," as Grandma often referred to us. And all of this was happening at the worst possible time, during the Depression.

All three generations suffered. We kids were under the constant surveillance of Grandma and Grandpa, who were critical of how we spent our days, how we spoke and dressed, and how we behaved. (In a good many ways, they never quite made it into the twentieth century.) Suddenly we were subjected to a completely new set of rules, which governed every aspect of our lives. The whole family had to go to bed at a set time every night and get up at a set time every morning. We all had to be fully dressed for the day before we ate breakfast. We all had to sit down at a properly set table three times a day, and we all had to eat what was served on that table. Generally Grandpa would choose the menu for breakfast because he was the first one up. If he decided he wanted oatmeal, then everyone ate oatmeal; if he decided he wanted pancakes, then everyone ate pancakes; whether he selected sorghum, honey, or molasses as the sweetener, all were required to accept his choice. We were allowed no say in the matter.

In addition, to reinforce the principle of "Waste not, want not," we were required to eat everything on our plates. If we didn't, the food was set aside and served to us at the next meal.

Generally, unless it was a Saturday and we had cousins visiting, there was no eating between meals.

Through this regimentation, the austere habits that Grandma and Grandpa had adopted and lived by for decades were imposed on us with a vengeance. And we often resented their severity. To be fair, I must note that it was those habits that made it possible for them to acquire four debt-free farms by the time we came to live with them. Now, there's an achievement not to be overlooked. Nonetheless, Grandma and Grandpa were what the locals called "land-poor"—people who owned a lot of land but had very little money. And even what little they had they tried to save. The only things they spent money on were tea, coffee, sugar, salt, white flour, cloth, and kerosene.

Years later I came to understand that there was a good reason for them to want to save money. They needed it to pay the taxes on their farms, three of which they had rented out to the families of their daughters. Due to the deepening Depression, they could never be sure if the rent would actually be paid. If the rent did not come in, there would be no money to pay the taxes and the farms would be lost. We children sensed, but could not really understand, the awful threat of that disastrous economy. I had to grow to adulthood before I could even begin to comprehend the impact of what was happening in those days—the disappearance of money and jobs, the loss of machinery and farms, the bank failures that took people's entire savings.

Though we didn't understand them, we children were seldom protected from the harsh realities of the period, and we certainly sensed that something terrible was happening. Indelibly stamped in my memory is the scene in my Aunt Hazel and Uncle Ernest's farm kitchen one wintry March morning when I was perhaps six years old. There I entered to find all the stalwart adults of my world—Grandma, Grandpa, Mama, my aunt and uncle—still and wordless as statues. It was clear that they had been crying. I had never seen adults cry. I didn't know they could cry. I was struck mute with a fear that grabbed me right in the guts. Though I was given no explanation at the time, in the days that followed I overheard enough to realize that Grandpa's brother and sister had each lost their farm, all of their machinery and all of their livestock, for reasons that were unfathomable to me. What can a child know of vast economic forces operating on a global level? I was stunned and afraid.

Grandma and Grandpa's lives were changed forever by the plunging economy. It has taken me a lifetime to realize that the Depression and its consequent tragedies were nearly as incomprehensible to the adults as they were to us children. Since they could not understand what was happening in the world, how could they explain the situation to us? Suddenly, unexpectedly, a family of five was now the responsibility of two old people who had thought they were heading into a comfortable, if frugal, retirement. They must have been scared to death.

In Garrison, then, we children were required to adhere to the rigid routines set down for us by Grandma and Grandpa. But our lives changed radically when the school year ended around mid-May, for that was when we left Garrison for the country. The move to the country provided our little family with a welcome separation from our grandparents, and them with a no doubt equally welcome respite from us.

The farm we lived on was directly across the road from the farm where Mama's sister, Aunt Hazel, her husband, Uncle Ernest, and their three sons lived. Unusual in Iowa, this proximity meant that there was much sharing and interaction between the two families. Feeling equally at home at both places, we cousins shared pets, leisure time, food, and chores. Indeed, the two properties were treated as one cooperative, if complicated, venture, though we maintained strictly separate households for eating, sleeping, and gardening. Each farm had its advantages. Aunt Hazel and Uncle Ernest's farm was equipped with all the necessary implements, the buildings were properly maintained, and the livestock were well housed in winter and in summer; but it had insufficient pastureland. Our place was older, and the house, the sheep shed, and the chicken houses were the only buildings habitable the year round. The ancient, though picturesque, barn had been allowed to fall into a state of disrepair, and provided proper shelter for horses, calves, chickens, ducks, and geese only during the mild months of summer and fall. However, the permanent and best pastures were on our side of the road.

Grandma and Grandpa visited the farms frequently in their very noisy Buick bringing food, household necessities, and goodies. On these visits they would stay the day, lending a hand wherever help was needed, and then return to their home in the evening. They did this for all four of their daughters and their families.

It is no exaggeration to say that Grandpa and Grandma were about as compatible as two people could possibly be. They seldom argued; they went everywhere and did everything together. However, there was one event—involving a gun—that must be chronicled, an event that was revived, relived, and recounted repeatedly during the time our family lived with them. It happened when they were young parents and lived on the farm that later came to be occupied by Aunt Hazel and Uncle Ernest. In those days guns were a part of farm life. Women as well as men learned to shoot. Every family owned at least three guns: a .22 rifle, and ten- and twelve-gauge shotguns. From early childhood we were taught to respect and care for guns. "The most dangerous gun," we were cautioned, "is the one that isn't loaded." That expression was drilled into us for reasons you will soon understand. One winter day Grandpa was in the kitchen cleaning his guns and Grandma was upstairs making beds. Grandpa accidentally discharged his "unloaded" gun. Grandma started screaming. Grandpa ran from the kitchen and started running up the steep stairs just as Grandma started to run down. They slammed into each other on the landing at the right-angled turn of the stairs, connecting with such force that they knocked each other to the floor, whereupon, in their panic, they began to shout at each other. No matter how many times they told the story, they still couldn't get over the fact that they had erupted in such outbursts.

"Why did you yell?" Grandpa would ask Grandma at the conclusion of yet another retelling of the event.

"I yelled because I thought you had shot yourself. Why did you yell?"

"I yelled because I thought that I had shot you!"

They rehearsed this frightening event so often and vividly that I sometimes believed I was there to witness the incident. They were never able to get beyond their fright for each other's well-being, nor were they ever able to see the burlesque humor in this event, which so entertained us grandchildren. Though there was a real possibility that the shot could have penetrated the ceiling and entered the bedroom, it turned out that it had lodged itself harmlessly in the doorsill between the kitchen and the living room. Curiously, Grandpa, who was so meticulous about everything, never repaired that doorsill.

Our move to the farm when school let out meant that the rigidly ordered lives dictated by our grandparents were now governed by an entirely different set of expectations: our mother's. Even though we had many more chores and responsibilities such as taking care of the livestock, preparing meals, and planting and tending gardens, we actually felt freer on the farm than in Garrison. In important ways our lives were more our own, and Mama often addressed and treated us as if we were adults—if only because she needed us to be.

We four children were almost too much for our mother. To a surprising extent, she simply let us go our own ways. She didn't mind when we went to bed or rose in the morning, if it was not a school day. She didn't care what, when, or if we ate. She didn't object if, in my nightgown, I trotted out to the henhouse to gather a couple of eggs and then, still in my nightgown, cooked a fried egg breakfast and ate it sitting outside on the sunny cellar door with my favorite cat. She ignored the niceties of setting places at mealtimes. Instead, she simply placed the food and utensils in the middle of the table and let us serve ourselves.

Mama almost never made an attempt to serve a balanced meal. If she had just taken bread from the oven around the middle of the day, our noon meal would consist of freshly made bread, homemade butter, whole plum jam, and a huge pitcher of milk. If, in the garden, she noticed that the sweet corn was ready, we had nothing but buttered sweet corn for supper. Further, she didn't insist that we all eat at the table or that we all eat at the same time.

Of course, she did insist that we all do our assigned chores. Since it was obvious even to us children that it was necessary to meet our obligations to make the family operate, we seldom failed to do so, but we were allowed to create our own routines for our workdays—as did our mother, who had some very odd ideas about such matters. She marched to a different drummer, so to speak. Her priorities did not match those of most sensible people. One day she might iron or bake, even though the temperature had reached 95 degrees, on the grounds that she could not be made more uncomfortable than she already was. Yet the next day she might rise at dawn to start weeding in the garden because she liked the cool of the morning.

The real surprise is that Mama was an indifferent homemaker. She could make great soup and bake superb cakes and pies, but she could never cook meat nor fry potatoes to anyone's liking. She would either overcook or undercook, oversalt a dish or forget the salt altogether. At my brothers' urging I gradually began taking over the everyday cooking for the family when I was not much more than eight years old. I apparently inherited a natural affinity for cooking from Grandma and, rather than feeling burdened by the responsibility, I felt honored. Throughout my life, my culinary skills have been a significant asset.

With the wisdom of advancing age, I have lately come to believe that Mama acted as she did because she was crushed by the stigma of her broken home and overwhelmed by the neverending burden of tending to and raising four active children. She coped the best she could, and certainly she had many gifts and talents. She loved being out-of-doors and could work for hours husking corn, shocking oats, and gardening. She had a remarkable rapport with animals, especially Grandpa's favorite, the horse. And she could play the piano and sing.

The chief effect Mama's unconventional life practices had on us kids at the time was our keen awareness that other children did not live the way we did. Though the realization that we were just outside the mainstream of society sometimes made us uncomfortable, it also made us stronger and reinforced our feeling of independence. Mama's loose routines also made us kids remarkably flexible in handling unforeseen events as we grew up. If things don't go as planned, adapt to the new development and get on with your life.

My parents

With all of her nonconforming lifestyle, Mama did some things spot-on. She was a tyrant when it came to learning, or anything else pertaining to school. She encouraged, nay, demanded, that we do our homework, that we do more in school than was asked of us, and that we participate in spelling, dramatic, and music (both voice and instrumental) competitions—though she rarely attended the plays, concerts, or other contests that we competed in. She was, in fact, quite reclusive. Her parental involvement was almost completely behind the scenes. However, for my lifelong pursuit of learning, and appreciation of music, I owe her big-time.

Beyond her, I owe these gifts to my grandfather, because it was he who had recognized similar gifts in my mother and encouraged them to flourish. Petite and pretty, studious and possessed of an exceptional memory, Mama was Grandpa's favorite child. (Grandma repeatedly sniffed that he had always babied her.) In an extraordinary move for a farmer, Grandpa had enrolled her and her sister Hazel at Tilford Academy in Vinton after graduation from eighth grade, because he wanted his daughters to continue their education and there was no high school in the area. When they graduated from the academy (the school he himself had attended as a boy), he sent them on to Iowa State Normal School in Cedar Falls to earn their teacher's certificates. Until her marriage, then, Mama taught at Monroe 6 in a one-room country school—the very one we would later attend.

Another debt I owe Mama, which went unrecognized and unappreciated until much later, needs to be noted. The day I learned this particular lesson was one of those bitterly cold winter afternoons when the roaring fire in the kitchen range provided the only heat. My mother had allowed her pet canary to fly free about the kitchen while she cleaned his cage. The beautiful yellow bird suddenly flew down and landed on the almost red-hot stove lid. He emitted one single, terrible scream that I can hear to this day. (When I read the startling first line of *Gravity's Rainbow*, "A screaming came across the sky," I wondered if Thomas Pynchon had experienced a similar event.) Without hesitation, Mama grabbed the stove lid handle and deftly tilted the mortally wounded creature into the blazing fire. I was dumbstruck. I knew how much she cherished Chicky. Looking straight at me, she said, "Don't think of yourself. Think of Chicky."

I never forgot this heroic example of unselfishness, and have used it to sustain me in making painful decisions when our family had to euthanize beloved pets. Don't keep an animal alive because you can't bear to suffer the pangs of bereavement. Think of the animal. This attitude makes the act bearable.

✳

Mama, Aunt Hazel, Uncle Ernest, Grandma, and Grandpa had a real gift for integrating us children into farm life. Working alongside us, they taught us how to perform the chores and execute the obligations that make a family and a farm work. Together we planted and tended gardens; harvested and canned fruits, vegetables, and meats; milked cows and fed calves; gathered nuts, morels, wild berries, grapes, and honey; cut wood; and harvested corn, hay, and soybeans. Thus we acquired an impressive store of what came to be identified as "assumed knowledge"—an education that is hard to match.

We had the whole outdoors as our world during the summers, because we always spent them on the farm. And under Mama's lenient, perhaps even negligent dominion, we kids felt unburdened. We were relieved of the disapproving and critical presence of our grandparents (though not one of us would ever have put it that way, for we respected them mightily). Despite the heavy responsibilities we bore, summers were the time we relaxed and felt appreciated. Winters under the eyes of our grandparents were much harder.

2

Great-Grandpa Jonathan

Old folks were ubiquitous in our world. As we were growing up we were surrounded by swarms of cousins, aunts, uncles, great-aunts and -uncles, grandparents, and great-grandparents. There was a saying in our family that no one ever died; people just dried up, were hung on a hook, and conducted their affairs from there.

I will forever remember meeting one of the oldest of the old folks—my grandfather's father—for the first and only time. Though he had lived most of his life in the Yankee Grove area, Great-Grandpa Jonathan had long since moved to Northern Iowa to live out his old age with one of his nine living children. His visit occurred early in the fall, after the oat harvest and before the beginning of corn-picking time, around the year 1930.

"Great-Grandpa is coming!" The announcement was on everyone's tongue. Jack, John, Avis, and I, along with our cousins Dean and Robert, who were almost like brothers to us, were all lined up on the freshly scrubbed porch of Aunt Hazel and Uncle Ernest's farmhouse. All the boys had on clean, blue denim bibbed "overhauls" and had combed their hair with water, a sure sign of a special event. My little sister, Avis, and I wore newly made gingham dresses, yellow polka dots on a blue background, with bloomers to match. Mama had put up our hair in rag curls the night before, another sign of an occasion. We were all barefooted.

"Keep your heads bowed during grace!" "Try not to get dirty!" "Keep your voices down. Above all, don't run into Grandpa!" Aunt Hazel's orders were stern.

Grandma, Mama, and Aunt Hazel had been cleaning and baking for days. In Iowa, the honor accorded a guest was gauged by the food the homemaker put on the table. Mama had baked bread with special care for this occasion. When the loaves were done, she removed them from their black tin pans, flipped them onto their tops, and returned them to the oven of the cast-iron kitchen range for extra crisping, thus ensuring an all-over tasty crust. And she made an especially large batch of honey-hickory nut cinnamon rolls in the nine-bun cast-iron pans. These had to be removed immediately after baking to prevent sticking, and we kids would sneak a few of the sweet, crunchy nuts that oozed down the sides. Aunt Hazel made her specialty, an angel food cake—high, white, and covered with a boiled whole-milk frosting. There were apple and cherry pies whose flaky crusts shattered at the first touch of the fork.

From the preparations and the reverence with which the adults spoke of Great-Grandpa, we children looked forward to his visit with the same awe and expectancy that the Israelites awaited Moses's descent from the mountain. Sitting in the lower branches of the sturdy box elder tree, we endlessly discussed his impending arrival. Several of the older kids hooted in derision when I asked whether or not we should address him as Great-Grandpa. (This was the beginning of my becoming aware of an undeclared and not strictly defined division between myself, my little sister, our young cousins, and friends on the one hand, and

my older brothers, cousins, and friends on the other, with age—
eight or nine years being the dividing line—the key factor in
one's identification. Throughout my early childhood, younger
children were referred to by older ones as the Little Kids, and we
Little Kids referred to them as the Big Kids.)

And then he arrived. Grandpa Arthur, who was his oldest son,
helped him emerge from the Buick with the isinglass curtains. He
looked exactly like one of the prophets pictured in Grandpa's
Sunday School pamphlet, *The Upper Room.* His gnarled hands
clasped a sturdy cane with a gold-clad crook; his body was slight
and frail; his head looked enormous because of his long white
hair and his immense white beard. His eyes, fierce and piercing,
focused for what seemed too long a time on each of us kids as we
were being introduced. A little frightened, we responded to his
questions and observations with unaccustomed sedateness.

Great-Grandpa
Jonathan Urmy

After supper, Great-Grandpa did something to me that was
so unusual and so remarkable, something that overwhelmed and
embarrassed me so much that I was never able to speak of what

occurred. Not everyone would understand such a reaction. That is, you wouldn't understand unless you came from a family of "hearty-handshake" Methodists the way I did. In a "hearty-handshake" Methodist family it wasn't considered appropriate behavior to show approval or affection toward people by hugging, and/or kissing, or, indeed, even touching. For instance, I recall an uncomfortable incident that occurred one winter Saturday night in Garrison. Our garrulous, outgoing next-door neighbor, who had dropped in for a chat, turned to us as she exited the kitchen door, saying, "Thanks for the great evening. Oh, I do love you folks." With that she quickly departed. Grandma stiffened in her chair. When the door was securely closed, she said quietly, "Well, we like her, too. But there's no need to say so."

Nor did this emotional austerity ease with the passage of time. Consider Grandpa's response to the safe return of my brother from five years of dangerous service in World War II. Having served in the fiercest battles of that war, Jack had been wounded, decorated, and pronounced a real hero. On first seeing Jack, Grandpa placed a hand on Jack's right shoulder, then, as if realizing that he was about to reveal some deep emotion, quickly withdrew it as he said ever so softly, "I'm glad you're back. I never thought I'd ever see you again." His eyes were slightly misty, but that was it. In our family, no matter what the circumstance, one's emotions were required to be kept private.

You could touch, hug, pat, or even kiss kittens, puppies, a favorite calf or horse, but you just didn't do it to people. If you achieved some prize in school like winning a music or declamatory contest, a spelling bee, or top honors in your class, you would be rewarded, along with some approving comments, with the old hearty handshake. It was a fact that we had no acceptable way to show affection toward people.

To this day I cannot explain Great-Grandpa's astonishing behavior to me on that first night of his visit, but after supper, when we were all gathered in the parlor (opened especially for this occasion), the old man sat himself down in a cherry rocker, hooked his heavy mahogany cane over one of its arms, then called me over to him and pulled me gently onto his lap. Startled by this unusual outward display of affection, I became rigid. As he softly stroked my shoulder, I lifted his great white beard, tucked my head under it, pulled my bare feet up, and allowed myself to settle, lulled by the loud ticking of the huge gold watch in his vest pocket. There I remained for the rest of the evening, listening to reminiscences of pioneer days in Yankee Grove, and gradually relaxing into the comfort of his warm lap and a long session of storytelling.

This was a fine entertainment for us all. Cousins and brothers sprawled on the carpet, half reclining on their scabby elbows, bare feet with bloody, stubbed toes sticking out into the middle of the room. The adults sat in chairs ringed around the room. Everyone gave the old man their complete attention.

Great-Grandpa recounted tales of bitter blizzards, the deaths of infants from whooping cough, diphtheria, and pneumonia. He remembered how Indians always came to winter in Indian Hollow in Yankee Grove, and he seemed happy when he was told the spring was still there, running clear and full. An avowed teetotaler, he was not so happy when he recalled that a tavern that had served as a stagecoach stop once occupied a spot near the home place in Yankee Grove. He described favorite horses and long-ago quarrels and chuckled over his naming a mule "Jake" after one of his stubborn neighbors. He gleefully recounted his victory over the Burlington, Cedar Rapids, and Minnesota Railway when it appeared that the railway was going to cut a sizeable corner from one of his fields, depriving him of access to this fertile land. Determined to fight the land grab, he sat vigil with his twelve-gauge shotgun until the powers-that-be decided to reroute the rail bed, leaving his field intact. Moreover, the curve that resulted meant that the train had to slow down so much to make the run safely that Grandpa Arthur and his brother Charlie were able to hop the slow-moving cars early every morning to ride to Vinton, where they were enrolled at the Tilford Academy. In the evening, they would return the same way they had come, hitching a ride on one of the railroad cars and hopping off as the train slowed for the fortuitous curve.

After all these stories, one of the boys dared to ask the question they had all been wanting to ask: "How did you lose half of your hand?" At this point I parted the coarse, white beard so I could watch the gesture he made with the thumb and index finger of his right hand. That's all that was left of his hand; the rest of it just slanted downward and was covered by a horrid, shiny, pinkish scar.

"Well, that happened when your grandpa was a boy. We had been watching an eagle that had been taking chickens and pigs for quite a while. He didn't take a lot; he'd just take one a day. I didn't mind the chickens so much, but he kept gettin' the little pigs. So one day he was a-sittin' and a-waitin' at the very top of that cottonwood tree there on the corner of the barnyard. That was his favorite place. I saw my chance so I got my gun and went upstairs to get a better shot out of the bedroom window. Now, I don't know exactly how it happened, but the gun exploded and it took half my hand right off."

We were mesmerized.

"Golly! What did you do with the part that was blown off?"

"Well, we just put it in a glass fruit jar and filled it with alcohol and buried it out there in the far corner of the strawberry patch."

"Do you think it's still there?"

"No reason why it shouldn't be."

Anyone who knows farm boys doesn't have to ask whether they went in search of the buried hand. Of course they did. But they never found it.

Those who were present often referred to Great-Grandpa's never-to-be-forgotten visit in later years. We discussed the stories he told, what he did or didn't say, the accuracy of his reports, his gold-bedecked cane, his physical condition, and the length of his beard. But no one ever mentioned his unprecedented display of affection for me.

3

Aunt Belle

During the winter in Garrison, Mama and we kids were frequent visitors at Aunt Belle's house on Saturday nights. Though Aunt Belle lived there with Grandpa's other unmarried sister, we never referred to it as Aunt Agnes's house.

The house was located on a corner just one block away from the Farmers Store, and a short walk from us. The kitchen occupied one half of the first floor of the house; a small living room and Aunt Belle's tiny bedroom occupied the other half. Aunt Agnes claimed the entire upper floor as well as the far end of the kitchen, where she sat in a large wicker rocker with built-in baskets on each arm. Her great Bible, always open, usually to the Old Testament, sat right in front of the rocker on a podium of its own, with a handheld magnifying glass holding down its pages. Aunt Agnes had a mass of iron gray hair which she cut periodically, though "cut" is a euphemism for what she did. She whacked it off, one-two-three, with a huge dressmaker's shears, but always left it long enough to hang down below her shoulders like a thick gray cape. She seldom combed it but piled it on top of her head every which way, which was somehow not unattractive.

Aunt Agnes had withdrawn from the family while she was still in her late teens, and living in Yankee Grove. Ever since, she had kept to herself, embroidering and reading the Bible. Aunt Belle was her sole link to the outside world. When we kids came in she would ignore us most of the time and continue her perusal of the Bible, looking down at it through her thick eyeglasses and the magnifying glass. From time to time, she would cross her arms over her ample breasts, look heavenward, and exclaim, "Oh, my soul!" Then she would hunch over the Bible and reread whatever passage it was that had startled her, and immediately there would be another outburst, always emphasizing the last word: "My soul! Oh, my soul!" Finding this hilarious, we kids would mimic her and giggle all the way home. Everyone generally understood that Aunt Agnes was "half a bubble off plumb."

Aunt Agnes was the oldest of eight surviving children, and Aunt Belle was the youngest. They were as different as night and day. Tiny and energetic as a hummingbird, chirpy and happy as a wren, Aunt Belle had a wry sense of humor and a sharp wit. When asked about her weight she would reply, "Oh, I weigh about a hundred, I guess, if I'm soaking wet and have a few rocks in my pockets." She always wore full-skirted, long-sleeved, high-necked, ankle-length gingham dresses of dark, flowered prints. On Sundays, for church, she had two good dresses, one for summer and one for winter. I never saw her in a new dress. Her hair, which she wore braided or in a bun, was a rich brown with only a few gray hairs here and there, even when she reached her eighties. Aunt Belle knew all about wildflowers and medicinal herbs, where to find them in Yankee Grove and how to use them; she could sing, play the piano (mostly hymns and popular tunes), grow flowers—and find joy everywhere. She was always ready to go on a picnic or a tramp in the woods, and best of all, she liked to take us children with her. Though she was of our grandparents' generation, she seemed like one of us kids, only with a lot more sense and a lot more money.

Aunt Belle

Saturday nights with Aunt Belle began in the kitchen, where we would make chocolate fudge, penuche (a brown sugar fudge), and popcorn. Aunt Belle grew her own popcorn and hung it, still on the cob, from the ceiling of her buttery. While we were cooking and eating, we would often learn poems or, if we were preparing for a Christmas or Easter program at school, practice a part in a play. Other times we engaged in word games and riddles. Can you crawl through a postcard? I can. It was Aunt Belle who taught us to fold and cut a postcard so that we could make a circle big enough to crawl through.

After we had gorged ourselves, we all had to wash our hands in the gray-striped enamel wash basin and, if it was really cold, we had to put on heavy sweaters in preparation for going into the living room for the next part of the evening's entertainment, which always involved some combination of the curio cabinet, the Victrola, and the upright piano. (The only source of heat in the whole house was the kitchen range.) During our hours in the living room, Aunt Belle and Mama would take turns playing the piano and we would all sing: "Way Out West on a Reservation," "Red Wing," "My Grandfather's Clock," "Put on Your Old Gray Bonnet," and "When You and I Were Young, Maggie," along with about twenty other of the *101 Favorite Songs.* I still remember all of the verses and the chorus of the first two songs mentioned, and some of the verses and choruses of the last three. I don't know another person who does.

If we sang hymns, which we frequently did, Aunt Agnes would stay up and listen to us from her wicker rocker in the kitchen; if we didn't, she would go upstairs. When I practiced nonreligious songs on the piano, Aunt Agnes would look agonized and moan for all to hear, "Oh, dear! I do wish Mildred would play a tune!"

The Victrola was a special beauty; over four feet high, its mahogany-red cabinet was polished to a soft, glowing patina. There were no fingerprints on it and there were never going to be any fingerprints on it, either; no one but Aunt Belle was allowed to touch or wind it. We listened, enchanted, to such selections as "Hello, Central, Give Me Heaven," "There's a Vacant Chair at Home Sweet Home," "Tell Mother I'll Be There," and "Life Is Like a Mountain Railroad." I can recall the first verse and chorus of these songs, too.

Some evenings Aunt Belle opened the bent-glass curio cabinet and allowed us to see and touch the wonders of its contents: Staffordshire dogs; fragile, bluest-eyed, pink-cheeked Meissen dolls; Haviland and Dresden plates, vases, salt cellars, and spoon holders. There was also a display of seashells that she had picked up when she visited California and Catalina Island, her only sojourn outside of Iowa. We never tired of looking at these marvelous treasures.

A few times she brought out the small horsehair trunk that had belonged to her mother, Harriet Turner (the woman we believed, accurately or not, to have descended from the *Mayflower* Turners). The trunk had a legendary quality, for Aunt Belle said her mother had brought it in a covered wagon all the way from Connecticut to Iowa. Among the precious mementos inside the trunk were fragile silk scarves, delicate lace collars and cuffs for a lady's dress, the softest, somewhat stained ivory-colored kid gloves to fit an impossibly tiny female hand, and best of all, letters and poems (mostly religious in nature) written by Harriet's father, who had originally been a sea captain. The script on these yellowed papers was in a large, firm hand and beautifully executed in a flourish of brown ink. Mama was allowed to hold and read the poems to us kids. I recall one that referred to dying, to trumpets sounding a call and a glorious entry into heaven accompanied by angels. I was too young at the time to appreciate the historic significance of the contents of this trunk; I merely wallowed in the pleasure of being allowed to see and touch.

After a Saturday night of such indulgences, we would leave Aunt Belle's warm kitchen to exit into the bitter cold and trudge the three blocks up the icy sidewalks to Grandpa's house, all five of us singing, not too loudly, but with spirit:

> "*Life is like a mountain railroad with an engineer so brave.*
> *We must make this run successful from the cradle*
>   *to the grave.*
> *Watch the curves, the hills, the tunnels. Never falter,*
>   *never fail.*
> *Keep your hand upon the throttle, and your eye*
>   *upon the rail.*"

It is probably difficult for anyone today to comprehend or appreciate the eagerness with which we anticipated an evening spent in the company of an ancient grand-aunt, eating candy and popcorn, telling riddles and singing hymns, but Saturday nights were a real treat for us.

After school, especially in the spring, if we were sent to the Farmers Store, we never missed an opportunity to walk by Aunt Belle's house, for there was always the chance that she would greet us from her screened-in porch: "Hey, go get your mom and let's go down to the quarry for a picnic!" That meant a weenie roast with marshmallows, bananas, Hershey bars, and Baby Ruths. You will notice that those are all store-bought goodies, all purchased by Aunt Belle, for we would never have been allowed to spend money on such luxuries.

The abandoned limestone quarry where we went for these picnics was a favorite spot. Accessed by walking east on the railroad tracks, it had an impressive bounty of fossilized lizards, worms, scallops, and fishes embedded in the rock. And we could wade on the smooth stones in the clear creek that flowed around the north edge of the quarry. On one such outing, we were crossing the trestle over the creek, which was still swollen by recent rains, when we came upon three young men shooting .22-caliber rifles at tin cans floating and bobbing in the swiftly flowing water below. They had assigned a much younger brother to wade into the water, retrieve the cans, and replace them in the water upstream. Time after time the young men aimed and fired but never made a hit.

Aunt Belle started to taunt them. "Missed!" she said dryly. "Missed again!" "Missed it a mile!"

She kept up her quiet comments until one of the men said in

exasperation, "You think you can do any better? Here, you try it!" He handed her the gun and three bullets, whereupon she took careful aim and sank those cans, three in a row. Then, grinning from ear to ear, totally pleased with her display of prowess, she handed the rifle back without comment, and without even looking at the young men.

My, we kids were proud of her. She had perfected her aim by shooting the English sparrows and blue jays that had dared to harass her adored house wrens. But how could those young men have known that?

Aunt Belle was the protagonist of another scene that I treasure to this day. She, Mama, my sister, and I frequently went for quiet walks the length and breadth of Garrison, which was all of about eight blocks long and five blocks wide. We walked in early evening, looking at the flower gardens and talking. I must have been about eleven years old at the time of this incident—a homely child who was painfully aware of being fat and dumpy, with fine, unruly hair that never stayed in place.

This particular steamy Saturday evening the four of us were walking up from the railroad tracks, having walked all the way down to the western tip of town to the Brick and Tile Factory. It was August and we were thoroughly enjoying the many flowers, which at that season included golden and bachelor buttons, foxgloves, Canterbury bells, seven-sister roses, intensely colored zinnias, and delicately blue lilies.

Suddenly I was aware that two sisters, a few years older than I, were advancing toward us arm in arm. Lillian and Marcia were Scottish beauties with shoulder-length, reddish-blond curls prettily arranged around their perfect, smiling faces. Their skin was pink, their eyes were sparkling blue, their arms and legs were slim and long. They wore pink, full-skirted pinafore dresses with an inset banding accentuating their incredibly slender waists. They had perfect figures. They were everything that I wanted to be.

I was walking ahead of our little group and, as the Wallace princesses approached, I stepped off the sidewalk into the dew-dampened grass to let them pass.

Aunt Belle saw this; she hurried up to me and asked, "Why did you get off the walk when you met those girls?"

I replied, as if it should have been clear to anyone, "Because they are the prettiest girls in town! And I didn't want them to get their feet wet!"

Aunt Belle grabbed me above the right elbow with both of her hands and shook me until I actually saw blue stars, roughly pushed me back onto the sidewalk, and growled between clenched teeth, emphasizing each word: "DON'T YOU EVER, EVER GET OFF THE SIDEWALK FOR ANYONE! YOU ARE AS PRETTY AS ANYONE! DO YOU UNDERSTAND?"

Though I didn't understand and didn't believe her, deep in my heart I fervently wanted to, and I have always loved her for what she said to me that night.

In the summertime Aunt Belle and Aunt Agnes grew flowers as well as vegetables. They quarreled so much over their flowers that they divided the garden plot and each tended her own. Their flowers were a delight to the whole town, but Aunt Agnes wouldn't part with a single blossom, while Aunt Belle loaded up every passerby with a bouquet of dahlias, lilies, cosmos, lupines, bachelor and golden buttons, zinnias, foxgloves, Canterbury bells, roses, violets, pansies, and forget-me-nots. Whatever was in bloom, she would share. "The more they're picked, the more they'll bloom!" Of course, she was right. She was the walking definition of a "green thumb"! When the pansy bed threatened to engulf the whole garden, she pulled pansies up by the handful and dumped them in the ditch alongside her property; without any care whatsoever, they took root and bloomed right there.

When Great-Grandpa Urmy died it was discovered that he had provided for these two daughters in a curiously cruel way. His will stipulated that an excellent piece of farmland would be left to Drake University in Des Moines on the condition that, in return, Aunt Agnes would be paid a set amount of money every year for the rest of her life. Surviving relatives darkly speculated that the details of this arrangement had been achieved in an unwholesome manner. According to family folklore, a university representative drove the old man away on outings on several different occasions. Apparently, it was on one of those occasions that the deal had been made. The details are far from clear and, for years, I listened to my elderly relatives mutter about this agreement, calling it a scandal. The will further required Aunt Belle to look after Aunt Agnes and to live with her in the house in Garrison that their father had purchased for them.

Aunt Belle was naughty and died of heart failure in her early eighties, leaving Aunt Agnes, who had never dealt with the world, alone in her little house. I use the word "naughty" because Urmy women traditionally didn't die until they reached their nineties. And indeed, that crusty old doll, Aunt Agnes, did live on into her nineties. The Drake University powers, tired of waiting around for her to die, filed a lawsuit pleading that they had already given her more than the land was worth, and sued to stop the required payments to her. The family, unaware of this, did not challenge the suit, and the payments were stopped in 1959, according to the records in the Benton County courthouse. Officials sold Aunt Agnes's furniture and carted her off to the Benton County Poor Farm, where she died in 1965. She is buried in the Yankee Grove Cemetery.

Once, before Aunt Belle died, I got up enough courage to ask her a very personal question.

"Aunt Belle, how come you never got married?"

She looked at me for a long time. She was standing by the kitchen stove, her delicate hands clasping and unclasping the stove handle, and she told me the following story:

"Well, I did have one beau. He told Art [her brother and my grandpa] to tell me Barkis is willin' and that he would be over Saturday night. [Mama later explained to me that this was a Dickens reference, alluding to the passage in which Barkis sends an oblique message to Clara Peggoty via David Copperfield that 'Barkis is willin'.'] Well, that made me so mad! I thought he had a lot of nerve asking me to marry him through Art like that! So when he came over Saturday night I wouldn't take his hat; I wouldn't take his coat. I wouldn't ask him to sit down. I treated him just as cold. I treated him so bad he never came back."

She stood absolutely still for a long time; then she continued:

"I'm kind of sorry I was so cold to him; he went and married Abbie Cross, made her a good home and was a good husband to her. They had a nice family."

She remained contemplative for a while and then continued, "It's been kind of lonesome sometimes." Talk about roads not taken.

4

Thanksgiving

Let me describe a traditional family get-together. The day before Thanksgiving the grand square oak table in the dining room had been extended by its six leaves, and the freshly laundered and ironed damask cloths were whitely, brightly, smoothly arranged over its entire length. At least two weeks before, we had washed and ironed the tablecloths, which were of sentimental value, having been purchased for my grandfather's mother by his father in 1867—the year Grandpa was born out in Yankee Grove.

On these occasions we used the real silver (polished with a bit of house flannel and Arm & Hammer baking soda) and the double set of Haviland china decorated with the pink moss roses. The whole family would be coming—aunts, uncles, cousins—so we placed the settings close together. Even so, there would have to be two seatings, with the men and the older boys (the Big Kids) eating first, followed by the women and younger children (the Little Kids).

Preparations and planning for Thanksgiving dinner began weeks before the event. In late September we collected the ground-cherries for pie and stored them, still in their little paper-baglike husks, in a single layer on the floor of the library, a cool, dry room on the north side of the house which was too cold to occupy when the weather began to turn. (Those we didn't store we made into sweet, translucent jam by boiling them with sugar and paper-thin slices of lemon. Grandma's golden rule of proportions I still recall: five cups of fruit to four cups of sugar.) Ground-cherries, for those readers unfamiliar with them, are small yellow fruits that develop inside a tan, papery covering much like the gaudy Chinese lantern. Indeed, the two are related; both are members of the nightshade family.

Also, in September, we identified two geese for special attention. They were given special food of cracked corn and were allowed the freedom to forage on the apples and sweet knotgrass in the orchard.

In early October, we targeted a few of the largest, most colorful pumpkins to be given particular care. Later, we would choose one of those to be made into pies. Still later the whole family gathered nuts in Yankee Grove. About two weeks before Thanksgiving, nearly everyone took turns cracking the nuts—a major enterprise. We would crack them outside on an anvil or, if it was too cold, we would go to the basement. It takes a long time to collect enough nut meats for the amount of baking we did. We stored these goodies in glass jars, each measured and identified: *1 cup butternuts for cake + ½ cup for frosting; 3 cups black walnuts for cake, frosting, and apple salad; 1 ½ cups hickory nuts for cake and frosting.*

About four days before Thanksgiving, the Big Kids, accompanied by us Little Kids, were dispatched to the cornfield to choose one of the pumpkins. Usually the golden orb was so large the Big Kids had to roll it into the kitchen and join forces to lift it to the wooden table. We sliced it clean through the center with our largest, sharpest butcher knife, and using Grandma's huge aluminum jam spoon, scraped the seeds out of the center right down to the firm flesh.

Again because they were strong, it was left to the Big Kids to slice the entire pumpkin into three-inch-wide crescents. After the supper dishes were done, we all sat around the table, trimming the rind off the slices and cutting them into two-inch pieces, which we put into the blue and white marbleized granite kettle that was usually reserved for making jams and jellies. Once the kettle was filled, we poured water into the kettle "until you could just see it through the pumpkin," and then set the kettle to boil on top of the Monarch iron stove. By the time we were ready for bed the kettle had started to boil, at which point we moved it to the very back stove lid where it would cook slowly most of the night. And that was the whole idea. Slow-cooked pumpkin was the best.

In the morning, Grandma would put the mixture through a colander with a heavy oak potato masher that Grandpa had carved by hand for her. She now had a thick, puddinglike pumpkin mixture. Into the great round crock, brown on the outside, ivory on the inside, went the whole orange-colored mass. On this Grandma would wreak her own special magic as we kids watched, chins in our hands and our eyes wide open. Whole milk, a pint of heavy cream, six slightly beaten eggs, salt, lots of freshly grated nutmeg, cinnamon, ground cloves, and sugar were added to the crock. Then she beat everything together with that trusty oversized aluminum spoon that had been used so often that the edge of its bowl was lopsided.

Presto. She had produced a wonderful filling for pumpkin pies.

Now she had to make the crusts. With a gray graniteware quart dipper Grandma dipped into the fifty-pound flour bin in the kitchen cabinet, added a pinch of coarse salt, and ladled several spoons of pure white lard into the mixture. Lard was kept in three-gallon jars in the basement. To this she added a few table-spoons of cold water and mixed everything together with the tips of her fingers until the mixture resembled coarse cornmeal. Grandma taught me how to keep the bottom of a pie crust from getting soggy. To this day I still practice this method and have taught my children and grandchildren to do the same when mak-ing any pie with a puddinglike filling. She beat one egg white until it was frothy, and with her fingers, spread a thin layer over the crust. Then she popped it into a 450° oven for ten minutes. When the crust was nicely browned, she removed it from the oven, poured in the pumpkin mixture, and returned it to the oven to continue baking.

Now might be a good time to explain about that wood-burning iron kitchen range. Ours had four large stove lids plus a small back one, an oven door that folded down and was made of a shiny white ceramic with the word *MONARCH* written in blue script across it, and a large reservoir attached to the right-hand side which we filled with soft water from the cistern for washing dishes and ourselves. The reservoir had another purpose, too. When the situation called for a quick, hot oven—say 450°, which was what was required for making crisp pie crusts—you achieved that by stoking a few fat large corncobs into the firebox. But once the oven temperature soared and the crusts had browned, how could you reduce it to the 350° needed for baking the pies? Easy. Just fill a kettle with cool soft water and, keeping an eye on the more-or-less accurate thermometer on the oven door, carefully pour it into the reservoir. Since the reservoir is attached to the oven wall, the temperature drops instantly. Now the pies can con-tinue baking at a moderate temperature. When the thermometer drops below 350°, you just add a few corncobs. You'd be surprised how skilled you get in controlling oven heat in this manner.

But let's get back to the planning for the Big Dinner. Two days before Thanksgiving several important tasks had to be completed. First, we had to remember to set aside about two quarts of heavy cream for the whipped cream to put on top of the pumpkin pies and maybe the devil's food cake, because cream that is fresher than two days old will not whip.

Next, those two fat, sleek, and arrogant geese had to be killed and dressed. Since we wanted to harvest their feathers for quilts, feather beds, and pillows, we had to keep them from getting bloody. Our technique was to place the goose under a wooden box which my sister sat on while my brother Jack reached under and guided the goose's head through a hole that had been drilled through one end of the box. Still holding the goose's head, while another person held on to the neck to prevent it from reflexively withdrawing into the hole where it might bloody the feathers, Jack swiftly decapitated the goose with a huge sharp butcher's knife.

Then Grandma picked the feathers off, holding the great creature on her gingham-aproned lap, its neck now tied with a clean white cloth so there was no dripping blood to soil the feathers. Quickly and surely, she ripped the downy feathers off in great handfuls and thrust them into a blue and white striped ticking bag.

Once the geese were clean, we set about making the dressing. Again our forethoughtiness made things easy. For two weeks we had placed every bit of stale bread in an open pan in the pantry to dry out thoroughly in anticipation of this event. Our round, fat Grandma was the acknowledged champion of dressing makers everywhere, and I watched her year after year prepare it exactly the same way. She put the necks, gizzards, and hearts of

the geese in water to simmer. She cubed the dried bread and sent
one of us out to the garden to collect some fresh sage. Sage was a
key ingredient and Grandma used several large bunches of it,
which she dried quickly in the oven, then crumbled into the
cubed bread. Next she would beat half a dozen eggs, add at least
one pint of heavy cream, a pinch of salt, some black pepper, and
the finely chopped giblets. The giblet broth was then put back on
the stove. This was crucial, because Grandma insisted that the
broth had to come to a rolling boil before it was poured into the
bread cubes—now covered with the eggs and cream. (This
"rolling boil" rule may explain why no one ever got sick from
bacteria forming in this mixture even though it always sat around
for hours and we had no refrigeration.) Once the broth had been
poured, she turned the mixture over and over with two large,
long-handled aluminum spoons, taking great care not to mash
the bread cubes, and continuing to turn them until they'd soaked
up all the liquid.

Some of the Big Kids waiting to hear "Dinner's ready"

By eleven o'clock on Thanksgiving Day the aunts, uncles, and cousins had all arrived. The uncles and the Big Kids usually stayed out on the front porch discussing cars, animals, crops, politics, and the price of hogs, soybeans, and corn. Then they would gravitate to the back of the house or, if the gathering was on a farm, to the horse barn, ostensibly to see a new foal or check out a new stall (and leaving the women and the Little Kids to do all the work). It was years before I discovered the real reason: Someone had stashed a bottle of Old Grandad in Old Jude's grain box.

The aunts and the Little Kids gathered in the kitchen. Each aunt would have brought her specialty. Green lima beans, mashed potatoes, apple salad, cabbage salad, bread-and-butter pickles, vinegary beet pickles, baked acorn squash, ground-cherry, apple, and raisin pies, devil's food and angel food cakes, charlotte russe, and jams of all kinds were unpacked and put on the table.

All of a sudden the kitchen was buzzing with laughter and chattering, questions and answers, orders and suggestions. Everybody pitched in. There were Wealthy apples to be peeled, cored, and sliced, boiled milk dressing to be assembled for that apple salad, gravy to be made, potatoes to be mashed, cakes and pies to be sliced, cream to be whipped, a goose to be carved. Even the littlest ones were pressed into service to bring in more wood for the kitchen fire or fresh water from the pump. They knew that they could get an oatmeal cookie for their efforts.

These people genuinely liked each other. Whenever they were together there was an atmosphere of merriment and good cheer, with lots of joking, poking fun, and camaraderie. I loved the kitchen at these times. Tongues worked as fast as hands. Talk flitted amiably from one subject to another and none of it ever seemed too trivial. Anything you had to report was considered interesting. Gossip, some of it whispered or delivered sotto voce, was eagerly dispensed. Do you know how frustrating it is to have some juicy tidbit and no one to tell it to? Now was the time to unload everything you knew. And so the chatter went:

Well, I finally finished my quilt. Your hair looks great. I'll bet you're glad to have that done. Hank Shadler's cow nearly died this week. Marian kept calling Dr. Englebert. Amy marcelled it for me yesterday. She doesn't care what she says over the telephone. I didn't get hardly anything done all day. She'd say "The calf's half out." Then she'd call and say, "It's out further yet. But the legs seem to be caught inside." Would somebody stir this gravy awhile? I don't know how she could talk like that on the telephone. I wish you had brought more of your scrumptious pickles. I hear Kate Bushel got married. Who to? Now, you don't have to listen in every time the phone rings, do you? The hired man. Someone sharpen this knife. My dill didn't do too well this year. Was it a shotgun wedding? I guess so. See if this is salty enough. I heard that if she didn't announce the wedding, a little one would real soon. (At this point there would be a rolling of eyes and a sidelong look to my cousin and me.) *"Little pitchers have big ears."*

Looks like Henrietta Weyman is trying to run the Ladies' Auxiliary this year. Well, let her. Somebody has to do it. I sure don't want to. Is that dressing for the apple salad ready yet? I hear Rufus Boyd is looking for a goat again. No! They had so much trouble with that last baby I didn't think they'd chance another. Can someone start carving the goose? Well, I hear this one came without being sent for. Just hand me the whetstone so I can sharpen this knife. Now they know they can keep the baby alive on goat's milk they probably won't have so much trouble with this one. Not?

You going to Melinda's funeral? Oh, I guess so. Put the cabbage salad and the apple salad on the table. Such a shame; leaving all those children. I love the print in your dress; where did you get the material? The oldest one is almost twelve, so she'll be a big help. JC Penney's, only thirty-six cents a yard. Oh, the serving spoons are already on the table. Well, they say Lou left her lying in bed for a week before he went and got help. Matt McBain said she knew Melinda was dying soon's she walked in the door. The men are going to want coffee with dessert so I'll put up the pot now. Said she smelled death in the room. Are you finished with the mashed potatoes? Ed said he'd heard at the pool hall that she'd used a lead pencil to try to get rid of this one. Everything's about ready. Then I'll pour the gravy. Kenny and Harold, go down to the barn and tell the men to come up for dinner.

PART TWO

Building Character

Barn for hay, horses, and cows

5

Building Character: Oral Influences

One way to take the measure of a community is to listen in on its use of language: the folksy sayings that knit us together, the colloquialisms that inform, guide, chastise, amuse, and entertain us.

Proverbs, adages, maxims, old saws, mottoes, and aphorisms, most with a definite country flavor, pervaded our existence. We were bombarded daily with pithy phrases and epigrams, largely didactic. They were part of the "Life is real, life is earnest" brainwashing that formed our character. Indeed, my whole life was, and still is, haunted by the image of old folks' faces, glimpsed through a foggy mist, mouthing their received wisdom and bleating their hoary truths.

To this day I can see the two mottoes I had penciled in two-inch-high block letters on the dirty-blue hard cover of my loose-leaf notebook: IT IS EASIER TO KEEP UP THAN TO CATCH UP and I HAD NO SHOES AND COMPLAINED UNTIL I MET A MAN WHO HAD NO FEET. I purchased the notebook when I was in ninth grade and continued to use it all through high school, replacing the sheets as needed. ("Waste not, want not.")

"An idle mind is the Devil's workshop," "Satan finds some

mischief still for idle hands to do," and "Improve your mind each day" translated into "Learn some Bible verses or a song or a poem, or read a book." In other words, if you have any spare time, fill it with something useful. It was a given in our family that when females gathered in a group for whatever reason, their hands would have to go as fast as their tongues. But the tongues did wag. There were several expressions regarding talking, and I have only recently noted that nearly all of them use the feminine pronoun. "What's on her mind is on her tongue," "She thinks with her mouth," "She's got the gift of gab," and "She's got a tongue that's loose at both ends." But the biggest talker of all was described by, "She's got a tongue that's loose at both ends and has a swivel in the middle."

I don't know where a lot of the family sayings came from: "Don't look for us until you see us coming." This comment was made in response to the question, "What time can we expect you?" or "What time are you coming home from the dance?"

"He always got the hind tit." We Little Kids used this expression to complain to the Big Kids about an unfair division of some goody such as pie or cake. "Why do we always get the hind tits?" The source of this phrase was right in our own barnyard. Animals that bear litters of several young, such as pigs, cats, and dogs, have two rows of mammary glands arranged from the inside of the armpit to the groin area in order to accommodate their newborns. The forward teats are larger and produce more milk than the last two, which are smaller and produce significantly less milk. In the scramble to get the best place at the table, the stronger, more aggressive animals latch on to the bigger teats, leaving the weaker, less agile to take the hind tits. The hind tit position had long-term consequences, for the less nutrition one got, the smaller and weaker one would be. Always. The expression referred to someone who was generally thought of as being a bit of a loser. Forever and ever.

"What you don't have in your head you have in your heels." I used this great expression on my own kids. When we were growing up, there was no way a mother could or would make a trip to school to deliver a forgotten textbook, homework, or lunch box. You went and got it or you did without. And if you got all the way out to the garden and discovered you had forgotten to bring a paring knife, you had to go back to the house and fetch it yourself. And how did you get there? Well, you got there by using "shank's mare"—your own two feet.

"Whistling girls and crowing hens will always come to some bad end." Grandma was the only one I ever heard use this expression and it was always directed to me. She wanted me to act like a lady and very much objected to my whistling.

"Sing before breakfast; cry before night." This pronouncement was directed only at children. Frankly, when I was young I never understood this one either, but perhaps it is meant to caution against expending all one's enthusiasm and high spirits early on, leading to a crash by nightfall.

To us kids, everything was "keen" or "swell." If it was "raining cats and dogs" we all ran home "lickety-split." We called each other "crybaby," "bawl-baby," and " 'fraidy-cat," and when we girls had a falling-out we called each other "snot box."

When adults met downtown at the post office or the hardware store, they would stand around "chewing the fat." When it was time to get ready to leave the house to go to an appointment you were told to "Get your trottin' harness on." And if you wanted to let your friend know that you were hurrying you would say something like "I'll be with you in two shakes of a lamb's tail," or if you could do something in a very short time, "I can whip up some biscuits in two shakes of a lamb's tail."

I grew up thinking that certain expressions were actually one word: agoodwoman, hardearnedmoney, agoodhardworker, alittleheathen, adrunkenbum, demonrum, and agoodwoolskirt.

Thrift and its associated virtues were the subject of many of our sayings.

"She can throw out more in a teaspoon than he can bring in with a shovel." This insightful observation describes a wasteful wife—one, say, who didn't wipe the inside of an eggshell with her forefinger to extract every last bit of the egg white, or one who made dusting cloths out of old cotton dresses and shirts instead of first salvaging the good parts to make dust caps, tea towels, or napkins. Still another example would be the wife who invested her husband's hardearnedmoney in purchasing raisins, dates, cinnamon, nutmeg, and other expensive ingredients to make a cake, only to forget to add the baking powder, thus producing a leaden mass that had to be thrown to the chickens.

The occasional wasteful wife notwithstanding, there was an unspoken, general agreement conveyed to us girls by the grown-up females we came in contact with that women were superior to men. This was a secret discreetly kept from the men, who were catered to in many ways; men were offered the first serving at the table, they were granted the best cuts of the meat, they received the first cup of coffee out of the fresh pot, they were assured that the last piece of pie would be theirs, and on and on. But the women knew who really ruled the roost.

The females were keepers of cleanliness, sobriety, manners, morals, and decorum. I recall a joke that appeared on the back page of the *Pathfinder* that was told over and over again by Mama and her friends: An Old Maid (that's what we called unmarried women in those days) was asked why she didn't try to find a husband. Her reply was, "I have a dog that growls, a chimney that smokes, a parrot that swears, and a cat that stays out all night. Why do I need a husband?"

In Garrison, women didn't smoke, didn't drink, and didn't swear. Children wouldn't think of swearing in the presence of adults any more than they would think of sassing them. Why? Simple. Getting your mouth washed out with soap wasn't just an idle expression. We didn't like the taste of Lifebuoy or Fels Naphtha.

Ladies in our family and of my acquaintance expressed surprise and shock by "Dear me!" "Mercy!" "Mercy, me!" "Good Lord a'mercy!" "My stars!" and "My Lord!" Grandma had three exclamations that she used over and over again: "Gosh all hemlock!" "Not on your tintype!" and "Not much, Mary Ann!" They all said "Landsakes!" long before Ma Perkins made that saying famous.

One woman of about thirty came pretty close to breaking the no-swearing restriction by substituting the word "dash" into her comments where a man might have used the word "damn." "Dash it all! I'm sick and tired of waiting for the mailman!" "You're dashed right I'm going to the dance tonight!" "He drives that dashed car like a dashed madman!" Of course, Tina was considered bold to use this racy word, but what could you expect from someone who was reportedly seen wearing four-inch-high heels and drinking gin rickeys out at the roadhouse on Highway 218?

It was accepted that adult men would use some coarse language. The favored bad words of my uncles were "damn," "hell," and "shit." They would occasionally use these even in the presence of their wives and children. Calling someone a damn fool was done so frequently that it was almost acceptable in mixed company. "Of course he got stuck. He was a damn fool for trying to drive down that mud road." They also said "bastard," and "son of a bitch." But I seldom heard these words.

One summer, in our perverse fashion, out of the earshot of the adults, we kids all became "shit sayers." Saying "The hell you yell!" and "You're damn right!" just did not elicit the same satisfaction as "Shit!" The Big Kids taught us Little Kids everything we knew about its use. First off, they used it as a term of address calling both each other and us Little Kids "dumb shits" and "shit asses." If we were inept at some activity, say, in connecting the straps properly to harness a horse, they would declare that we didn't know "shit from Shinola." If we did something they found objectionable, they told us we were in their shithouse or on their shit list until further notice. If they caught us in a lie, we were told to "stop giving us that shit." If we objected to some dictate from them, they would simply dismiss our complaints with "tough shit." In a way that adults would never understand, we Little Kids did not take offense at these comments. We recognized that to be so addressed was a subtle welcome into the larger community of kids. We enjoyed a sweet sense of belonging.

Oddly enough, given how much we loved saying "shit," when we needed to empty our bowels we used a euphemism, saying we had to "take a dump." And if we somehow acquired loose bowels, we said we had the "carbolly-marbolly shoot-the-shoots" or, for short, "The carbolly-marbollies."

If a man caroused around during the night, he was guilty of "doing God knows what!" Such words were spoken sotto voce, implying dark, unspeakable deeds, and they always kicked my imagination into high gear. When uttered in the same conversation as the following—"He's going to hell in a handbasket!"—

and applied to a local Beau Brummel, these two observations could only mean that the man was guilty of all kinds of locally defined sins: drunkenness, laziness, and hanging around roadhouses, bars, and pool halls. This expression is still in use. I recently noted a bumper sticker that read "Where are we going and what am I doing in this handbasket?"

References to sexual matters were rare and exceedingly circumspect. When Shorty Long married an unusually beautiful girl, she was referred to as "a looker." "She can put her shoes under my bed anytime." That's what the young men said of "the looker" from Keystone.

At least in our family, the big "F" word, used so ubiquitously among today's youth and adults that it serves as a noun, verb, adjective, adverb, and even as a participle, was strictly forbidden. The Big Kids told us Little Kids this was a very bad word, but they didn't tell us what it meant. I vividly recall the only two occasions in my early childhood when I heard it. The first time was when Grandpa had made his way up to the front of Old Jude's stall to place a pan of oats in the bin on the right side of the manger. Both Old Jude and Grandpa were retired, but Grandpa was helping out with the chores. For reasons no one has ever been able to explain, that fractious horse took the collar of Grandpa's heavy sheepskin jacket in his teeth and held the old man high enough off the barn floor that he couldn't get away. Grandpa wasn't hurt, because he was protected by the thickness of the heavy sheepskin, but he found himself in a ludicrously helpless position. Dangling with the tips of his heavy work shoes barely scraping the floor and arms flailing, Grandpa became exceedingly agitated. Old Jude just held him there and would not put him down. Then that mild-mannered, clean-minded model of probity called his horse a "fuckin' bastard"! Needless to say we kids relished both the comic spectacle and the dreadful language, but we didn't dare laugh in his presence. We rushed outside of the barn where we collapsed in the straw stack and laughed ourselves helpless. We reported this incident over and over to our friends.

The other memorable time I heard the word was when the family was gathered one chilly Saturday morning in Grandma's kitchen in Garrison and news came that Mrs. Donleavey had given birth to her ninth child. This family had a baby every year; in fact, the arrival of a new Donleavey baby was the signal that spring had arrived, too. Uncle Ernest, chuckling to himself and addressing no one in particular, said, "There goes old Pat Donleavey again! Fucking himself out of a place at the table." Stern glances went all around but we kids just went right on playing dominoes and pretended we hadn't heard. We didn't want the old folks to know that we knew that word.

I never heard the currently favored expression indicating that a man enjoys an unusual degree of intimacy with his mother. Was it even in existence in the thirties?

Medical matters were another source of idiosyncratic sayings in our community. If someone from town asked Grandpa how Grandma was, and he responded that she was still "doctoring," that word conveyed significant information: It indicated that the ailment was severe enough to require professional advice from a medical practitioner. In our time, in our town, one didn't "doctor" for trivial matters. The locals must have been the despair of the medical profession, for you had to have a full-blown case of pneumonia, a temperature of 104 degrees, a broken bone sticking out of your arm or leg, or be at least six hours into labor past a nine-month pregnancy before anyone ever thought of calling a doctor. Is it any wonder that a few of those dedicated doctors succumbed to alcoholism?

Our family used a quaint expression that is worthy of preservation. The old codgers, and we were surrounded by many, deemed it weak in character to give in to an illness. Most of the time they would fight like fury to avoid taking to their beds. To succumb thus was considered a demeaning defeat by men and women alike. So, instead of going to bed, they would place two tall-backed wooden kitchen chairs face-to-face with each other, forming a kind of chair-couch in front of a warm stove. Wrapped in a soft wool quilt, they could recline there and recuperate without guilt. When such an incident occurred and a friend inquired after their health, an old codger might reply, "I've been sick-a-bed on two chairs." This comment would be delivered with a wry smile, both parties chuckling with the instant understanding that the illness had been quite unpleasant but nothing too serious.

My grandma was the source of many of the colorful homespun sayings that I remember so well. Though she had little formal education and I never saw her read a book, she could be quite eloquent. And she could also on occasion use language that was a real surprise coming from the mouth of a genteel Victorian lady, which is what she was. Grandma wore bloomers that buttoned just below the knee and dresses that reached to her ankles, and I never heard her refer to her leg as anything but a "limb." While she never went to the extreme of covering the legs of the piano with fine embroidered cotton, long-legged panties as she reported that her missionary sister had done, she was generally quite prim.

Once I deliberately used the word "shit" to shock her. She looked at me with distaste and said, "Now you have in your mouth something I wouldn't even hold in my hand." Yet she herself made use of the word when it suited her. Her impatient response to us kids moaning about something that we didn't have but wanted was, "Well, wish in one hand and shit in the other and see which one gets full the quickest!" Another time, tired of listening to us kids make "if" excuses, she exploded into our wailing with "If! If! I don't want to hear anymore about if! The dog would have caught the rabbit if he hadn't stopped to shit!"

She also contributed a riddle that we quickly passed on to our classmates. "What's born stingless, flies wingless, and sings till it dies?" That Grandma would even admit the existence of flatulence was a total surprise to us; I guess that's why I still remember this. I can't imagine where she learned such coarse expressions. She didn't get them from Grandpa. Just as he never used the cuss words that my uncles frequently indulged in, I never heard him tell an off-color joke.

Hers was a no-nonsense, pull-up-your-socks approach to life, and it was her happy pragmatism that has stayed with me throughout the years. It was she who would say to us, "Wait on yourself. Your friends will like you better." And better yet: "If you're looking for a helping hand you'll find one at the end of your arm." Grandma liked to have the family visit but she would coax them to leave with a cheery "Well, I was glad to see you come and I'll be glad to see you go!" or "It's ten o'clock. I'm t' home and I wish you were!" No one ever took offense.

Along with Grandpa, Grandma provided the solid, practical commonsense guidance in the lives of us children. She took the development of our character seriously and insisted that we improve ourselves. One of her more important observations was that it was impolite and unacceptable to visit your ill temper on those around you. If you wake up feeling at odds with the world, direct your attention outside of yourself, see what the world requires of you, and then get busy. The chances are that in a very short while, your grumpiness will soon be displaced by a feeling of goodwill. Her understanding of the psychology of moods was so keen that years later when I read the following passage from William James, I felt as though I'd encountered a soulmate of my grandmother's:

> *The voluntary path to cheerfulness, if our spontaneous cheerfulness be lost, is to sit up cheerfully, and act and speak as if cheerfulness were already there. To feel brave, act as if we were brave, use all our will to that end, and courage will very likely replace fear. If we act as if from some better feeling, the bad feeling soon folds its tent like an Arab and silently steals away.*

Grandma may not have been educated, but she certainly had sound instincts.

Though all of the grown-ups related how tiny and petite she had been when she and Grandpa married in their teens—they said that Grandpa could encircle her waist with his two hands—I never remember her as anything but my short, roly-poly, round, soft Grandma. And it was this small, fat Grandma who could make the daylight fly; her attitude toward work was relentlessly cheerful and infectious. On mornings when she felt especially ebullient, which was most of the time, she would give a humorous commentary that went something like this as she splatted joyfully down the hall in her bare feet, rapping on every bedroom door. "Get up, everybody! Everybody up! It's Monday, wash day; Tuesday we iron and bake bread; Wednesday we can tomatoes; Thursday we do mending and baking, and Friday we have to clean house and bake again! My goodness, the week is almost gone already and you're not even out of bed yet!" She could use up your whole week in less than three minutes.

Grandma stated her position most succinctly: "I'd rather wear out than rust out!" She was the master practitioner of the pithy epigram, and of the virtues that such epigrams expressed.

Grandpa and Grandma Urmy

6

Building Character: Literary Influences

For us children, building character, developing a sense of responsibility, and above all, improving one's mind constituted the essential focus of our lives. Childhood was generally considered to be a disease, or, at the very least, a disability, to be ignored for the most part, and remedied as quickly as possible. The adults thought of reading as part of the cure. Practically everything we were given to read was for the purpose of supplying examples of how we were to behave.

We were a family of readers, with the exception of Grandma, who had not gone to school beyond the sixth grade. Our attitudes were formed by songs, poems, books, and magazines. The *Cedar Valley Daily Times*, the *Des Moines Register*, *Capper's Weekly*, *Collier's*, *Woman's Home Companion*, the *Saturday Evening Post*, the *Pathfinder*, the *Christian Herald*, the *Christian Science Monitor*, and later, *Reader's Digest* were all part of our literary fare.

Although we didn't read the Bible early on, we were being prepared for it through exposure in Sunday school and by Grandpa's ample use of quotations from it, especially when we were misbehaving. I recall cringing in shame and fear when Grandpa would criticize the behavior of my oldest brother for some transgression I could not understand by reading from Ecclesiastes about there being a time for every matter under heaven and a time to put childish things behind him. His perorations usually ended with his reading one of the verses about how "God will bring you to judgment." He could reduce my brother to tears and induce in me all manner of unnamed terrors.

Along with *Aesop's Fables,* we were given Ben Franklin's essays to read from the very earliest, Ben being one of Grandpa's favorite people along with Jesus Christ, Mark Twain, Joe Louis, Franklin Roosevelt, and Abraham Lincoln. According to the older folks, Old Ben said everything best. What he said was as if chiseled in granite: Don't cry over spilt milk; Waste not, want not; Willful waste makes woeful want; A stitch in time saves nine; Don't pay too much for your whistle; Take care of your pennies and the dollars will take care of themselves; Don't put off till tomorrow what you can do today; A fool and his money are soon parted; and, perhaps the most instructive of all, Hunger is the best pickle. The essays containing these sayings seemed so relevant to the way we lived that it was hard to believe Ben Franklin had written them two hundred years before. What he had to say was just so sensible; Ben was talking to *us.*

One room in the house in Garrison was designated the library. Located on the north side of the house, it became a temporary storage space for jars of jelly, pears, and ground-cherries when the weather turned cold. The rest of the time it was a quiet spot for reading, well stocked with books my grandfather thought appropriate for us. The library contained a huge safe, a handsome mahogany bookcase with a bent-glass door, one chair, and, among other books, an 1890's set of *Encyclopedia Britannica.* Along with the Beacon Readers for beginners in school, we had the more challenging Young and Field Literary Readers, compiled for the fourth through the eighth grades. These were anthologies that included essays from famous writers, selections from the Bible, and Greek and Norse mythology presented in the language and style of educated people. We also had a selection of novels. *Little Women, Little Men, Freckles,* and *A Girl of the Limberlost* captivated me. I read these novels at least twice, as well as works by Dickens, Zane Grey, Lewis Carroll, Booth Tarkington, and Harold Bell Wright.

One whole shelf was devoted to the Horatio Alger series; there must have been over twenty volumes and I read them all. They were an inspiration to me and I blithely overlooked the fact that, for some peculiar reason, the heroes were always male. By contrast, we were forbidden to read *Peck's Bad Boy,* Nick Carter detective stories, and *True Story Magazine.* We read them anyway by sneaking them outdoors and then hiding them in the huge lilac bush. But we felt an immense guilt and shame about even this mild form of disobedience.

Besides having the library in our home, we were blessed with the loan of books from the library of the local physician. He allowed my brothers to borrow his books when they delivered the weekly *Saturday Evening Post* to his home. Through his collection we became familiar with the Radio Boys, the Bobbsey Twins, and Nan Sherwood.

Without knowing it, the adults in our lives practiced a most productive kind of behavior modification. After our chores and household duties were done we were given "permission" to read. In other words, our elders positioned reading as a privilege—a much sought-after prize, granted only to those goodhardworkers who earned it. How clever of them.

We read and learned poetry, a lot of it didactic. Grandpa gave my brothers a subscription to a magazine, *Boys' Life,* which was filled with inspirational poems that were easy to learn. I remember the first verse of one:

> *Standing at the foot, boys,*
> *Gazing at the sky.*
> *How can you get up, boys,*
> *If you never try?*

And so it went. Then there was this one:

> *Somebody said that it couldn't be done,*
> *But he with a chuckle replied,*
> *That "maybe it couldn't" but he would be one*
> *Who wouldn't say so till he'd tried.*
> *He buckled right in with the trace of a grin*
> *On his face. If he worried he hid it.*
> *He started to sing and he tackled the thing*
> *That couldn't be done,*
> *and he did it.*

We all learned that, and then my eldest brother found a parody of it which we happily chanted:

> *"Somebody said it couldn't be done,*
> *And the odds were so great, who wouldn't?*
> *He tackled the thing that couldn't be done,*
> *And what do you know? It couldn't!"*

Grandpa gave Jack a hard knuckle rap on the head for teaching that one to us Little Kids.

We read about Gunga Din as an example of dedication and

duty and memorized Kipling's "If." Another poem that I took to heart and still remember is the one called "Which Loved Best" by Joy Allison:

"*I love you, Mother,*" *said little John;*
Then, forgetting his work, his cap went on.
And he was off to the garden swing
Leaving his mother the wood to bring.

"*I love you, Mother,*" *said rosy Nell.*
"*I love you better than tongue can tell.*"
Then she teased and pouted full half the day
Till her mother was glad when she went to play.

"*I love you, Mother,*" *said little Fan.*
"*Today I'll help you all that I can;*
"*How glad I am that school doesn't keep!*"
So she rocked the babe till he fell asleep.

Then stepping softly, she took the broom.
And swept the floor and dusted the room.
Busy and happy all day was she;
Helpful and happy as a child could be.

"*I love you, Mother,*" *again they said,*
Three little children going to bed.
How do you think that mother guessed
Which of them really loved her best?

In this literature of our youth, the virtues of responsibility, hard work, honesty, and goodness were always rewarded. From the books and poems I read, I learned that it was up to me to make my own success. If I just applied my own will and determination, my own wits and wisdom, I could get what I wanted out of life. I was also responsible for my mistakes and failures. I was the master of my fate. I knew this was true because everything I read carried that message. As it says in Matthew 7:16, "Ye shall know them by their fruits. Do men gather grapes of thorns, or figs from thistles?" The implicit answer is "No," and I was exposed to no literature that contradicted the Bible, that indicated one could gather grapes from the thorn or figs from the thistle. The idea that good actions are rewarded, and bad punished, is a comforting fiction. As a child I needed to believe, and I honestly did believe, that life was like that. Even when confronted early in childhood with irrefutable evidence to the contrary, I tried to cling to the blessed and sustaining conviction that, somehow, life was fair. The literature I read told me so. I had plans to make a better life for myself, and I wasn't going to let a little thing like reality interfere.

7

Building Character: Religious Influences

We were, of course, a churchgoing family, and it would have been unthinkable for us children not to attend Sunday school when we were living in town. Although Grandma and Mama, neither of whom had any close friends outside of the family, attended church only sporadically, Grandpa always went, and took us with him. Like him, we children genuinely looked forward to the fellowship of church, and to frequent repetitions of the comforting belief that there existed a benevolent Being who watched over us.

The religious sentiment that pervaded our lives wasn't just a Sunday thing. If a farmer working in the fields saw a funeral procession going by on the road, he would stop his team or his John Deere tractor, and stand in respectful silence with his hat over his heart until the last car had passed. When we saw the moon for the first time at night, we would say, "I see the moon and the moon sees me. God bless the moon and God bless me." Then we would make a wish, assured that it had a pretty good chance of being granted if we had made a reasonable request. We said grace at the evening meal and a prayer before we went to sleep. "Now I lay me down to sleep, I pray the Lord my soul to keep. If I should die before I wake, I pray the Lord my soul to take." My sister and I would guard against the awful possibility that we might die after going to bed by also reciting,

> *"Little Lamb, who made thee?*
> *Dost thou know who made thee?*
> *Gave thee life and bid thee feed*
> *By the stream and o'er the mead;*
> *Gave thee clothing of delight,*
> *Softest clothing, woolly, bright."*

Then, with no apology to Blake, Mama repeated the question and supplied her own answer, which she taught us to repeat in unison:

> *"Little Lamb, who made thee?*
> *Little Lamb, God made thee!"*

For reasons that are not at all clear to me now, we found these lines comforting.

Some wag has described the Protestant hierarchy as follows: a Methodist is a Baptist who learned to read; a Presbyterian is a Methodist who went to college; and an Episcopalian is a Presbyterian who's made the social register. There were three churches in our little town of under five hundred people— Church of the Brethren, Methodist (where most of my family worshipped), and Presbyterian—and there were three more in the immediate surrounding rural area. Most, if not all, had been organized between 1858 and 1876. One would think that six churches ought to have been enough for such a small community. Even so, some souls, including Aunt Belle, journeyed all the way to Vinton, the county seat, seven miles away, so they could worship with a congregation that identified itself simply as the Christian Church.

Garrison developed on the side of a hill, and the geographical placement of the churches, from the top to the bottom, tended to reflect the social status of the parishioners—though the townsfolk would have reacted in horrified denial if anyone had ever pointed that out. There were no Episcopalians, while the Presbyterian and the Methodist churches were each located about halfway up the gentle slope, with the Presbyterians being on slightly higher ground than the Methodists, and the Brethren down below.

> *Lord, lift me up and let me stand,*
> *By faith on Heaven's table-land.*
> *A higher plane than I have found,*
> *Lord, plant my feet on higher ground.*

So goes an oft-sung hymn.

In 1926, because of a dwindling congregation, the Presbyterians voted to abandon their white clapboard church with its stained glass windows and join the Methodists in their solid red brick structure with its impressive bell tower and inspiring steeple. The Presbyterian church was later sold, torn down, and replaced by a private residence.

Most of the leaders of the community were members of the Methodist church. The banker, the postmaster, the principal of the school and nearly all of the teachers, the butter-maker at the creamery, the managers of the Garrison Supply Store and the Farmers Store, the blacksmith, the druggist, the agent at the railroad station, and the doctor were all Methodists, along with the owners of the pool hall, the barber and beauty shop, the Grain and Lumber Company, the hardware store, the grain elevator, and the Brick and Tile Factory. All of these people were considered to be pillars of the community; all were held up to us kids as examples to be followed.

Methodist church where Millie was baptized

Can you blame me for growing up thinking that Methodists were the epitome of success and society? It came as a real shock to discover, later in life, that not everybody held Methodists in the same high esteem as we did.

The special sense of security bestowed on me by belonging to this congregation was so strong that I always felt uneasy if I went to someone else's church. Once, I accompanied Aunt Belle to a mother-daughter banquet at the Christian Church in Vinton. After grace had been said, but before the food arrived, I noticed several ladies were going around the tables whispering something into the ear of each of the seated mothers and daughters. When it was my turn the lady whispered into my ear, "Are you a Christian?" So aware was I that I was in alien territory that I hastily responded, "No, I'm a Methodist!"

The Church of the Brethren was a simple, low-ceilinged, white clapboard construction, which was way down at the lower end of town, not far from the Brick and Tile Factory. Generally, it drew its congregation from the less educated segment of the community. We who belonged to the church on the higher geographical plane of Garrison felt just a tad superior to those who worshiped at the church at the lower end of town. Remember the hymn? While I never heard anyone say so, we enjoyed this subtle sense of superiority. Some called the parishioners Dunkards or River Brethren after their ritual of baptizing by total immersion, which was mildly disapproved of, as was their practice of ordaining as pastors ordinary members of the church whose sole qualification was that they had persuasive preaching powers. By contrast, a minister in the Methodist church had to have a minimum of four years of college. Further, the Brethren held tent revival meetings in the summer where hellfire preaching and loud praying ensued. Some of the more reserved Methodists, including our family, tended to think it was in poor taste to engage in such flamboyant emotional displays.

One steamy August evening, out of sheer curiosity, I joined an older friend of mine at one of those revival meetings. By the time we got there at seven o'clock, the congregation was already seated on the wooden folding chairs arranged in rows under a decrepit canvas tent that had been set up in a pasture near the church.

The service began. After the preacher greeted the flock, said some prayers, and delivered his sermon, we all sang some hymns. Following that, individual worshipers stood up and contributed short prayers.

At a certain point my friend Ruth stood up, head thrown back, eyes closed, and started addressing the Lord, her voice rolling out over the assembled sinners. Apparently everyone knew about Ruth. She was a charter member where praying was concerned. She never missed a revival meeting and people would say, "That Ruth Fyke! Boy, can she pray!" But I had never seen her in action.

On and on she went, recounting to the Lord how man wasn't rotten but his condition was, how sinful she was, how evil we all were, how we had fallen and how we had been helped up again, how all of us miserable sinners (she used those two words over and over again as if they were one word) were ever grateful to the precious Lord who would lead us into the ways of righteousness.

Her recitation of our sins was delivered in a kind of primitive rhythm with "Oh, Lord" interspersed with every pause and clause and at such a decibel it was as if she thought the Lord Himself was perched just over the hill. She carried on for such a long time that the rest of the assembled sinners got fidgety and began to stare at her. I was mortified. First of all, where did she get the nerve to cite me as such a sinner when I always, well, nearly always, tried so hard to be good? And how could she carry on in public like that?

Since I automatically exempted myself from the assembly (after all, these people weren't modest Methodists) I looked for a way to extricate myself from such an embarrassing display. I dropped to the grass on my hands and knees and started to creep down the row and out of the tent. My actions startled Ruth, and for a moment she interrupted her perorations. The preacher was quick-witted enough to take advantage of this brief pause to shout "Amen!" The congregation responded with their own "Amens" and started to sing.

I crept right on out of the tent and skedaddled home to the

sound of "Bringing in the Sheaves!" echoing out behind me through the hot summer night. That was the first and last revival meeting I ever attended and neither Ruth nor I ever mentioned it again.

The singing we did in our own church services was a good part of what I enjoyed about them. I especially loved the hymns: "The Old Rugged Cross," "Rock of Ages," "Someday the Silver Cord Will Break," "Let the Lower Lights Be Burning," "Sweet Hour of Prayer," "In the Garden," and many, many others. However, I was always troubled and a bit embarrassed by the crass materialism of "I'm the Child of a King." Why did God value all those houses and lands and the silver and gold? Nevertheless, I joined the congregation in the unabashed listing of all those riches. My naturally positive nature resonated to the solidly optimistic hymns we sang. We rocked the very rafters in our melodic assertion of the sunshine in our souls today and the wonderful words of life! I counted my blessings and named them one by one, promised not to yield to temptation, and was gladdened to learn how to keep the joy bells ringing in my heart. I am pretty certain that I can, even today, sing the first verse of at least forty hymns.

Churchgoing also gave me an excuse for getting all gussied up in my best clothes. Grandma made dresses for my sister and me out of cotton or wool, and our Sunday dresses had organdy or satin inserts in the yoke. If Grandma saw a style she liked in JC Penney's, she would create a pattern to copy it, for she liked our good clothes to be in the height of fashion. Avis and I were proud of that.

My sister and I had Sunday-best patent-leather "Mary Jane" shoes, which we polished with Vaseline to keep them from cracking. These were purchased for us once a year in the fall at the JC Penney's in Vinton for ninety-eight cents. Grandpa had heard that old J.C. would not hire anyone who used tobacco products, and that's why his store got most of our family's business.

In addition to the neatly ironed dress, the black patent-leather shoes, and the white ankle socks (long lisle stockings if the weather was cold), I wore little white cotton gloves and carried a purse containing a comb, a handkerchief with tatting decorating the edges, and one penny and one nickel that Grandpa gave to me. The penny was for Sunday school; the nickel was for the church collection plate. Not infrequently my sister and I would spend the penny on jawbreakers and bubble gum at Mrs. Quackenbush's sandwich shop located about a block from the church. We committed no such crime with the nickel, because during church service we sat in the pew beside Grandpa, who would be watching with his eagle eyes to see that we made our proper contribution. Since the money was "for the heathen" and since Grandma referred to us as "littleheathen," we joked that the penny went for its intended purpose. Deep in our guilty hearts, though, we knew that we were doing something quite wicked.

Sunday school started at ten o'clock before the church service. Besides providing us with a defense against Grandma's criticism of us as "littleheathen," we liked going because it gave us a chance to be with our friends. We would assemble in the noisy, concrete-floored church basement each week, the bigger kids sitting on wooden folding chairs, we little kids on small, bright red enameled chairs with rounded backs. Services were conducted by the minister's wife, assisted by the mothers of my friends. These minor saints did their best to teach us to pray, to sing, and to believe in the New Testament.

We learned the Twenty-third Psalm and the Lord's Prayer, and I'm afraid that more than a few of us recited, "Our Father who art in Heaven, Howard by Thy name" and were comforted that

"Surely Good Mrs. Murphy shall follow me all the days of my life." I know that I was embarrassed into uncharacteristic silence once when, on reading from a hymn book at Aunt Belle's house, I noticed that the words were "Weak and sinful though we be," not "We can sing full though we be," as I had been singing. I never told a soul of my discovery. When, years later, I heard about the little boy who came home from church and told his mother that he had sung all about a bear who was cross-eyed and whose name was Gladly, I harbored no doubt that the story was true. What understanding could a seven-year-old boy have of "Gladly, the cross I'd bear"?

During those mornings in Sunday School, the butter-maker's wife accompanied us on the black upright piano as we belted out our repertoire of children's hymns, which included "When He Cometh" (always sung on Children's Day), "Jesus Loves Me," "Jesus Wants Me for a Sunbeam," and "He Loves Me, Too." This last one proved problematic to me.

> God sees the little sparrow fall,
> It meets His tender view;
> If God so loves the little birds,
> I know He loves me, too.

I had questions. Why did He permit the sparrow to fall in the first place? What good does it do the sparrow if He allows it to die? I had seen lots of baby birds fall out of nests and I had never once observed that God was around to help them back to warmth and safety. And if He loves His little jewels so much, how come He didn't repair the heart of the blue baby that was born to the Kearneys? To my mind, the birds and the blue baby were being unreasonably abused. What happened to "As ye sow, so shall ye reap"? Mostly I was upset that so many good people had so many bad things happening to them: not just the blue baby born with a hole in his heart, but another baby, stillborn; the farmer, a nearby neighbor, killed when an angry bull pushed a John Deere tractor over on him; the fine fourteen-year-old son of my aunt and uncle drowned in a lime quarry near Garrison. I began to sense that all was not proper between God and Man and to further observe or conclude that God didn't exactly play fair.

After Sunday school, at eleven o'clock, we children emerged from the basement to join the congregation upstairs for church services. The highly polished oak pews gleamed and the bright, eastern sun illuminated the handsome stained-glass window all red, blue, and gold, featuring a long-haired, sweet-faced, grown-up Jesus. I yearned to be a part of this world and sublimated my doubts about the fairness of life in exchange for the comfort that enveloped me when the grown-ups smiled, greeted me warmly, and treated me with respect.

The children presented programs to the adults at Thanksgiving, Easter, Mother's Day, and Children's Day, but the Christmas programs were the real highlights of the year, suffusing the community in a flush of goodwill and merriment. We youngsters recited poems, put on plays, sang carols, made costumes, and got to stay up late. One program I remember with particular vividness included a partial reading of Dickens's *A Christmas Carol.* At the end, the Kearneys' two-year-old blue baby was carried onto the stage in the arms of one of his sisters. Everyone knew that this fragile boy, who had entered the world crippled by the hole in his heart, could barely speak above a whisper. The noisy congregation fell silent and leaned forward as he delivered his line: "God bless us"—pause to inhale—"everyone!"

The highlight of each Christmas program was the arrival of a properly outfitted Santa Claus with a sack of goodies to be distributed to the children. We all knew that the jolly man in the red suit and the white beard was the owner of the Standard Oil filling station. He was the fattest man in town and needed no stuffing materials. He knew everyone, and if you asked him for an extra bag of candy for a sick brother or sister, he would give it to you because he would already have heard about the illness. Inside the brown paper sack there were ribbons of slick candy, peppermint pillows, cherry, strawberry, lemon, and grape hard candies (some filled, some not), and jellied orange slices rolled in coarse sugar. Sometimes there would be chocolate drops, the old-fashioned kind with heavy white centers and a thin covering of bittersweet chocolate. Along with all of the candies there would be pecans, peanuts, and Brazil nuts in the shell, and, to top it all off, a Delicious apple and a navel orange. Remember, this lavish revelry occurred in midwinter during the harshest weather and the worst depression of the century, when grown men were selling apples on the streets to get enough money to feed their families, when one thought twice before spending even a dime, when poverty firmly strangled hope. The camaraderie and exquisite joy of an evening like this are all but impossible to convey today.

Then two events occurred that rocked our close community and contributed mightily to my skepticism. Two bankers absconded with all of the funds from the Garrison Bank, and a gentle reverend was murdered by a trapper who delivered a wallop to the back of his head with the butt of a shotgun. The reverend, who disapproved of killing animals for fur, had sprung snaggletoothed steel traps illegally set by the trapper to catch muskrats in that part of Platt Creek that ran through his farm. His two intelligent and charming daughters were my classmates in country school. I listened spellbound to the adults' graphic description of how the force of the blow popped the victim's eyes from their sockets and how he suffered for days before he could die. The bankers who only stole money were sentenced to serve twice the amount of time in jail as the murderer who had killed an innocent person— a man who was not only a reverend but also a loving husband and father. These two catastrophes and the disparity between the punishments nearly shattered my belief in the moral order of the universe as I had arranged it to my childish satisfaction.

When I was in seventh grade I felt even closer to losing my trust in a beneficent God presiding over a well-ordered universe when the mother of a classmate died after a self-induced abortion of her eighth or ninth pregnancy. Whispered words—"lead pencil" and "gangrene"—aroused questions, but there was no one who would offer answers. Why did God take Martha's mother? God wanted her in Heaven. But Martha and her brothers and sisters need her here now. When you grow older you'll understand. But I need to know now.

Many years later I knew immediately that I had found a poet who could speak for me when I discovered Emily Dickinson's haunting lines:

I shall know why—when Time is over—
And I have ceased to wonder why—
Christ will explain each separate anguish
In the fair schoolroom of the sky.

I tried my best to get along with adults and learned early on not to push them when they were explaining God's ways to man. The minister and his wife looked downright pained at my observations that a really good person would be unhappy in Heaven because of the knowledge of all those poor souls burning in Hell.

Wouldn't a really good person want to be sent to Hell to relieve that suffering?

Grandpa refused to engage in any religious discussions with me when I was a child. Years later, after I was married and discovered that one could have a beaker or two of Scotch whiskey without going to Hell, I discussed his near-total abstinence with him.

"But, Grandpa, even Jesus turned the water into wine at the wedding!"

"Well, I know He did! And that's the only thing I ever held against Him!"

It's probably a good thing that Grandpa wasn't alive in 1961 when a tornado toppled the bell tower of the church during Sunday morning worship. Two men were killed (one a cousin) and several worshipers were severely injured. Even Mama thought God had a little explaining to do on that one.

While the mysteries of faith still compel me, and I share the universal longing for certainty, what I have observed in the course of life has driven me far from organized religion. I have yet to arrive at either a final rejection or a final acceptance of what I was taught in those early years. But even as I continue to search for signs of a concerned and caring God, the comfort, hope, and inspiration that church provided me when I was growing up nourish me to this day.

8

Thrift

Use it up; wear it out; make it do; do without."
"Willful waste makes woeful want."

During the thirties, in Garrison and on that Iowa farm where land was plentiful but money was almost nonexistent, we never wasted a thing. We were raised in the habit of thrift. It pervaded our lives. This was partly due to the Great Depression and partly due to the fact that Grandma and Grandpa never completely made it into the twentieth century. They provided the example to us kids.

Imagine, if you will, the effect of observing Grandpa treat a toothache. He never considered going for professional help, for that would have meant investing time, energy, and gas to drive the fifteen-mile round-trip to Vinton to the dentist, who would then charge him four dollars for the visit. Grandpa's solution was to climb by ladder to the topmost shelf of the kitchen cupboard and retrieve a tiny, square, brown glass bottle bearing a bright red skull and crossbones and measuring no more than one and a half inches high. After carefully removing the glass stopper, he would dab some of the carbolic acid on a snippet of white cloth and, using a toothpick, touch it precisely to the root of his aching tooth. Whether that tincture destroyed the nerve or simply deadened the pain, I don't know, but it seemed to work.

Throughout our community there seemed to be a quiet competition to see who could be the most thrifty. When we broke an egg, we ran our forefinger inside the shells to retrieve every last bit of the white. We then placed the shells in the warming oven of the wood-burning kitchen range. When they dried to a proper brittleness, we tossed them to the chickens to increase their consumption of calcium. It was commonly thought that to toss undried shells to the chickens would encourage them to eat fresh eggs.

The desired complexion in those days was as pale and creamy as possible, which wasn't easy to achieve given all of the time we spent working out-of-doors. My mother, like most of the women around us, protected her skin from the sun by wearing a sunbonnet on her head and pulling long cotton stockings over her arms. Her fine white skin was her greatest vanity. We used tomatoes, both ripe and unripe, to soften and whiten our cheeks and hands. If sunbaked faces were out, freckles were even less desirable. So unpopular were freckles that it was considered acceptable to invest ten cents in a large lemon and another ten cents at the drugstore to buy some borax to eliminate such blemishes. The recipe is simple and amazingly effective, but I have decided not to include the precise proportions, for I think the ingredients are too harsh. Many females of the day applied a poultice of cooked warm oatmeal to their faces, neck, hands, and arms to effectively bleach and soften skin.

To eliminate pimples and cleanse our skin when we were teenagers, my sister and I would ritually slather a lightly beaten egg white onto our faces and allow about thirty minutes of drying time, during which we were not allowed to smile, laugh, or talk. Then we would wash the mask off with cool, fresh water. You know what? I still indulge in this beauty treatment now and then.

We also used a slightly beaten egg as a shampoo to make our hair shiny. There was only one precaution to follow: Always use cool water to rinse. A cousin once forgot this important step, rinsed with water warm enough to coagulate the egg in her hair, and ended up having to invest a couple of hours combing out the scrambled egg with a fine-toothed comb usually reserved for looking for nits.

At the end of a shampoo, we girls always used a couple of tablespoons of apple cider vinegar in the soft water rinse. It gave a bright, glistening shine to our hair.

We put to good use that ultrathin membrane that lines the inside of the eggshell. We kids frequently got wood splinters or slivers in our fingers, our feet, and sometimes on our butts. Breaking a fresh egg, we would carefully peel a small portion of the white membrane out of the shell and place it on the splinter. Usually, by the next morning the splinter would have been drawn to the surface, ready to be plucked out. Also, when placed on boils and pimples, the drying egg membrane produced a whitehead which could be pricked with a red-hot needle, releasing the infected matter. The adults used these treatments, too.

For larger or neglected boils, we had at hand still another remedy that did not require money to be spent at the drugstore or, God forbid, at a doctor's office. We pulled a fresh red beet from the garden, cut it in half and scraped it with a tablespoon until we had a handful, clamped it over the boil and covered the area with a white cloth bandage. The cloth bandage came from strips of worn-out sheets, of course. Again, usually, but not always, the drawing power of the beet would do its magic in a matter of a day or a night. If not, we just repeated the application.

Vinegar, salt, peroxide, and baking soda (Arm & Hammer, what else?) constituted a large part of our stock of drugs, and, with the addition of Bon Ami and wood ashes, our household cleaning supplies as well.

With baking soda we relieved our occasional bouts of indigestion, brushed our teeth, kept the silverware shining and the glassware bright and free from soap and hard water spots, and soaked the year-long accumulation of dust from the ninon curtains whenever spring cleaning rolled around. We also used baking soda to make a poultice for relief from the stings and bites of honeybees, yellow jackets, hornets, mosquitoes, and flies.

A never-fail recipe to remove any yellowed stains on trays, dishes, tables, or countertops was to mix equal parts of Bon Ami and cream of tartar into a paste with hydrogen peroxide. Apply the paste to the discolored area, leave on for thirty minutes, and then rinse thoroughly with clear water. I continue to use and recommend the recipe to this very day. It's extremely effective for discolored countertops in the bathrooms and the kitchen.

Vinegar was another useful item. Besides using it in canning and pickling, we mixed it with warm water and scrubbed the wooden furniture, floors, and stairs to make them fresh and shiny. We also mixed it with an equal amount of table salt, spread it on the bottoms of copper-bottomed pans, and, after a few minutes, gently scoured away any discoloration, leaving the copper gleaming. We wouldn't think of spending money to buy a commercial cleaner.

We were thrifty in ways our kids nowadays can't even imagine. Recycling was simply second nature to us. On the farm, we not only recycled but reused all bottles, paper bags, jars, and tin cans. The jars and bottles were used for canning, pickling, and other kinds of storage. The tin cans held everything from nails and paper packets of seeds for the next planting season to marbles, crayons, and dominoes. We also planted our geraniums, begonias, green peppers, and tomato plants in them. The seedlings we cultivated indoors gave us a head start on spring planting. We even rolled up last year's calendar, tied a ribbon around the middle, slipped the ribbon loop over the closet rod, and created another dress or shirt hanger.

We were taught that if you bought something it should last forever—or as close to forever as we could contrive. I think one of the cleverest tricks was how we extended the lives of socks. When the socks of the biggest child developed holes in the toes, Grandma, using her dressmaker's shears, would cut off the end, sew it closed on the sewing machine, and pass the socks down to the child next in size. When the socks developed holes again, she would repeat this until the sock had been passed down to the child with the smallest foot. You think that was the end of those socks? "Not on your tintype!" as she would have put it. She cut the ribbed tops off of those socks and they did duty sewn into the ends of sleeves of fall and winter jackets and coats to keep out the bitter cold.

Of course, there were times when the socks developed holes in the heels. This repair called for painstaking darning, always done by females and nearly always done during their so-called leisure time. But there was a limit to how often socks could be darned, and when they had been "all darned out" we were resourceful to the end. We cut them into small squares and tossed them into the shoe-shine box to be used for buffing cloths. Or we cut them lengthwise into two-inch widths and clamped them into the reusable mop handle designed for this purpose. We used a dry mop made of woolen socks for dusting and a wet mop of cotton ones for washing floors.

Years later I heard the story of the New England ladies who, when asked where they bought their hats, replied, "We *have* our hats!" I knew exactly where they were coming from.

In the kitchen there was no end to ways to save. During the spring and summer months when all hands were working hard at plowing, planting, and harvesting, we frequently had bacon for breakfast. After slicing the slab down to the rind, we removed the bacon strips, leaving a twelve-inch-square piece of fatty skin that we used to grease the hot iron skillet before we dropped in the pancake batter. After it had served in this way for a few days it was cut up and tossed to the pigs or the dogs. It probably goes without saying that we saved all of the grease left over from frying and used it to flavor the dressings that we put on everything from salads to biscuits.

We wouldn't think of washing a skillet that had been used to fry chicken, pork chops, hamburgers, or steak without first putting a quarter cup of water into the drippings, scraping the browned goodies from the bottom of the pan, and pouring the tasty liquid into a jar, where it was kept until we needed it to add to gravies, or to make a dressing for potatoes, green beans, or lettuce. I am saddened when I observe present-day cooks failing to make use of these drippings. They're missing the best part.

Grandma was the premier saver. Among her half-dozen needles, she had a fine one that was about one and one half inches long, which she used for quilting and turning cuffs and collars. (In the thirties, when the collar of a man's shirt became frayed you could extend the wear by simply removing it from the shirt and turning the frayed front to the unworn back. Since the introduction of channels for stays, you can no longer do that.) She kept all of her needles stuck into a red felt pincushion which she had owned since just before God. Anyone was welcome to use any of her needles with the single exception of the tiny quilting needle, her treasure. Then one day the needle "turned up missing," as she expressed it. She questioned the whole family; you would have thought she had lost her wedding ring. Finally, she calmed down, sat at the wooden kitchen table, and gingerly started pressing the sawdust-filled cushion onto the hard table edge. In a few minutes, from the depths of the pincushion she had pressed not just her precious tiny needle, but five others in a variety of lengths and thicknesses which had long since disappeared from use. Words could not describe her delight when she flashed her newly found hoard to the family.

Grandma kept her buttons in an oblong metal box covered by a weighted hinged lid bearing the picture of a horse-drawn sulky, and in capital letters, the name of the universally beloved horse, Dan Patch, who had died in 1916. The vintage box contained all sizes of mother-of-pearl buttons, from teeny buttons for a newborn baby's dress to huge buttons for a mother's blouse. There were also green, black, red, white, blue, brass, and silver buttons. There were even eight exquisite ceramic buttons of pink rosebuds with apple green leaves. For as long as anyone could remember, folks had been cutting buttons from worn-out clothing and popping them into that box. When we were really young, if we got sick enough to stay home from school, we were allowed to play with the buttons in the button box—a real treat.

After Grandma's death, when we were going through her things, the whole family got a huge teary laugh when one of us dug up a large multicolored ball of threads and string from the bottom of the woven reed sewing box she'd received from her sister, who'd been a missionary to China. Affixed to the ball by a black-headed pin was a small crumpled note on which she had written with a dull lead pencil: ALL ENDS—NO GOOD. It was her equivalent of "Pieces of String Too Short to Save."

Grandpa was no piker when it came to extending the useful life of an item. I still remember how he repaired the huge blue and white enamel canning kettle when it developed a hole in the curve just above its bottom. First he cut short a small smooth-topped bolt, just a tad larger than the hole, thrust it through the hole from the inside, and tightened a tiny washer and nut onto the outside. I marveled at his patience as I watched him painstakingly pound the washer to fit the slight curve of the bottom of the kettle before he installed it. Years later, when my husband and I were university students, we utilized this identical maneuver to repair a hole in the housing of the water pump of a Sears washing machine. Grandpa was visibly pleased with us when we reported that to him.

Equal ingenuity went into the production of wax. Yes, wax! Among his many accomplishments, Grandpa was a successful beekeeper. The hives he'd stationed out under a grove of plum trees provided us with wax as well as honey. During that decade, the winters were unbearably cold while the summers were punishingly hot. After draining the honey, Grandpa simply set the dry honeycomb on some hardware cloth spread over an empty Folgers coffee can and placed it in the sun. Sometimes it took a whole month to melt, at which point he would mold the wax into a ball that he could comfortably hold in his hand.

We kids dreaded the Saturdays during the winter when each of us had to take a turn at the numbing task of holding on to one end of the heavy linen thread while Grandpa held on to the other and, with maddening, deliberate thoroughness, waxed the cord with his homemade ball of honeycomb. This waterproof cord was used to repair gloves, shoes, jackets, caps, our single baseball, and even the harness for the horses.

Oh, and about those gloves. Cotton work gloves, which were bought in packages of a dozen, were indispensable for such chores as corn husking, plowing, splitting and stacking wood, pitching and hauling manure, and driving horses. Of the eleven people on those two farms, only one was left-handed. That meant that every now and then we would end up with about a dozen left-handed gloves, since the right-handed ones developed holes far more rapidly. It was Grandpa who solved that problem by the simple expedient of turning the left-handed glove inside out, thus creating a right-handed one. This procedure works for leather gloves, too.

Making do was another thrifty habit. If you didn't have a regular sharpener or whetstone handy and you discovered your knife had dulled, everyone knew that all you had to do to restore a quick, though temporary, razor-sharp cutting edge was to whet your knife on the unglazed rim of the milk crock. I still use this trick from time to time.

Every once in a while my children make fun of me for my "make-do" efforts. Not too long ago they called to ask if I could provide them with a level so that they could hang pictures on the walls of an apartment they had just moved into. Knowing that time was of the essence, I drove over to their apartment with an oblong perfume bottle almost full of water taped flat to a yard-stick, and showed them how they could use it as a level. For some reason they found this makeshift device fall-down-and-slap-your-hand-on-the-floor hilarious.

The clincher for thrift is what became of the horse, Old Mike, after his death. It happened around 1912, long before my time. Apparently he had been retired and was allowed to graze in the orchard and on the grasses of the woods, generally living a well-earned life of leisure. He'd become a family pet; his only real job was to take my mother in a surrey to the rural school where she was teaching.

Then, at the age of twenty-nine, in the middle of an exceptionally cold winter, which had caused him to grow a luxurious coat to protect against the brutal weather, Old Mike died. Grandpa skinned him and sent his hide to a tanner in Muscatine, Iowa, who made it into a truly handsome robe backed by black wool and trimmed with green felt. Grandpa told me that he had paid fifteen dollars to have this done. That robe was used in the car in the winters by Grandpa and Grandma until after their deaths, by Mama wherever she needed it, and then by me to place on the floor in front of the living room fireplace after I grew up, married, and had children. Sometime around 1980 it started to shed a lot of those lovely dark brown hairs, and I finally had to abandon Old Mike.

9

Medicine

Since professional medical care was all but absent from our lives, children as well as adults knew a great deal about home remedies. If, for example, one of us kids was attacked by bees of one kind or another—stings from wild honeybees, bumblebees, yellow jackets, sweat bees, and hornets were a regular part of life on our farm—we all knew enough to apply baking soda, black mud, or earwax to relieve the excruciating pain. If we developed a canker sore on a tongue we knew just the thing to do: Harvest a green pepper from the garden, chew it well, but don't swallow it. The chewed pepper relieved the smarting pain in an instant. We still resort to this instant cure when anyone gets a mouth sore. In the wintertime when we lived in Garrison and there were no green vegetables, we used a crystal of alum to relieve canker sores, but green peppers taste better than alum and I'll take the green pepper cure over alum any day.

Perhaps because of our storehouse of knowledge, parents were remarkably complacent about all the injuries that were a routine part of the lives of free-range farm children—cuts from knives (which even six-year-old kids routinely incurred), stone bruises caused by bare feet on rocks, blood blisters, and all the bloody, oozing scrapes on knees, arms, elbows, and thighs. When one of us kids received a scratch, cut, or puncture, we didn't run to the house to be taken care of. Nobody would have been interested. We just went to the barn or the corncrib, found a spiderweb, and wrapped the stretchy filament around the wound. It stopped the bleeding and the pain, and was thought to have antiseptic qualities. Generally, healing occurred without further attention. Skin has got to be one of God's greatest creations.

We took care of ourselves for more serious injuries, too. Every home in our area had Vaseline, lard, baking soda, boric acid, salt, camphor, alum peroxide, Vicks, Mentholatum, tincture of iodine, and, some few years later, Mercurochrome. The peroxide may have been the most commonly used of these remedies. Because we went barefoot all summer it was not unusual to suffer cuts from double-bitted axes, broken glass, barbed wire, or rusty nails. If we got cut or stepped on a nail, we "bubbled the poison out" by pouring a bit of peroxide on it, and it usually healed in a couple of days. Local lore also maintained that a chaw of tobacco applied to a deep cut could draw out the poison. We sought relief from the painful throbbing of stone bruises by soaking the foot in extremely hot water twice a day. But there was nothing to do about blood blisters. They just disappeared by themselves, though they were sometimes painful for a very long time. It was a miracle that none of us kids ever broke a bone, and we rarely developed life-threatening infections.

One truly frightening day out in Yankee Grove, when my brother slashed his leg with a glancing blow of his ax, I saw my grandfather burn his handkerchief to get fresh charcoal to apply to the cut to stop the bleeding. Grandpa did one of his horses that same courtesy when the animal got fearfully entangled in some barbed wire and suffered deep wounds in his fetlock. Not one of us ever received a tetanus shot, though for a couple of weeks one summer we discussed, in appropriately funereal tones, the death of a neighbor's horse from lockjaw. The animal developed the infection from a barbed wire injury and had to be put down.

I myself developed a quite serious infection one summer. I remember whimpering all night, half awake and half asleep, from a fearful pain coming from the toe pad beneath my big toe and the one next to it. When I showed it to Mama the next morning, she responded in an uncharacteristic manner. She actually sprang into action. Pointing to a distinct red line running from between my toes almost up to my knee, she diagnosed blood poisoning. Did she call a doctor? No. In a trice, she poured boiling water into the white enameled foot pan and, once it had cooled somewhat, had me soak my foot for a very long time. When she was satisfied that the stone bruise was soft enough, she used a razor blade to cut a tiny gash deep into the tough, swollen, bluish area, until lots of bloody pus oozed out. The pain diminished immediately. With that she poured the ubiquitous, all-purpose peroxide on it, and wrapped my foot in a bandage made from worn-out white sheets or shirts. After several days of soaks followed by the deft use of the razor blade to keep the wound open and a post-nick flush of peroxide, the red streak gradually disappeared.

During that period, I was a bit of a celebrity, for blood poisoning was something that Big Kids and Little Kids alike knew was a serious enough matter to warrant the attention of adults. Further, I had the distinction of being granted official layabout status. In a family where Industriousness was second only to Godliness, this was a highly desirable state, and I had come by it honestly. Had I been suffering as a result of a gluttonous indulgence in green apples or a casual disregard of an unstable pile of wood, such carelessness would have elicited no solicitousness whatsoever. But this condition was not my fault. By common consent of the adults, I was exempt from all chores and all family responsibilities, and was permitted to reign in the high-backed rocking chair in the kitchen and read to my heart's content. My enforced sloth was the envy of all of the kids.

Many of the home remedies that were the order of the day came from a thick, heavy book called the *People's Home Library*, an impressive compendium of lore on the treatment and medication of people and livestock, and on domestic science or cooking and household management. Now in an exceedingly dilapidated condition, it has been in our family since 1920, and is currently in my possession.

In almost any gathering of women, some part of the conversation focused on a debate about the various remedies. Was the best sassafras tea made from the bark, the root, or the actual wood of the tree? Should the onions for a chest poultice be baked or fried? And which would draw a splinter out the quickest—the delicate membrane from the inside of an eggshell, or a piece of salt pork?

Much discussion was devoted to the efficacy of the popular patent medicines. I recall several: Carter's Little Liver Pills, Dr. Pierce's Pleasant Pellets, Dr. Pierce's Golden Medical Discovery and Lydia Pinkham's Vegetable Compound. All of these creations were praised and widely used. A search in the *People's Home Library* yielded the formula for Lydia Pinkham's concoction. Among other things, it calls for partridge berry vine, cassia, cramp and poplar bark, unicorn root, sugar, and alcohol.

The *Home Library* also reveals the recipe for Dr. Pierce's Golden Medical Discovery. Besides honey, tincture of digitalis, and extract of acrid poisonous lettuce (herba lactucae virosae, popularly known as "false opium" because the milky juice of the lettuce possesses opiate or soporific qualities), that miraculous remedy contained alcohol (64 percent) and laudanum (opium). Now note this: Dr. Pierce's miracle medicine was recommended for "chronic weakness and other complaints of women," which meant that three times a day, ailing females were dosed with a slug of alcohol, tincture of digitalis, a dash of laudanum, and an opiate-like extract from wild lettuce. Oh, joy! Oh, rapture unforeseen!

Tucked among the pages of this tome of household helps, I discovered a separate quaint publication: a slim forty-five page booklet describing, among other things, various maladies and their cures. Entitled *Memorandum and Discount Book Designed for Farmers, Mechanics and All People,* the booklet measures three and a half inches by five and a half inches and was published in 1884 and 1885 by the same man, Dr. R. V. Pierce. Dr. Pierce also created and sold some of the patented medicines referred to in the *People's Home Library* and operated The World Dispensary and Invalid Hotel in Buffalo, New York.

Fortunately I had the foresight to make and keep a copy of the booklet, but it wasn't until my own children were grown that I took the time to peruse the contents to see why we kids were not permitted to view its pages. Among the forbidden items is a brave, solemn, and, to the present-day reader, hilarious, discourse on "a startling weakness...a nervous and general debility, the baneful and ruinous results of Certain Solitary Indiscreet Practices of the Youth of Our Land." Dr. Pierce catalogues the results of "these vices" as follows: "a desire for solitude, languor, mental anxiety, gloomy forebodings, melancholy, impaired memory, physical debility and indigestion." The list goes on to enumerate the debilitating drain such vices make on the "vital fluid" or "life principle." The good doctor then issues this comprehensive indictment: "To this secret drain on the system may be attributed the cause for a large proportion of all cases of palsy or paralysis, apoplexy, epilepsy, softening of the brain, convulsions, insanity and loss of nervous and muscular power." The modern reader's response is likely to be a lighthearted, "But I was cautioned only that it would make me go blind."

The intimate tone of Dr. Pierce's booklet assures the reader that all of his communications are "sacredly confidential," that all medicines he prescribes are vegetable-based, perfectly harmless, fast-acting, and effective, and that there is no reason to consult with other doctors. Advertised in the *Memorandum and Discount* booklet, for those men seeking this delicate information, are additional publications by the good doctor. *The People's Common Sense Medical Adviser* could be purchased for one dollar and fifty cents; the pamphlet *Abuse of the Male Reproductive Organs and the Diseases to Which It Gives Rise* could be had by simply sending a stamp for postage.

All of us kids came down with pinkeye, chicken pox, red and German measles, and mumps at one time or another. My brothers suffered most from chicken pox, while I nearly died from the red measles when I was seven or eight years old. I was ill for over a month, and "out of my head" for half of it, but I have several distinct memories from that shadowy time. I was permitted to sleep in a bed alone; my aunt from the farm across the road placed a bouquet of beautiful pink peonies by my bedside; and every time I regained consciousness, Grandpa would be at my side offering a spoonful of scraped apple and urging me to eat. Apparently the doctor had been summoned but he said that my left lung had collapsed and that he had no way of treating that condition. After I grew up, my aunt told me that Grandma probably saved my life by forcing me to lie on my right side so that the left lung would reinflate.

Colds were a part of life in the winter and were treated the old-fashioned way by rubbing the chest with Mentholatum, or Vicks VapoRub. Earaches were sometimes relieved by having an obliging uncle blow warm tobacco smoke into the ear and then plugging it up with cotton. Anyone, young and old, who developed a severe upper respiratory infection could look forward to having a flannel packet of hot, fried yellow onions and goose grease placed on the chest. This poultice was considered the ultimate in cures but we kids all hated it, for the smell enveloped you like a thick cloud the next day at school, inviting unkind remarks from classmates.

When we had a long bout with a cold, we were made to eat onions baked in ashes—a treasured remedy of the oldest generation. After the fire had been banked for the night, an ancient great-aunt would bury whole, large, unpeeled yellow onions in the ash box of the kitchen range, where the residual heat lasted long enough that the onions would be totally cooked through by morning. Everyone who was coughing was offered a portion for breakfast. The old folks loved them; all of us kids hated them.

What we kids loved was Aunt Belle's horehound candy and cough syrup. We all swore that these concoctions worked. Years after I grew up, I asked Aunt Belle to give me the recipe. Take a double fistful of horehound pulled from the garden, she always said (I could never pin her down more specifically about the amount). Then:

> Put the horehound, either fresh or dried, in a pot with
> three cups of water, and boil for twenty or thirty minutes.

Let the pot set until cool, then strain the leaves out. Add enough water to what is left of the horehound liquid to make three cups. Place in a pan with seven cups of brown sugar. Stir. Boil until a hard, but pliable, ball forms when one half teaspoonful of it is dropped in very cold, but not ice, water. (Modern cooks will remove the syrup from the heat when a candy thermometer reads 250° to 266°.) Pour into a buttered cookie sheet with a rim. Cut into one-by-two-inch squares when partially cooled. Roll in granulated sugar. If you want horehound syrup instead of candy, simply reduce the boiling time.

Some of the home cures we used sound like voodoo, none more so than our various wart removal remedies. I think there is no way to convince anyone who had not been a participant in the procedure that such treatments could work. But I personally had an amazing success with one of the wart removal rituals. When I was about thirteen years old, I served as the hired girl to a farm family of six children. Both hands of the eight-year-old son were covered with ugly warts. I had heard Aunt Belle describe how to cure warts, so with unwarranted assurance I offered to remove the offending blemishes from Melvin's hands. He agreed to do as I said. Following Aunt Belle's instructions, I peeled a medium-sized potato, took it out into the middle of the dirt road that ran by the farmhouse, placed it on a flat stone that we had put there, and stomped the potato flat. Then we went back to the house and—this part was considered crucial to the healing process—agreed not to look at the stone or to visit the site for two weeks. The theory was that as the potato on the stone disintegrated, the warts would vanish. Each day we looked at Melvin's hands. By the end of the first week the warts started to disappear. By the fourteenth day his hands were completely smooth. Believe it or not, this is a true story.

Another such event took place when my husband and I were at the University of Iowa and I took him to Van Horn, a tiny town in Benton County, to introduce him to my grandfather's oldest sister. We found her weeding in her garden decked out in a voluminous print dress covered by a checked gingham apron, up to her waist in larkspur, foxgloves, Canterbury bells, snapdragons, lilies, and zinnias. Delighted to see us young folks, she threw back her sunbonnet and started chatting. About the first thing she noticed was that my husband had three large warts on the side of his index finger. Without pausing in our conversation, she removed a dressmaker's straight pin from the right side of her apron, handed it to my husband, and said, "Now, you don't want those warts, do you? Here, you take this pin and give your warts to me." Without missing a syllable that garrulous old doll continued our discussion with no further reference to the matter. About three hours later, on our way back to the university, we were both astonished to discover that the three warts had all but disappeared. Within a few days, there was not a sign of them. I have no logical explanation to offer for the success of this strategy or for the one I myself used. All I know is that they worked.

When I was a child it was assumed that virtually all conditions could be treated by a home remedy. We children heard our parents discuss everything from how to remove freckles on faces and brown spots on hands (apply white vinegar or boiled oatmeal) to how to handle the body of a person who had just died (begin by stuffing cotton balls or cloths into all orifices). We children never had any firsthand experience with human dead bodies, but we certainly found that bit of information fascinating.

In a very real way we felt that possessing such a large treasure chest of knowledge about taking care of ourselves, from birth to death, was empowering. Many, many years later my family reaped the benefits of all that down-home wisdom when our two-year-old son had the misfortune to swallow a bobby pin while he was being cared for by a baby-sitter. By then I was living the antiseptic life that was considered normal in those times. I had left the farm, embraced the germ theory of disease, accepted the verifiable fact that doctors were necessary and reliable, and considered myself several notches more sophisticated than my country cousins, who were still relying on home remedies. Immediately after the baby-sitter told us about the bobby pin, my husband and I rushed our son to the university hospital. In the fluoroscope, we watched the pin being thrown at the pylorus— the opening from the stomach into the small intestine—over and over again. There was a real danger that the pin would perforate the stomach. But the surgeon was hesitant to perform major surgery, which would necessitate general anesthesia, on such a young child. The decision was to wait two weeks, and fluoroscope the child every day to check on the position of the pin. Day after day we watched the pin being thrown hundreds of times at the opening; day after day we were disappointed in noting the failure of the pin to pass out of the stomach.

The situation was now getting dangerous, for we surmised that the stomach acids had dissolved the thin plastic that coated the metal pin, which meant that we could no longer take comfort that the coating might offer a tiny bit of protection against the threat of perforation. About ten days had passed and surgery appeared inevitable. Then I got a bright idea: Call back to Garrison and see if one of the old codgers could come up with a solution. It was Aunt Belle who suggested we feed Greg mashed potatoes and sauerkraut. It turned out that Greg loved mashed

potatoes and sauerkraut, and it also turned out that very young
children do not readily digest sauerkraut. On the magical, mysti-
cal third day, the bobby pin, entangled in the undigested sauerkraut, was pulled through the pylorus and passed safely through
the intestines and out of the body. It was the most beautiful
bowel movement I have ever seen. Of course, the happiest part of
all was that a two-year-old escaped the trauma of general anesthesia and major surgery.

I thought I had a pretty thorough knowledge of home remedies from my childhood, but in my early twenties and newly married I learned about yet another from my European-born
mother-in-law. I arrived at her house for a visit, suffering from an
acute upper respiratory infection, a weakness that had plagued
me all through my early teens. The dear lady at once saw my mis-
ery and announced that she had a cure for me. Putting me into
bed, she had me lie on my stomach with my blouse off and
hauled out a worn, soft black leather bag filled with small glass
bottles—twenty-four in all. While she held four or five of the tiny
bottles in one hand, she used the other to dip a fourteen-inch-
long, cloth-tipped wire into alcohol and set the cloth on fire.
After she put the flame to the mouth of each of the bottles to
burn off the oxygen and create a vacuum, she quickly clamped
the bottles to my upper back. She repeated this process until all
twenty-four bottles were securely attached to my back. Highly
amused by this antiquarian procedure, known as cupping, my
sixteen-year-old sister-in-law, my husband, and I periodically
erupted into giggles and laughter while my very serious mother-
in-law was doing her work. But as soon as she covered me with a
heavy flannel blanket, I fell asleep as if drugged and slept through
the night. The next morning my health was greatly improved. I
must also add that the bruise-blue polka dots that the vacuum

bottles had left on my back remained there for weeks. I've gotten a lot of mileage out of this story, for I am the only person I know who has had the benefit of such a remedy. We still have the cupping kit and will give it to a medical museum.

And there you have it. We may no longer rely on foxglove, May apple, ginseng, burdock, goose grease, fried onions, and other natural substances for our ailments, but there is much valuable relief still to be found in home remedies, even if we have no idea how they work.

My own present position on home remedies is much like that of the Irish lady who, when asked if she believed in fairies, replied, "Of course not! But they're there all the same!"

10

Chores

The continuity and stability of family life was absolutely dependent on the fact that all of us kids did the chores that were expected of us. Both in Garrison and on the farm, our duties were posted on a hook behind the kitchen range. Usually two of us were assigned to each task, and tasks were rotated. We were responsible for setting and clearing the table; washing, drying, and storing the dishes; getting wood and corncobs up from the cellar or in from the woodpile; carrying drinking and cooking water in from the windmill; filling the reservoir with soft water from the cistern; and carrying out the slop. Ugly word, that. Since we had no indoor plumbing, we had to dump our waste water into a five-gallon bucket. In town, when the bucket was full, the slop was carried out to the edge of the property and dumped into a large drainage ditch behind the garage; on the farm, it was carted down to the hog house and dumped into the swill barrel, where it would eventually be ladled into the troughs for the pigs to drink.

There were sure consequences for neglecting to do one's chores. For instance, fuel for the kitchen stove had to be brought in the night before so that Mama could start a fire in the morning and the day's cooking could begin. That meant that every night someone had to gather small and medium-sized sticks from the grove behind our house. If Mama discovered there was no kindling, the kid who had forgotten to gather it the night before was rousted out of bed forthwith and made to go out and get it.

It was Grandma who insisted that we all learn to start a never-fail fire. Here's her method:

> Loosely crumple a half sheet of newspaper and place it in the firebox. Lay about twelve sticks the size of a pencil in a teepee pattern over the paper, and place four dead sticks about half the size of a man's wrist over all. Now top the whole pile off with two or three dry white sticks of split maple or other hardwood about eighteen inches long, and touch a lighted match to the crumpled paper. (We used Blue Diamond matches, kept in a glass jar in the cupboard.) A quick, bright fire is guaranteed.

When the snow kept us from gathering dead sticks, we had a secret weapon. Grandpa, ever one to plan ahead, kept kerosene-soaked corncobs stuffed in an old Folgers coffee can on the floor behind the kitchen stove, always ready for use in a pinch.

In our early years, all four of us kids would help with the after-supper cleanup in Garrison: clearing the table, filling the dishpan with warm soft water from the reservoir, scalding the draining dishes with boiling water from the gigantic stainless steel teakettle, washing and drying the dishes, and putting them away in the kitchen cabinet. In the winter, we even did the dishes at the noon meal, which we called dinner. We ran home the three blocks from school, ate, washed and dried the dishes, and ran back to school—all between twelve and one o'clock.

A serendipitous outcome of this dishwashing activity was that all of us kids became excellent spellers, for Mama used our time at the sink to test us on the list of one thousand words that were on each year's *Des Moines Register*'s statewide spelling contest.

On the farm, children were drafted into the workforce early. Even the youngest could pull radishes, pick and shell peas and beans, harvest strawberries, and help wash vegetables. Tiny tots were taken along to the garden whenever an adult went, and they simply followed the example before them. They seemed to have a natural inclination to be useful and, of course, the praise they received encouraged them no end.

My sister and I found washing the take from the farm garden to be a special delight. Immediately after harvesting the vegetables we would go to the windmill, which was not far from the house, pump fresh water onto them, and clean them with a brush that we kept hanging on the pump along with the tin cup for drinking. On the green grass by the mill we would husk and desilk the sweet corn, look over the oak leaf lettuce for tiny jade green inchworms, remove the tops from the carrots and radishes, and scrub the new potatoes; then we would rewash everything and tote the dishpan of veggies, spanking clean, to the kitchen. We didn't have to clean up our leavings, because the sheep and the two retired horses that had the run of the huge yard would soon make short work of the garden debris.

Not all chores were this pleasant. As we got a little older, all of us kids, from the littlest to the biggest, were assigned to pull milkweed, morning glories, and button weeds out of the oat, corn, and bean fields. If left unhindered, morning glory vines would seriously entangle the plow, and the button weed would impede the growth of other plants, especially the soybeans. We could work only two or three hours at this backbreaking job. Our backs ached, our hands grew sore, and we sweated profusely even though we wore straw hats to shield us from the furious Iowa sun. My perhaps faulty memory of this onerous task was that we received a nickel for a bushel basket of weeds.

Another group endeavor was handpicking green beans for the canning factory in Vinton. The only bad part of bean picking was that we couldn't start until midmorning, after the sun was hot enough to have dried the dew, because an unsightly rust would form on the beans if they were picked while they were still damp, making them unacceptable at the canning factory. Other than the heat we all enjoyed bean picking, Little Kids and Big Kids alike. Of course the Big Kids largely ignored us Little Kids, but they tolerated us and we got to listen to their jokes and their conversation, which seemed quite interesting and grown-up to us. The absolute best part of our efforts in the bean fields was that we were paid twenty-five cents a bushel: a veritable fortune.

Another activity we all did together, Mama included, was shocking oats. The men and Big Kids used a horse-drawn binder to cut and tie the fully ripe oats into bundles or sheaves tied with twine. Standing six or eight bundles cut side down and close together, we topped the shocks off with an odd sheaf. Grandpa insisted the protective capping sheaf be placed with the oat heads facing west since that was the direction most of the wind and storms came from and they would not blow off so easily.

During one of those summers in the thirties when the temperature was cruelly hot—the thermometer would register 112 in the daytime and fall to only 95 at night—Mama had a novel idea about when to do the oat shocking. As we were finishing our supper one night she said, "Look, there's a harvest moon. What say we all go out and finish shocking oats? There're not many bundles left, and we won't have to scorch doing it tomorrow."

So we all trekked out to the forty-acre field that lay just beyond our house yard, and shocked oats beneath the moon. In Iowa, a giant full moon in August is magic. It truly "doth shine bright as day," just as the child's poem says. I have nothing but happy memories of that evening and several others like it during those fierce summers of my youth.

Though certain work was usually thought of as man's work, on our farm, everyone, male, female, and kids, lent a hand to get the job done. Women, if circumstances required, could be counted on to help load hay into the haymow, shock oats or wheat, and don a corn-husker and work gloves to handpick a field of corn that had become too rain-soaked to accommodate the heavy McCormick Deering mechanical picker. The same was true of "women's work." There were times when men helped women can meat, assisted in an extra-heavy wash, lent a hand at making apple or plum butter, and took a turn at the churn. When work needed to be done, it didn't matter whether the worker wore pants or a skirt.

Haying, the term we used for harvesting red and white clover, timothy, and alfalfa (food for our livestock), was sheer hell for everyone involved. And in our family everyone was involved: men, women, Big Kids, Little Kids. Choosing the right day to mow was crucial, for at least three consecutive days of hot, dry weather had to follow. Hay that had too much moisture in it would mildew, and the animals would not eat it. Even worse, spontaneous combustion could occur, causing the entire stash to smolder, blacken, and nearly catch fire, totally ruining the winter's food supply. This happened on a neighbor's farm, much to the fascination of us Little Kids. For about a week, black wisps of smoke emanated from every crack and crevice of the barn. It was such an eerie, awesome sight that the entire county turned out to have a look.

Once the weather conditions were deemed propitious, the men and one of the Big Kids would cut the hay with a horse-drawn mower. Another Big Kid would follow with a side delivery rake, an implement designed to cast the hay into a long row called a windrow. Now it was time for earnest prayer. Dear God, please, please, for the next few days let the sun shine, let the humidity be low, and don't let it rain. Please, please, please.

After a few good drying days, the real work began. Since the barn on our little farm was outdated and dilapidated, and we were in residence only half of the year, the hay was stored in the fine red barn on our aunt and uncle's farm directly across the road, where it was needed to feed the horses and cattle all winter. A hay-loader, which was attached to the back of a horse-drawn wagon called a hayrack, gathered the hay from the field and conveyed it onto the wagon. When the rack was sufficiently full, one of the Big Kids drove the wagon to the barnyard across the road where the hay would be transferred to the mow or loft—a sheltered space that exists inside and at the top of the barn, similar to the attic of a house.

Often one of the women performed the activity called "stick the fork." Standing at the edge of a load of hay, the fork sticker would step aside as a murderously heavy hay fork plummeted from the peak of the barn, gravity driven, deep into the hay. Next, she secured a latch that locked the load onto the fork and shouted a signal to the Big Kids stationed in the upper reaches of the barn that a forkful of hay was ready to be delivered.

This was the moment when another horse-drawn vehicle—the

sturdy, two-wheeled cart that supplied the power to lift the hay from the rack into the mow—went into action. The intricately designed link between the cart and the hay fork was a double length of rope, threaded through a series of strategically placed pulleys, which ran from the hay fork at one end, up to the peak of the mow, across the full length of the interior of the barn, front to back, and down the exterior wall to the ground where it was tied to a huge iron hook attached to the back of the cart. When we heard the shout indicating that the fork was set, one of the Little Kids down in the barnyard would say "Git up," the Big Kid who was driving the cart would guide the patient retired horses away from the barn, and we Little Kids would walk barefoot in their wake, ready to play our assigned role in the farmyard pageant.

Once the hay fork reached its destination high in the mow, one of the Big Kids up there would holler and we Little Kids stopped the team on its outward journey, about fifty feet from the barn. At that point, a second shout from the Big Kids signaled the fork sticker to pull the rope that tripped the latch on the fork, releasing the hay, which the Big Kids distributed using giant pitchforks. Of all the rotten tasks that were part of haying, being assigned to that windowless, almost airless, excruciatingly hot loft was the worst. We Little Kids were frequent witnesses when the Big Kids staggered out of its dark confines, exhausted and near to passing out. We hurt for them.

But we had our own trials to bear. Each time the horses came to the end of their little journey from the barn, this was our cue to detach the rope and hook from the cart so that the horses could turn around and go back to the starting place without becoming entangled in the rope. Carrying those items back to the barn was onerous work for us, for the iron hook was heavy and the rope irritated our hands and arms. The scorching sun beat down on us all day long as we trod back and forth in the dusty barnyard, and there were times when I thought I might faint. However, we did have a proud sense of achievement, knowing that we were doing our part in this important venture.

The whole family worked all day in this manner until all of the hay from the fields had been gathered and as much of it as possible stored in the mow. The hay that could not be stowed there was stacked in the barnyard.

When dusk came after a day like this, Mama would fetch a steaming kettle of water from the kitchen stove and bring it out to the porch where, during the summer months, we set up a washing station which consisted of a wooden bench, an enamel wash basin, clean towels, a mirror, and a pail of fresh water for drinking or to temper the hot water. She started with us girls, giving us a soaping from head to toe and sending us, towels and nightgowns in hand and naked as jaybirds, across the grassy lawn to the windmill. Once there, Sis and I pumped pails of refreshing cold water and doused each other all over until we fairly tingled. After we dried ourselves, we donned our cotton nighties and ran back to the house and up to bed. We would be dead to the world in minutes.

Then the boys soaped themselves at the basin and they had their turn at rinsing with the cool, clean water from the mill. It was an altogether satisfying closure to our day.

When Grandma learned of this audacious ceremony, she tore into us, using her favorite term "littleheathen." "A body'd think you had no upbringing," she proclaimed. "They'd think that you'd been peed on a stump and hatched by the sun."

Grandma's displeasure merely reinforced our child-centered belief that all was as it should be. The exhausting labors of our day, the soothing soaping with warm water, the exquisite drenching with the cold fresh water, and the donning of the clean cotton nighties at the end of the ritual bonded us so completely to one another and to Mama that there was no room for such a critic. Grandma was, quite properly, outside of our summertime world.

Getting a chicken ready for the supper table was another of those jobs that we kids could do. As a matter of fact, preparing meals was part of the daily chores. From the age of about eight, all of us kids, boys and girls alike, knew how to snatch a chicken by both legs from a feeding flock, having lured it to the spot with a pan of cracked corn, and then how to quickly dispatch the frantic fowl with a hand ax. We had several methods, but the preferred one was to grasp the legs and the wing tips in the left hand, lay the head of the chicken on the chopping block, stroke the top and the back of the head gently a couple of times, and then deal the fatal blow with the ax. The stroking has a hypnotic effect on the bird, soothing it so it will remain absolutely still. Once the head is chopped off, you release the chicken, allowing it to flop wildly about the barnyard until it stops of its own accord. And now you know the origin of the expression "running around like a chicken with its head cut off."

All of us kids knew how to proceed with readying the chicken for supper once we'd killed it. Before you ever went out to the barnyard to select the unfortunate fowl, you had made sure that there was a teakettle of boiling water ready for the next step. While you waited for the chicken to stop thrashing around you poured the boiling water into a galvanized bucket. Then you grabbed the chicken by the legs and dipped the body up and down in the water. Once this was done, you simply stripped the smelly, wet feathers from the fowl. The next part of the job required the help of one of the other kids. Taking a double layer of newspaper, one of us lit a match to it while the other held the naked chicken just high enough over the flame so that the hairs were singed off. This singeing required great care but it had to be done. At this stage you brought the chicken indoors for the disjointing.

Now, with a sharp butcher knife, you cut through the rear end and drained the intestines out onto a clean cutting board. Here you had to separate the gizzard, the heart, and the liver. You learned how to carefully cut the bubble of green bile from the liver without rupturing it, or else its vile taste would ruin the liver. You also learned to cut open the gizzard and skillfully peel the inside membrane away without spilling the malodorous contents. The giblets were much sought-after at the table when suppertime came. We ate a lot of chicken and that is why everyone had to know how to prepare one for the table. Our favorite supper was fried chicken, fried potatoes, salad with sour cream, corn on the cob, and thick slices of tomatoes.

The traditional chores for boys on a farm are fairly familiar, but the duties required of girls are not so well documented. By and large, housekeeping chores were done weekly: Girls were expected to make beds, do dishes, set the table, prepare meals, sweep, dust, mop, and wax floors, and do the washing, ironing, and mending.

On our hands and knees we mopped the kitchen linoleum, slathered paste wax over it and, still on our knees, polished the floor to a bright shine with a worn-out cotton blanket. We cleaned the upstairs hardwood floors with a soft cloth, slightly dampened with a combination of vinegar and water. During the wintertime when it was too cold to spend much time upstairs because we had no central heating, we dusted those floors with a mop made out of strips of wool from worn-out socks, shirts, and scarves.

I still find charming our method for cleaning during those winter months when the stairs collected a lot of dust bunnies in the corners. Shaking a vegetable brush dipped in water, we would thoroughly dampen an opened newspaper, which we placed on the second stair from the top. Then, with a goose wing, we would carefully scrape the dust from the top step onto the wet newspaper and proceed, step by step, to the bottom of the stairs. The dampness caught the dust bunnies and kept them from flying up into our faces. Today I use this method for cleaning ashes from the fireplace.

Let me explain the goose wing. We saved the wing tips from all the geese we ate, because the stiff, glossy feathers were remarkably efficient at removing ashes and dust particles from the tops of the kitchen range and the potbellied living room stove as well as the bunnies from the stairs.

Windows were so public that we invested considerable energy in keeping them clean. Here is how we did that: Coat the glass with a thin paste of Bon Ami (the "hasn't scratched yet" product) and allow it to dry to a powdery coating; then, remove the residue with crumpled sheets of the *Cedar Valley Daily Times* or the *Des Moines Register* and keep rubbing until the windows shine. Having sparkling windows was as important as having a snowy wash on the line by ten o'clock on Monday morning. Bon Ami worked great on car windows, too.

Besides making the world go around, those folks who did their assigned chores were identified as "goodhardworkers." They were respected, held up as an example to others, greeted with a smile and a hearty handshake, and privileged to enjoy a feeling of goodwill throughout the community.

Those who did not have quite the dedication to the work ethic that most of us subscribed to were not held in such high esteem. Here is a song we used to sing to mock them:

"*I don't work for a livin';/I get along all right without.*
I don't toil all day/I guess it's because I'm not built that way.
Now some people work for love,/and they say it's all sunshine and gain.
But if I can't have sunshine without any work,/I think I'll stay out in the rain.
Oh, give me a nail and a hammer, and a picture to hang on the wall.
And give me a tall stepladder, for you know that I might fall.
And give me a couple of waiters and a barrel of good old bad ale.
And I'll bet you I'll hang up that picture, if somebody'll drive the nail."

Then repeat the first four lines.

My earliest memories seem to begin in the early thirties; that era may or may not have been the beginning of the dreadful competition to have the brightest wash, the cleanest windows, and the shiniest linoleum, a competition cleverly foisted on the American woman by advertisers trying to sell products. Though there was a sweet innocence to the way we entered so enthusiastically, if mindlessly, into that competition, these many years later I am glad to see healthy signs of rejection of so much wasted energy. There is a story currently making the rounds about a newly married young woman who complained to her mother that she couldn't stay with her husband because of the four-letter words that he used. She cried that she had never heard such language in her parents' house and just couldn't be expected to put up with it. After much gentle coaxing from her mother she repeated the offensive four-letter words that so shocked her: cook, bake, wash, iron, dust!

11

Farm Food

W hat shall we have for dinner?" was the question we always asked after we had eaten breakfast. "What shall we have for supper?" was the question we always asked after we had eaten dinner. Meals were mostly prepared by women and the Little Kids, both girls and boys.

Meal preparation demanded a ceaseless dedication of time and energy that is not readily apparent. So let's have a look at the basic steps necessary to get dinner on the table. First of all, wood and corncobs had to be brought into the kitchen to make a fire for cooking, and a pail of hard water had to be fetched from the windmill for drinking, boiling vegetables, and making coffee.

Let us say that for a midsummer meal we had decided to have salad with a sour cream dressing, little new potatoes with butter and cream, peas, sliced tomatoes, corn on the cob, and pork chops. This was an unusually easy meal, for the main course, the meat, had already been fried, covered with fat, and stored in the cellar during last fall's butchering, and required only that you take an iron skillet with you to the five-gallon crock in the basement, scrape the fat aside, fish out the pork chops, and give them a thorough heating in a hot oven. For the vegetables, a couple of kids, along with an adult, would be dispatched to the garden with a paring knife, a pail, a kettle, and a huge dishpan. There we picked the peas, the tomatoes, and the lettuce and placed them in the dishpan. Relying on the feel of the corn in our hands to select ears that were full and firm enough to eat, we snapped them from the stalk and placed them in the pail. Then, we dug the potatoes. Afterward, we carried our harvest directly to the windmill, where we washed everything with freshly pumped water.

Meanwhile, someone would have gone outside to fetch the sour cream, butter, and heavy cream from the cistern, which served as our icebox in the summers because the temperature in its depths was much lower than in the pantry. We stored our perishables there by putting them in a huge enamel kettle, which we attached to a twenty-foot rope and carefully lowered into the coolness below. Heavy two-by-twelve-inch planks separated by one-inch spaces covered the opening to the cistern. When we wanted to retrieve something, all we had to do was pivot one end of a plank up and over, and haul up the rope, which was secured to the pump at the base. Until electricity was extended to the rural areas, which didn't happen until sometime in the mid-thirties, this arrangement served us well.

Further preparation in the kitchen required only that we make the sugar, vinegar, and sour cream dressing for the salad, slice the tomatoes, and boil the potatoes and corn.

This was the amount of work that went into the making of an incredibly simple noon meal. You will note that I have not included a dessert. Cookies, pies, or cakes had to be baked at another time. And I have not even reminded you that the dishes had to be washed, dried, and stored in the cupboard after every meal. Further, don't forget that you had to plan, prepare, and serve supper just a few hours after you finished dinner.

I must admit that, at times, we found the inevitability of having to put a good meal on the table three times a day a bit wearying. To accomplish this feat, there was a clear need to plan ahead, to develop gardening and cooking skills and, in general, to cooperate. I have been amazed and amused how these valuable skills benefited me in unforeseen and unpredictable ways later in life.

It should be obvious by now that the center of all activity in those days was the kitchen. It was where we gathered for companionship and for a variety of work and leisure-time pursuits, where we ate all our meals, and where people entered the house most of the time. Just about the only time people entered a farmhouse through the living room door was when the whole family gathered for holidays and Sunday dinners—and, of course, for funerals.

On our small farm, the kitchen took up half of the first floor of the house. A bushel basket of red corncobs and a sturdy oak box filled with split wood stood beside a cast-iron cookstove, which had a water reservoir attached to one side. On the right side of the kitchen, against a wall, was a handsome dark oak kitchen cabinet that was a marvel of utility, having two separate tin-lined bins that tilted out from the base for easy accessibility. One held fifty pounds of flour, and the other twenty-five pounds of sugar. The cabinet also had many drawers, one of which was deep and large enough to hold four loaves of bread. In addition it had shelves for plates, cups, saucers, bowls, pots, and pans; a narrow shelf for spices; and a heavy enameled shelf that pulled out so that you could roll out piecrust or bake a cake. You can still occasionally find such items in antique stores. I find myself irresistibly drawn to them.

The left half of the room contained round-backed wooden chairs and an oblong wooden table covered with an oilcloth patterned in cheery pastel posies or cherry clusters. We had the luxury of a new oilcloth once a year; we usually purchased it in the spring at JC Penney's department store. Two very large glass lamps, which provided the only light for the entire house when darkness fell, graced the tabletop. Their wells had to be filled with kerosene and their fragile chimneys cleaned every single day. Nearby was a sort of reading nook, where a three-shelf wooden bookcase with an attached magazine rack was flanked on one side by two comfortable high-backed rocking chairs and a small handmade footstool, on the other by two windows that let in enough light to read by in the daytime. This area always appeared to be in a state of inviting disarray, littered with copies of the *Cedar Valley Daily Times, Capper's Weekly, Collier's,* the *Pathfinder,* the *Christian Herald,* and whatever books we were reading at the time.

At the far end of the kitchen, on the cooler, northern side of the house, was a pantry or buttery where we regularly stored food—leftovers, jams, bread, milk, and home-canned fruits and vegetables such as apples, peaches, red cherries, tomatoes, peas, beans, and carrots.

There were many good reasons for being in the kitchen—light, warmth, food, drink. The teakettle was always on the stove and there was nearly always some leftover coffee in the gray graniteware coffeepot. All in all, the kitchen had just about everything to make one comfortable.

I think it is a universal trait to wallow in memories of the tastes, fragrances, and textures of foods from one's childhood. Proust probably wasn't the first to celebrate this phenomenon on paper, but he is certainly the one who became famous for launching an entire novel with a description of a well-remembered fragrance—that of the madeleine. The smell of bacon is what brings back a flood of memories to me, and the closest I come to Proust's experience is the joy that comes over me when I conjure up the taste of a sandwich made of homemade bread spread with smoked bacon drippings, topped with the thinnest slices of crisp red radishes freshly harvested from the garden, and sprinkled over with coarse salt. Bacon fat was as important in our kitchen as chicken fat is in a Jewish kitchen. In those days we saved all of the grease left over after frying bacon to use for frying bread, eggs, and potatoes, and often to flavor vegetables. Of course, that was long before we had any knowledge of cholesterol.

Another simple treat we enjoyed—which my kids looked down upon until they tried it themselves—was walnut-sized red potatoes, sliced and topped with a razor-thin shaving of cold sweet butter, sprinkled with coarse salt and freshly ground black pepper.

We welcomed spring with real enthusiasm at least partly because we were starved for fresh vegetables. In the winter months we relied on home-canned goods—tomatoes, corn, corn relish, green and yellow wax beans, chili sauce, and dill pickles, as well as cherries and peaches—because we ran out of fresh vegetables and fruits, with the exception of potatoes and apples, by the end of January. As soon as the snow melted and the dandelions started to grow, we rushed outdoors with a sharp paring knife to harvest a whole dishpan of the tender new greens, which we carefully washed several times to rid them of soil and the tiny bugs and worms that you could be sure you'd find. Usually two people co-operated in this operation, because it was absolutely essential that there be no little beasties remaining on the leaves.

Once they were clean, we placed the greens in a huge kettle, added water, salt, pepper, ham hocks, or about a pound of bacon cut into two-inch squares, and boiled the mixture for about thirty minutes. Then we added little new potatoes and continued the cooking for another twenty minutes. We all considered this dish a delicious treat.

As with the early harvesting of the dandelion greens, we also rushed the season by digging parsnips as soon as we could put a spade in the ground. Preparing parsnips required only washing, peeling, cutting into quarters, and frying in bacon drippings until they were nicely browned.

In my files, I note a recent article by Craig Claiborne citing a report from the United States Department of Agriculture about psoralens, a toxin contained in parsnips. Tests have revealed that the chemical causes cancer and mutations in laboratory animals, and may be deleterious to the health of human beings. Neither peeling nor cooking reduces the concentration of psoralens. The article concludes that one ought to eat parsnips in moderation and that "man should not live by parsnips alone." We have eaten parsnips all our lives and do not seem to have suffered. Of course, we never ate an abundance of parsnips, as we ate them only in the early spring season, so we were—unwittingly—following the advice of the article.

At the same time we dug spring parsnips, we could also dig the first horseradish. The person digging was required to cut two inches off of the top of the root and instantly replant it in the ground where it would grow a new root and ensure a harvest for the next year. Tears streaming from our eyes, we grated the horse-radish by hand on a wooden table set up outside of the summer kitchen. When we had a bowlful, we added a bit of white vinegar, and a tad of sugar. It would keep in small glass jars for a month or so. The item supplied commercially in the markets today bears but a faint similarity to the newly harvested and freshly grated horseradish, which is frighteningly strong but rapidly loses its strength. It tastes fabulous on such foods as pork chops, sausage, and fried eggs.

Spring also meant fresh, tender lettuce leaves. We planted oak leaf lettuce early and protected it so we could indulge in a truly fine dish called Wilted Lettuce. Here it is:

> Pick, wash, and dry a large bowl of oak leaf lettuce. In an iron skillet, fry about eight slices of bacon until crisp and brown. Crumble the bacon, but not too much, over the lettuce. Pour the fat out of the skillet, leaving three tablespoons in the pan. Add one half cup water, four green onions or scallions, one tablespoon sugar, and three tablespoons of apple cider vinegar. Bring the mixture to a boil, all the while scraping the brown bits from the bottom of the skillet. Pour the boiling mixture over the bacon and lettuce, which will wilt the lettuce. Stir and serve immediately with some good bread.

Iowa was and still is corn country. We ate a lot of sweet corn, and in our younger years, we particularly savored the blue sweet corn for which Grandpa was famous. In the late spring, corn on the cob served right after it was harvested became a staple in our diets and a never-fail spirit lifter. Not only did we eat it at home but we developed an efficient way to serve it at family and church gatherings and picnics. Here's how: Place about three quarters of a pound of butter in a large-mouthed, two-quart Mason jar, and pour three cups of near-boiling water over the butter; it will melt and float to the top. Dip the hot ear of corn into the jar and quickly remove it. It comes out completely saturated with butter, ready to be salted and eaten. Now step away and make room for the next parishioner.

Scalloped corn was another favorite, and the recipes that are found in just about every good cookbook today are exactly the ones we used many years ago on the farm, so I will not include one here. It's a fine dish, worth reviving.

These days when there are two ears of sweet corn left uneaten, I am tempted to throw them away. Who wants to eat cold corn? Then I remember the tasty Corn Oysters of my childhood. Here's how to prepare:

> Slice the kernels off the cooked sweet corn. (Two ears will yield about two cups of kernels.) Add a quarter cup of heavy cream and stir. Mix one teaspoon baking powder, one teaspoon salt, and a dash of freshly ground black pepper with three tablespoons of flour and add to the corn mixture. Beat two large eggs and add to the corn. Place two tablespoons of vegetable oil—you can use bacon drippings if you want to—in a cast-iron skillet and heat until oil sizzles. Then, drop heaping teaspoons of batter into the oil, let brown, turn, and let that side brown. Remove from pan, drain on paper towels, and eat immediately.

One of our favorite corn dishes was succotash. I was under the impression that my mother had invented succotash because of the haphazard way she seemed to just toss in the ingredients without measuring. I have since standardized the recipe as follows:

> Place a quarter cup of finely diced onions and two tablespoons of butter in a large skillet and cook for ten minutes on moderate heat. Do not brown. Add four cups of white or yellow sweet corn cut from the cob or frozen. Add two

cups of green lima beans and half a cup of heavy cream, two teaspoons of sugar, salt, and black pepper. Heat, stirring often, until cream begins to thicken. These days I often add a half cup of chicken broth in place of the heavy cream.

Succotash could also be made out of reconstituted dried corn in the winter. We prepared corn for out-of-season use by scraping the kernels from the cob, depositing the creamy mess onto clean cotton pillowcases, covering it with gauze to keep the insects away, and stirring it twice a day. We let it dry for days in the sun, waiting until the kernels came to resemble popcorn, at which point we stored them in two-quart jars. Treated in this fashion, corn will keep for months. Besides using the dried corn to make succotash, we also used it as the basis for a fine savory dish we made in the winter months. We soaked the dried kernels overnight, drained them, added a ham hock and more water, and cooked until the corn was soft.

For the most part, breakfast was a routine production of oatmeal, bacon, and eggs, or simple, quick pancakes. Feeding and watering the chickens, making school lunches, and other such chores meant that no one could afford to dawdle. There was so much to do. But now and then, usually on Saturday or Sunday morning, there was time to indulge ourselves in the luxury of making these buttermilk pancakes.

Into a large bowl sift together two cups flour, one teaspoon baking soda, 1 teaspoon salt. In another bowl, add two and a half cups of buttermilk to two beaten egg yolks and beat thoroughly. Add to dry ingredients and beat well. In a smaller bowl beat two egg whites until they hold their peaks. Using an up-and-over motion, gently fold half the whites into the wet mixture. Now lightly fold in the remaining half of the whites. Heat two tablespoons of butter in a large cast-iron skillet until it is too hot to touch and add a serving spoon of batter to form a five-inch pancake. Depending on the size of the skillet or griddle, you can expect to make one, two, or three pancakes at the same time, or you can use two skillets. Bake the pancakes at moderate heat until they are bubbly on top and brown on the bottom. Using a metal pancake turner, turn each pancake and bake until brown on the remaining side. You may have to add more butter to the skillet to bake the rest of the batter. Transfer to waiting warm plates, spread with butter, syrup, or jam, and serve immediately. If you have a generous soul who volunteers to do all of the baking so that the rest of the diners may eat the very instant the pancakes come hot out of the skillet, you are blessed.

One of the great ways to create a quick lunch was to cut about a dozen dead-ripe tomatoes into a skillet, season with fresh basil, salt, pepper, and a tablespoon of sugar, and bring to a boil over medium heat. Add about six slices of slightly dry bread torn into small chunks and pour a cup of heavy cream into the pan. Bring almost to a boil and serve immediately. Very satisfying.

In those days we put cream on just about everything. We added cream to cooked, dried lima beans; to fresh, green lima and snap beans; to yellow wax beans; to peas, cooked carrots, and onions; to turnips, carrots, and new potatoes mashed together; to corn on the cob and to corn cut from the cob. And, best of all perhaps, morel mushrooms were doused in lots of cream after first being browned in butter.

I learned early how to use cream to create a gourmet dish out of wild game. Especially in the fall when the harvesting season was over, part of our meat supplement consisted of quail, ring-necked pheasant, and wild duck. These wild birds, with practically no body fat, are stringy and have a gamey taste. Cream is a wonderful complement to them. Here is how we cooked pheasants, which are tiny, requiring four or five of them to serve six or seven people.

> Disjoint four ring-neck pheasants, sprinkle with salt and pepper, add two onions cut in half, two carrots cut in four-inch pieces, and place in a large Dutch oven. Pour in heavy cream to just barely cover the birds. Cover the pot with the tight-fitting lid and place it on the very back of the stove. Keep a slow fire burning and turn the pieces once or twice, and in about four hours you will be able to serve a superb dinner to the family. You can follow the same directions to cook eight quail or two rabbits.

Of course, if you were of a mind to, you could easily substitute butter for cream in this recipe, as in many others.

This was the thirties, and it was a time when we could count on nature's bounty for many of our treats. In the fall we were able to gather a great variety of nuts. In the spring and summer we could pick ruby red currants, wild plums both yellow and red, wild cherries, wild red and black raspberries and blackberries, wild grapes, and crab apples from the bushes and trees that grew along the roads and fences. We ate the plums, currants, and berries as a snack on the way home from country school, and we gathered more of them to take home to make pies, jams, and jellies. Every farmwife reveled in her jelly cupboard. Adding pectin made from crab apples to the juices of wild grapes, cherries, and plums was the process used to create jewel-colored jellies. Our secret flavoring agent for wild cherry jelly was two tablespoons of crushed pits wrapped in a small cotton bundle and added to the juice. (It might enlighten you to know that, like apple seeds, cherry seeds contain cyanide and will kill you if eaten in large quantities.)

Mashed potatoes were a staple at threshing, haying, corn shelling, and family dinners. We developed a fine way to make them ahead of time. After we had added the butter, cream, and broth to the potatoes, we added about half a teaspoon of baking powder to the mixture and poured it all into a casserole, or just let it sit in the pot. About thirty minutes before the men came in for dinner, we would place the potatoes in the oven. The baking powder made the dish light and puffy.

What can you do with leftover mashed potatoes? Add beaten eggs, grated onions, and salt, form into patties like thin hamburgers, and fry them in bacon fat or oil until they are crispy and golden brown.

These days, growing up in households where both parents work, children have a limited chance to learn how to prepare simple foods. Let's remedy that. Fresh fried potatoes are delicious; here's how to make them:

> In a large heavy-bottomed skillet—I recommend a cast-iron one—place two or three tablespoons of vegetable oil, heat to very hot, and add fresh, thinly sliced potatoes. Of course, on the farm we used tasty bacon fat. If you want to live dangerously, go ahead. Now sprinkle coarse salt and freshly ground black pepper on them. Stand by with a long-handled pancake turner. Don't touch them until they are nicely browned on the bottom—about ten minutes. At

this point, gently scoop the slices up and deposit them upside down into the skillet. When they are crisp and brown, serve immediately. These are a special treat.

And unless you grew up on a farm, I'll bet you didn't know that by mashing about five slightly overcooked turnips with three slightly overcooked carrots, and adding a bit of butter and salt, you can make a surprisingly tasty dish. Serve hot. The family will love it.

Notice that all these recipes contain only those ingredients that are commonly found on the farm, in the countryside, and in the home cupboard. Remember, there was a serious depression at the time. Our mothers competed to create interesting, tasty food out of what was at hand, and their gentle competition resulted in some wonderful recipes.

Here is the recipe for a dessert we called Cotton Tops.

> Blend five tablespoons of butter or Crisco with a cup of sugar. Add one egg and beat together. Sift together one and a half cups flour, half a teaspoon of salt, two and a half teaspoons of baking powder, and four tablespoons of cocoa. Add this mixture alternately with two thirds cup milk. Pour two thirds full into greased muffin tins and bake at 350° for twenty minutes. Frost with powdered sugar icing.

And here's how we made a delightful, thrifty main course dish we called Porcupines:

> Mix one pound of ground beef with half a cup of uncooked rice, salt, pepper, and a little milk. Form this mixture into oval-shaped balls about three inches long. Place in an

oblong Pyrex baking dish and pour one and a half to two cups of fresh or canned tomatoes on top. Bake in a 350° oven for an hour and a half. The cooked rice pokes out of the ovals like porcupine quills. It's a fun dish. A child can make it.

Another thrifty oddball recipe, which Grandma said she got from her own grandmother, was for carrot marmalade. With oranges and money in short supply there was no way we could possibly make orange marmalade, but we did grow marvelous carrots and, combined with just one orange and some honey, which we almost always had on hand, they made a very tasty marmalade.

> Cut up two cups of raw carrots, one large orange, and one large lemon; remove the seeds but leave the peel on; put through a meat grinder (nowadays, you would use a food processor). Then mix with one cup of sugar and half a cup of honey. Place in a straight-sided saucepan, cover, and simmer for ten minutes. (The cover is to ensure that the granulated sugar dissolves thoroughly.) Remove the cover and continue simmering and stir frequently for about forty-five minutes. Pour into sterilized jelly jars.

We did not bother to hot-pack this jelly because we ate it too fast for it to become moldy. I need to interject here that even if we did find mold on top of a jelly we never discarded it. We simply scraped off the mold along with the top half inch of jelly, tossed it into the garbage, and ate the rest.

Apples were abundant in the thirties in Iowa and nearly every farm boasted an apple orchard containing Early Harvest,

Wealthy, Whitney, Wolf River, crab, and Greening apple trees. I'm sure that the present day Granny Smith was developed from the Greening of our day, though my memory is that the Greening was larger and more juicy and flavorful than the modern Granny Smiths. The Wealthys and the Greenings would keep in the cool basement until early February.

We used apples from our orchards in many of our favorite dishes, including Grandma's unique recipe for quartered apples, which was a variation on old-fashioned applesauce. So many of my friends have asked for it that I offer it here. The apples keep a long time and are fabulous with any kind of pork dish.

> In a large shallow pan or skillet place two quarts of water, six cinnamon sticks, two cups sugar, and two thinly sliced lemons, and bring to a slow boil. Quarter, core, and peel about a dozen apples; place the quarters in the simmering sugar water so that they are not crowded. Simmer gently for seven to ten minutes. Stand by with a slotted spoon. When the quarters turn translucent, test for doneness with a toothpick—or a straw yanked from the kitchen broom. (The germ theory of disease wasn't taken all that seriously in our house; it was just too bothersome to deal with.) The apples should be just barely done. Remove each quarter when it's ready and place it in a pretty compote dish (if you are going to consume it within a few days). When the syrup has completely cooled pour it—cinnamon sticks, lemon slices, and all—over the apples.

There is one recipe that has created wild enthusiasm among my friends, my friends' friends and friends of my friends' friends, and that is Grandma's apple cream pie. Because I think you will really love this treat and because of the current concern about cholesterol, my version of the recipe calls for pie crust made with vegetable oil, which I have been substituting for the lard used in the original. Here's how to make crust for two large one-crust pies.

3 cups all-purpose flour
3/4 cup vegetable oil
1 1/2 teaspoons salt
3/8 cup skim or whole milk

Blend all together with a fork, and form into two equal balls using your hands. Roll out between two sheets of wax paper. Peel the top paper off the dough using a spatula. With the paper side up, carefully fit the crust into the pie pan. Now carefully remove the wax paper. If the crust tears, don't worry. Using your fingers, carefully paste over the hole. Take care not to stretch the dough. Unlike the old-fashioned lard dough, you can handle this mixture as much as you like. You will probably never make the old-fashioned dough again.

Note: the following recipe is for one ten-inch pie; if you want to make two pies, double it.

Combine three quarters of a cup sugar with three table-spoons flour and one half teaspoon salt. Stir. Add three tablespoons of this mixture to the dough-lined pie pan, and pat it gently but firmly into the crust with the opened palm of your hand. This little trick promises a crisp under-crust when baked. Set aside the remainder of the sugar mixture.

Peel, core, and cut into eighths six Granny Smith apples. Add two tablespoons of lemon juice if the apples are not tart enough. Arrange apples in the crust, sprinkle with the remainder of the sugar-flour mixture, and dust liberally with cinnamon. Pour a half pint of heavy cream over all and sprinkle one tablespoon of sugar on top of this wonderful creation.

Place in 450° oven for twelve minutes, then reduce the heat to 350° and bake about one hour or until the apples are done. You should test for doneness with a toothpick—or a straw drawn from the kitchen broom if you are as indifferent to the dangers of germs as we were.

We made another fine-tasting apple dish when there wasn't time to make a pie. It is called Apple Candy Pie.

Fill a medium casserole about three-quarters full of peeled, cored, and sliced apples. If the apples aren't tart enough, add a tablespoon of lemon juice. In a separate bowl, mix one cup of flour with one cup of either cane or brown sugar, one heaping teaspoon of cinnamon, and four tablespoons of soft butter. Frequently we would add three quarters of a cup of chopped hickory nuts. These days we use pecans. Blend with that stirrup-shaped hand blender until mixture looks crumbly. Sprinkle on top of the apples. Do not stir. Bake in a 350° oven about forty-five minutes. Then turn oven to 450° and brown quickly. You can serve this hot, cool, or warm and, of course, if you like, you can pour cream on top.

I still have in my files a faded four-by-six-inch, batter-besmeared index card that was once white but is now eggshell brown in color. The writing, in lead pencil, is barely discernible. If the health department authorities were to note it, I'm sure they would declare it a health hazard and seek to have it destroyed to prevent possible contamination, but to me it counts as one of my treasures because it gives directions for the delicious applesauce cake that I made almost daily when I was a hired girl working for a family with six children. I was just over thirteen years old, so that makes this card about seventy years old.

> To make applesauce cake, cream one and a half cups sugar with a half cup butter. Add one egg and beat. Mix the following dry ingredients: two and a half cups of flour, half a teaspoon salt, one teaspoon each of cocoa, nutmeg, cinnamon, and baking powder, two teaspoons of baking soda. Measure two cups of applesauce. Beating after every addition, alternately add the applesauce and the dry ingredients to the wet mixture. Finally, add two thirds cup of raisins and three quarters cup of chopped walnuts or pecans. Pour into greased and floured 13X9X2" loaf pan and bake in 350° oven for forty-five minutes.

Apple salad was featured at almost every Sunday dinner in the fall of the year. Black walnuts or hickory nuts were always added to the apples and were a must. Generally we cracked the nuts and picked out the kernels the night before while we listened to *The Grand Ole Opry.* Since the dressing or sauce has to be room temperature, we made that ahead of time, too.

> In a small heavy-bottomed saucepan, mix one and a half tablespoons of cornstarch with half a cup of sugar. Gradually add one cup of whole milk and stir. Bring to a

simmer slowly, stirring constantly until mixture thickens. Simmer at least two minutes, remove from heat, and add two teaspoons of vanilla. Place cover on pan and allow to cool. When it's time to eat, peel, core, and chop about a dozen tart, crisp apples and place in a large bowl. Add the nuts and cooled sauce. Stir and serve. Incidentally, we also poured this sauce over apple dumplings, and we sometimes made it with pure cream instead of whole milk.

Could consuming apples in such great quantities and so many different versions be responsible for the longevity of Iowans?

Another ubiquitous item at the Sunday dinner table was cabbage salad.

Choose a fresh head of cabbage that is tight and firm, and feels heavy in the hand. With a sharp knife, shred finely. For a crispy, crunchy salad, do this the day before and place the shredded cabbage in a plastic bag along with ice cubes. Drain well and pat dry with paper towels. Add two large carrots, finely grated, and two tablespoons of yellow or white onion, grated extra-fine. Mix the following: one cup of mayonnaise, half a cup of sour cream, one or two tablespoons of apple cider vinegar, and a tablespoon of sugar. Pour over the cabbage and stir.

Early on we used to make our own mayonnaise, but about the middle of the thirties, Miracle Whip and Hellmann's hit the market, and ever since I have used one of those for convenience.

Bread was a staple, and every female knew how to make good, crusty loaves. Here is a wicked recipe for quick biscuits guaranteed to please.

Place two cups of flour, one teaspoon of salt, four teaspoons of baking powder, and a scant tablespoon of sugar in a bowl and stir. Pour as much heavy cream into the bowl as needed to make a very thick consistency. Drop by the heaping tablespoonful onto a pan and pop into a 350° oven. Bake about twelve minutes or until the biscuits are a heavenly golden brown. Serve immediately.

As you already know, a farm family had to plan ahead, and we did that in the bread department. We mixed the flour, salt, sugar, baking powder, and butter together until it looked like coarse cornmeal, put the mixture in a glass jar, and stored it in the coolness of the buttery. When an emergency arrived, all we had to do was to add milk or cream, drop the biscuits onto a pan, and pop them into the hot oven.

Just about everybody these days makes bread, so no one needs a recipe from the thirties, but Grandma's unique topping for kuchen deserves to be remembered. She just lopped off a big handful of the bread dough after the first rising and flattened it into a six-by-twelve-inch shallow pan. While the dough was rising for the second time, she prepared the following concoction:

In a heavy-bottomed saucepan, mix three quarters cup sugar and one and a half tablespoons flour with one cup of heavy cream. Cook over low heat, stirring constantly. When thickened, add one teaspoon vanilla, let cool, and pour over the bread dough. Sprinkle heavily with cinnamon and sugar just before you put it into a 350° oven. Bake about forty minutes. If you like, you can place apples or berries on the loaf and then pour on the topping.

The boys used to go hunting on Sunday afternoons. The rabbits, red timber squirrels, ring-necked pheasants, wild ducks, and quail they brought home made for a welcome addition to our regular fare of pork, beef, and chicken. Generally they used a .22 rifle, but my brother John developed a unique method of hunting that is worth reporting.

When the wheat and oats have been harvested, an eight-inch stubble remains in the field. A light covering of snow on top creates many protective hiding places, much like tiny tents. These are called forms and are a perfect camouflage. Sitting with its head toward the opening, a rabbit can safely hide, rest, and sleep. We all knew that when a rabbit senses approaching danger, it will frequently freeze rather than run. We also knew that a rabbit will leap forward when it does try to escape. John's ploy was to walk casually among the stubble, all the while keeping an eye out for a resting rabbit. When he spotted one he would continue his walking at the same steady pace, giving no indication that he had a victim. About two steps past the form he would suddenly drop back, ready to grasp the rabbit by its head and its powerful hind legs the moment the animal lunged forward from its hiding place. It will come as a surprise to many people that rabbits not only kick but they also bite. Quick action is called for at the point of capture. With one hand grasping the rabbit by the hind legs, John would deliver a sharp whack to the back of its head with the other hand, killing it instantly. Rabbits have weak necks. Everybody knew that, too.

You may have heard the expression, "There's more than one way to skin a rabbit," but on our farm there really was only one way to do it and even us Little Kids knew how. While someone holds the animal by the head, you take a hefty folding knife and run the sharp blade in a circle just at the base of the neck. Now, with both hands, firmly grip the fur at the shoulders and pull the skin down the body. Presto! The skin turns inside out and all you have to do is cut the skin at the back feet. The one who captured the rabbit gets to keep the left hind foot as a good-luck piece. Every Big Kid carried one.

It took at least two rabbits to make a meal for our family (Grandma and Grandpa, Mama, and the four children) because there are only three good pieces to each one: the saddle of the back and the two hind legs. Since rabbits have almost no fat, we always fried them in bacon fat and served them with a rich brown gravy.

We were not very creative in preparing the many meats we ate, with the possible exception of making the absolute best head-cheese in the whole wide world, which occurred only at butchering time. Preparing the head for cooking usually fell to us Little Kids. Just as we were never permitted to see my uncle deliver the fatal sledgehammer blow to the head of the hog, we were never permitted to see him sever the head from the body of the butchered porker. Somehow it just appeared, partially submerged in cold water, in the largest dishpan we had. We children were provided with small handheld brushes, a couple of toothbrushes, several clean washcloths, and a box of baking soda: Arm & Hammer, of course. Someone had already scraped the hairs off; I have no idea how that was done. It was our job to douse the creature with baking soda, and scrub the head until it was pink and clean. The truly repulsive part of the endeavor was that we had to thoroughly clean the ears and brush the teeth with the baking soda until they were completely free from any debris or dirt. This was where the toothbrushes and washcloths came in handy. We had to turn back the lips and ears, dust with the soda, and have at the orifices with the brushes and the washcloths. Can you see a five- to ten-year-old child of today turning to such a task?

After the head was thoroughly cleaned, the adults carried it to the barnyard and placed it in a huge iron kettle placed over a fire built exclusively for this purpose. It was up to us Little Kids to maintain a steady fire. It is my opinion that all children are, by nature, pyromaniacs, and we loved this task. After boiling for a half hour, the water was drained and replaced with fresh water from the windmill, along with onions, carrots, and a bit of sage. For the next three hours, by adding fresh wood to the fire, we Little Kids kept the kettle boiling until the meat started to fall off of the bones. Then the adults took over again. After allowing the head to cool on a cutting board, they pulled away the succulent, lean meat and a lot of the pink, tender skin. They cut the morsels into bite-sized pieces and placed them in a large kettle, with about a quart of the strained liquid combined with white vinegar, salt, black pepper, a bay leaf or two, a few leaves of sage, and a dash of red pepper. This concoction was boiled for about an hour, poured into a heavy, flat-bottomed crock (ours was a heavenly blue color with a two-inch collar) and allowed to cool in the buttery. By morning the gelatinous broth had set, with the little chunks of meat suspended within it. The small amount of fat contained in the rich broth floated to the top and served to cover and preserve the headcheese. To serve, you carefully scraped aside the cover of fat, sliced the cheese straight through to the bottom in quarter-inch slices and served with freshly ground horseradish. Nothing in the present-day market comes even remotely near the flavor, texture, and heaven of this homemade headcheese.

As I reminisce on butchering, I realize that we often ate meat three times a day, partly because in the early thirties we had no refrigeration, and partly because at butchering time there was so much of it available. We loved all cuts of meat, tenderloin, chops, ham, and sausage, but we didn't like pork liver. We didn't like its mahogany color, we didn't like its texture, we didn't like its taste, and we didn't like its size. So we consumed the fried slices reluctantly and with loud complaints.

It turned out that even adults could get too much liver. In those days, pastors were poorly paid in money and, to supplement those meager salaries, parishioners took it upon themselves to contribute such items as apples, pies, cakes, and dressed chickens. So it is not surprising that sometimes the pig liver, which was so large that it filled a medium-sized dishpan, would be transported to the parsonage of the Methodist church in Garrison. The delivery usually occurred on a Saturday night when farmers came to town to do their weekly trading. I remember one November Sunday when the reverend, a bachelor, trying to restrain a sly smile, preceded the sermon by thanking the members of the congregation for their generosity in providing him with a bounteous supply of meat for his table. He reported that when he had awakened that morning he had found five dishpans full of liver on his back porch. A guilty giggle rippled through the assembled group over his announcement. Later, some of us entertained ourselves envisioning the good reverend, on his knees, offering his retiring prayer that evening: "Dear God, thank you for your infinite wisdom in creating the pig, not with four, not with three, not with two, but with one liver. Amen."

Just as you are not likely to be scrubbing the head of a dead pig, you are not likely to be faced with the challenge of preparing a turtle for frying, but permit me to describe the procedure. The Big Kids would occasionally bring home a snapping turtle from a fishing excursion to Platt Creek. A turtle can withdraw its head,

legs, and tail into a perfectly tight box, making an almost impen-
etrable fortress. You have to wait patiently; when the turtle feels
calm enough, it will extend its head. This is the time to poke it
gently; when it gets irritated enough, it will clamp its jaws around
the stick. Now you can draw the head forward and chop it off
with a butcher knife or a hand ax. Be warned: The reflexes in the
legs can continue to be operative for a few hours after the
beheading. This can be disconcerting. Next, place the turtle on its
back and run a sharp knife around the shell where it joins the
skin. Pull back the skin on the legs to the feet. Remove the lower
part of the shell by hacking or sawing through the bridges which
join the two shells. Insert a sharp blade under the shell and lift it
off. Remove and discard the entrails. The rest is easy. Lift the four
quarters out of the upper shell and place in a bowl filled with
water that has a cup of coarse salt dissolved in it. Allow to set for
a few hours or overnight. Drain, rinse, and dry the meat, dredge
with flour, and fry it the way you would chicken. Do I have to say
it? It tastes like a free-range chicken.

When I told my own children that we used to make our own
marshmallows they wouldn't believe it could be done, so I must
include our original recipe for all to try. The only change is that
where we used to beat the mixture with a slotted spatula, today I
would use an electric mixer.

> To make marshmallows, mix a quarter cup of cornstarch
> with a half cup of powdered sugar. Sift together into a small
> bowl. Lightly but thoroughly butter an eight-inch cake
> pan. Now sprinkle one tablespoon of the cornstarch and
> powdered sugar mixture into the pan. Be sure to coat the
> sides as well as the bottom. Add a pinch of cream of tartar

and one teaspoon vanilla to two thirds cup of granulated sugar. Place one third cup water in a small saucepan, add one and a quarter envelope of Knox's unflavored gelatin to the water, and let stand for five minutes. Now add the granulated sugar and place over low heat. Stir until the gelatin and sugar come to a full boil. Pour the mixture into the large bowl of an electric mixer and add half a cup of light corn syrup and a quarter teaspoon of salt. Turn the mixer to high speed and mix until the mixture will hold a peak. Pour into the prepared pan and let set for two hours. Cut the sheet of marshmallows into quarters and sprinkle with the remaining cornstarch and sugar. Invert on a baking sheet. Dip a sharp knife into a glass of near-boiling water, cut each quarter into nine pieces, and roll each piece in the cornstarch and sugar. Place on a cookie rack covered with parchment paper and allow to dry.

These tasty treats will keep for several weeks in an airtight container. If you have kids around, they will keep maybe one hour.

A recipe for a totally outrageous luxury goody worth resurrecting follows. Known to us as Ting-a-Ling, it contains a surprising number of store-bought ingredients, and for that reason I think it must have been created near the end of the Depression.

Take one pound of German sweet chocolate and two squares of bittersweet chocolate, and melt them together in a pot or bowl placed over hot water. Then add to the pot two cups each of Rice Krispies and cornflakes, one cup each of coconut and hickory nuts, walnuts, or pecans. Mix well, drop by the teaspoonful onto a cookie sheet, and place in the refrigerator to harden.

The foregoing recipes and practices describe how we put food on the table during the Great Depression. Domestic Science and Home Economics have long since vanished from the school curriculum, and it is no longer practical to cure and smoke your own hams or make your own butter or headcheese, much less your own marshmallows. However, I do feel that the knowledge of how to fry potatoes, make a piecrust, and dress a chicken encourages self-sufficiency and creates a sense of confidence in one's ability to cope with life. Indeed, I want my own family to be aware of the foods, the ingenuity, the knowledge, the skills, and above all, the everlasting work that was required to survive when resources and supplies were limited.

But most of all I want them to enjoy the kinship of souls that is created when everyone gathers in the kitchen to prepare a meal together. Although cooking today is vastly easier, there is still nothing like putting a good meal on the table to make people feel they have done something meaningful.

12

An Especially Pleasant Chore

During the months we spent on the farm, we kids were sent to get the cows from the pasture for milking every afternoon at four o'clock. There was a general rule that two or four could go, but never three. The wisdom behind this was pretty sound: If a disagreement occurred, two would likely gang up on a third and it would be two against one, whereas if there were four there was a good chance of an even two against two.

The cattle and the working horses were grazed on twenty acres of permanent pastureland which contained a fairly steep hill going down to a slough and connected at the corners, checkerboard-style, to the hazel brush. Fenced off from the other fields by barbed wire, these parcels were never put under cultivation and thus represented a soul-nourishing stability for us kids, unlike the rest of the farm where crops were rotated every year. For instance, where we would see a cornfield one year, we would see a soybean field the following year. Only the pastures and the hazel brush never changed. They were there forever.

In case you don't know, a hazel brush is land that is covered by a growth of hazel, a bush that can grow to twelve feet tall yielding sticky clusters of easily harvested reddish-brown nuts enclosed in leafy husks. Our hazel brush also contained twenty-foot-tall wild cherry trees, three of them so densely overgrown with wild grape vines that they looked for all of the world like green castles. They provided a natural haven. Taking sandwiches and books, my sister and I would climb to these treetop towers when we wanted to escape the world for a lazy afternoon. Except for Mama, who accompanied us kids there on picnics, adults rarely invaded the area of the hazel brush.

The hazel brush was also graced with a few black walnut trees and a single gigantic elm that we regarded almost as a shrine. Here was where we picnicked, and here was where we could always find morel mushrooms in the spring. Some few years ago I took my husband to introduce him to the hazel brush and especially to that elm. I measured the circumference of this grand tree to be approximately fifteen feet and rejoiced that, undoubtedly because of its isolation, it had escaped the blight that has killed almost all of the elms in the Midwest.

Once when I was alone and harvesting hazelnuts, I reached for a cluster and found myself staring into the beady black eyes of a mouse-sized bat the color of a red fox. Not having any gloves, I took off my bloomers, gathered the little beastie from the bush, and ran home with my treasure, which had never been seen on the farm before. After a few days, we returned it to the hazel brush. We never saw its like again.

It was about a fifteen-minute walk from the house to where the cows usually congregated. Inevitably, Wordsworth as well as Whitman and Tennyson do insinuate themselves into my thoughts when I think of the journey I took down the lane and across the pasture to fetch the cows, for what could be more easy and natural than the connection between those poets and these scenes from my childhood? For me as for Wordsworth, the memory of nature is so soul-restoring that even today, when "the world is too much with me, late and soon," I relive that trek in my inward eye.

I always choose a late afternoon in May as the scene of my reverie. First of all I banish the companions who would certainly have been with me and proceed alone. The air is pure and refreshing; there are no man-made sounds or smells. Of course I am barefooted. You can't commune with Mother Earth with shoes on your feet. I follow the deeply rutted, dusty path worn by the cows down to the end of the narrow lane where I first encounter the tender, cool grasses of the pasture. A dozen locust trees adorned with their clusters of ivory-colored blossoms are all abuzz with a congregation of honey and bumblebees. The rich sweet fragrance is almost overwhelming.

Following the cow path angling to the left, I head for the sharp decline toward the slough. On the right, about halfway down the fence line of cedar posts, the dearest deep-down freshness of a crab apple tree in full bloom captures my eyes with a startling cloud of Renoir-pink blossoms. There is a robin's nest almost hidden in the branches. The sheer grandeur of this giant pink bouquet inspires me with what Walt Whitman describes as the spirit of nature twining with my soul. There was and is something wondrous about this tree. How did it get here? It's the only crab apple tree on the whole 240-acre farm.

Some knowledgeable reader will accurately observe that the locust trees do not bloom until long after the crab apple; but in my mind's eye I like to have them bloom at the same time—and after all, it's my reverie.

Soon after entering the pasture, I see the cows awaiting my

arrival, across the slough and up the hill, huddled under the half-dead cottonwood tree. I shout from a distance, "Ca-boss, ca-boss!" which gets the lead cow moving homeward, soon followed by the rest of the herd. Their thirst and their full udders prompt an orderly trek across the slough, up the hill, down the lane, and across the road to the barnyard.

Once I focus long enough on this peaceful scene, I invariably find that my equanimity has returned. Often I fall asleep. What a tonic memory can be.

13

Water Windmill

In the thirties, every farm depended on the windmill to pump water from the ground. On our farm, the water for household use was pumped directly into buckets and carried into the kitchen. Water for the animals was first pumped into a large storage unit called a supply tank, which was located next to the windmill in the orchard not far from the house. The supply tank was in turn connected to a much smaller tank in the barnyard, which was located on a slightly lower elevation. This intelligent arrangement allowed us both to protect the water supply from being contaminated by waste from the livestock, and to take advantage of gravity, because the water flowed through a buried lead pipe that ran down a gentle slope straight into the stockyard tank.

Yet another of the invariables in the daily round of chores assigned to us kids when we were in the country was to see to it that the tank in the barnyard was full before the cows and horses were brought up from the pasture. We controlled the level of water in the stock tank with a float on a short wire, not unlike that found on a toilet. But we had to be careful that the tank not be full to the point of overflowing, because the area around it had to be kept as dry as possible to prevent any mishaps involving the animals. Having been without water all day, the livestock would aggressively shove and push to get a drink as soon as they got back to the barnyard. If the ground around the tank was muddy and a cow or horse slipped and broke a leg, it had to be shot.

Country windmill

In order not to be wasteful, we also kept a watchful eye on the water level in the supply tank. There was a short pipe sticking out at a right angle to the side of the tank about one foot from the top; when we noted water trickling out of it we knew that it was almost full and someone—anyone, because this was a responsibility we all shared—had to go out and take the windmill out of gear to stop the pumping. One of us was always having to put the wheel in gear or to take it out of gear because water did or didn't need to be pumped. We also had to take it out of gear if the wind was blowing too hard, because there was a real danger that the wheel could be damaged or actually blown off the tower. As you drive through the rural areas today, you will likely see windmill towers with the wheels in tatters and the blades bent or missing, the result of just the kind of negligence we were constantly warned against.

Though we could generally depend on the wind for power in Benton County, there were times when it died down and my uncle had to engage a small, noisy, gasoline-powered engine to pump the water for the livestock. If we were abandoned by the wind when we went to fetch water for household use, we kids had to uncouple the windmill shaft from the top of the pump and use the pump handle to raise water manually. The shaft was so heavy two kids had to work together, first to uncouple it from the pump, and then, after we had filled the pail with water, to put it back onto the pump. At this point there was the ever-present danger of mashing the skin between the index finger and the thumb, which caused the bluish blood blisters we all suffered on occasion. They hurt like crazy and sometimes we cried. But we accepted this injury as being just as inevitable a part of life as the need for water.

14

Milking and Other Nightly Chores

During the fall months when we were still living on the farm, we had to make it back home from school by about four-thirty so that we could change out of our school clothes and start the evening chores, which included feeding and watering the pigs and chickens and gathering eggs, activities that even the Little Kids could do. After we collected the eggs in pails, we carried them to the cool cellar where we placed them, one by one, in crates especially designed for eggs—twelve dozen to a crate.

We used this pleasant time to catch up on the day's events. One early evening we were on our way to the cellar with the eggs when we fell into a discussion of the lecture on centrifugal force that had been presented in school that day. Our cousin Robert, who was just about old enough to be a Big Kid, spoke.

"I bet I can swing this pail of eggs in a circle over my head without spilling any." He was carrying a three-gallon bucket piled high with eggs.

"Betcha you can't."

"Betcha I can. Centrifugal force will keep the eggs in the bucket."

"OK. Try it then."

"Watch this."

And, indeed, he would have been successful except that he hadn't counted on the fact that the weight of the eggs forced him to step backward as he initiated his overhead swing, and the bucket hit the clothesline right behind him. Both families had scrambled eggs for supper and for breakfast, and the Big Kids and the Little Kids took scrambled egg sandwiches to school for lunch the next day. While we kids teased him unmercifully, the adults were uncharacteristically sympathetic, perhaps because the mess had been created in the interest of science.

Women and Little Kids on the farm typically did the feeding and watering of the animals, but milking was generally considered to be the lot of the men and the Big Kids. In our family, the milking was done in the cow barn on our aunt and uncle's farm across the road, because that's where all of the cows from both families were sheltered. Every farmer knew that to maintain their production rate, cows had to be milked pretty much at the same time every morning and evening. Milking was a duty that permitted no days off. There were no exceptions.

After each milking was done, the cream had to be separated from the milk, another task for the adults and the Big Kids. We Little Kids liked to be present for that. We could catch pitchers of cream and milk for household use and fill a pan with milk for the cats and dogs.

Our separator was a handsome scarlet De Laval with a shiny stainless-steel tub atop it like a bulbous crown. One of the Big Kids would start cranking the crooked handle to get the mechanism whirring at a moderate, measured pace. It was considered an honor to turn the separator handle. Steady was the order, for if the turning were too fast or too slow, the separating would not be accomplished efficiently, and too much cream would be left in the so-called skim milk—an inexcusable waste, for cream could be exchanged for hard cash, a scarce commodity at our place.

Once the mechanism rose to a proper speed, one of the Big Kids poured a couple of buckets of milk, warm, bubbly, and fresh from the cow, into the tub on top of the separator. The cream flowed out of a small spout and was added to the contents of the five-gallon stainless-steel cream can, while the skim milk streamed from a larger spout into pails that we lugged to the pig trough.

The dogs and cats, who were given a communal pan of milk to share, could always be counted on to appear on time for the pouring, and for a while we had one cat, Cleopatra, who used to show up during the milking. Sitting on a ledge about eight feet away from my uncle, her mouth wide open in anticipation, she would be rewarded with squirts of warm milk straight from the teat. The milk that didn't make it into her mouth soaked her from head to toe, but we all swore that she wore a big smile on her face. Afterward, it always took her twenty minutes of intensive grooming to lick her fur clean and restore it to a shiny gloss.

Once a week the five-gallon can was placed by the side of the road to be picked up by the Cream Man and trucked to the Garrison Creamery. The person in charge of making the butter there was a highly esteemed member of the Garrison community known—of course—as the Butter Maker.

Occasionally, a farmer would get a whole can of cream returned to the farm with the contents of the can tinted an apple green. This coloring meant that some foreign body, usually a dead mouse, had been found in the can, making it unusable for making butter. The harmless dye was placed in the polluted cream so the farmer would not remove the mouse and return the contents to the creamery. The green cream was usually fed to the chickens and pigs. In its heyday, Garrison butter became famous for its delicate fresh flavor and was shipped to faraway markets, but those days are long gone. In 1971, with the help of yearly grants from the Iowa Arts Council, the creamery was converted to a successful theater known as the Old Creamery Theater Company. In recent years the troupe moved to Amana, and, at this writing, the creamery building is being dismantled, its bricks being salvaged for future use.

One of the by-products of the Garrison Creamery was a vast amount of buttermilk. We used to buy it for five cents a gallon, but sometimes we made it ourselves if we were churning our own butter. Big Kids and Little Kids alike took turns at the churning; the one who was doing the honors when the first flecks of butter appeared was rewarded with the first glass of the tasty buttermilk. With chemicals of all kinds added, little of the buttermilk produced today bears any resemblance to that of my youth. I know that sounds like a trite and truculent observation, but I will compound my truculence by adding that the current generation will never know the sublime taste of the tomatoes and the strawberries we picked sun-ripened from the vine and ate on the spot.

In the spring, after the separating was done, the newly weaned calves had to be fed. Young calves are adorable creatures with soft eyes and silky coats, and the oldest of the Little Kids and the youngest of the Big Kids joined forces in this delightful chore, which usually took place at twilight. We filled small galvanized pails with warm skim milk and, submerging our hand in the milk, palm side up with three fingers protruding, we angled the still-warm, tasty liquid to the calf's mouth and wiggled those fingers. The calves would pull and suck with surprising strength, slurping up the milk around our fingers. Occasionally a calf would wrest the bucket from our hands and end up with its head in the pail and the bail hooked over its ears. Then all of us had the fun of trying to catch the bewildered tyke as it blindly bawled and kicked its way around the pen. After a few days, the calves would no longer need our fingers to entice them but would drink straight from the pails.

The separator had to be cleaned twice a day. We did only a perfunctory cleaning after the evening milking, tossing a couple of pails of fresh water into the tub and letting the water run through it. But every single morning of the year that beastie red De Laval had to be completely disassembled, and all its parts, including a large number of cone-shaped metal disks, had to be scrubbed and washed in hot, soapy suds, rinsed with scalding water, and stacked to dry. Of course, disassembling the separator in the morning meant that there was the equally inevitable chore of putting the whole thing back together again before the evening's milking. I think there were something like forty of those disks, but so onerous did I find this chore, I can't recall exactly how many.

Developing a sense of responsibility? Building character? Yes, of course, we were.

15

Wash Day

Nowadays, with computerized washing machines and automatic water temperature controls, we don't give the family wash a second thought. I note that my children and grandchildren change clothing from the skin out every single day and throw every item, including the bath towel used only once, into the hamper. I'm sure they would be amazed to learn that in my day men, women, and children put on clean clothes on Monday morning and were expected to wear them for the entire week, because laundering those clothes was a major undertaking, with every member of the family called upon to contribute.

Though Monday was the official wash day throughout the farm community and in the town of Garrison, preparations usually started Sunday night, when all of the dirty clothes were collected, sorted, and given special scrutiny. The boys were expected to empty the pockets of their shirts and "overhauls"—the ubiquitous bibbed pants made of blue denim. All men and boys wore them; women and girls almost never did. Mama would turn the pant and shirt pockets inside out and brush away the chaff, dirt, alfalfa seeds, and barley beards. All the clothes were then put to soak in a large galvanized tub of cool water.

If we were in Garrison, the next step was for a couple of the Big Kids to bring the copper oval-shaped boiler up from the cellar and place it on the Monarch kitchen range. Here was where real cooperation began. We Little Kids would pump cistern water into three-gallon galvanized buckets and the boys would carry them, two at a time, to fill both the boiler and the reservoir that was permanently attached to the kitchen range. We used cistern water—which is rainwater collected and stored in a cistern usually thirty to forty feet deep and lined with stones—because rainwater, unlike well water, is soft. In fact, there is a saying in Iowa that the well water is so hard you have to bite it out of the cup. Everyone uses it for drinking and for cooking, because it tastes fabulous and makes great coffee. But since it doesn't allow suds to form and is harsh on the skin, hair, and clothing, soft cistern water is always used for washing.

The laundry soap was also prepared on Sunday night. Using a tin cabbage slicer, Grandpa shredded one and a half bars of P&G, Fels Naphtha, or our own homemade brown soap into a green marbleized graniteware pan kept exclusively for this purpose. After adding a little water to the pan, he placed it on the back of the warm kitchen range and by morning we would have plenty of soft soap ready for the washing machine.

Since the stove had to be kept fired up to heat the wash water, wash day always meant beans for supper, because we could leave them to cook untended on the back of the hot stove. So while Grandpa made the soap, Grandma and I picked over a couple of pounds of navy beans. After discarding the tiny rocks and shriveled beans that we always found, we placed the remainder in a big iron pot. The next morning we would throw in a couple of car-rots, an onion, a small slab of bacon or a ham hock, and a few potatoes. Except for an occasional stir, the bean pot required no further attention.

Once the wash water was brought to a boil Monday morning, the heavy, awkward, round wooden washing machine was moved into the kitchen and Grandpa filled it with the water from the boiler and added the soft soap. All the clothes were washed in the same water, and were washed in order of whiteness and cleanli-ness: white clothes and bed linens first, followed by hand and dish towels, then the colored clothes, and finally the men's work socks, shirts, and overalls. In order to operate the washing pad-dles, once a batch of clothes was put in, someone alternately pushed and pulled a shoulder-high lever which was attached under the tub by some intricate arrangement of worm gears. Push-pull, push-pull, push-pull: fifteen minutes for every load. We all took turns at this task until it was time to leave for school, and then Grandpa manned the lever.

Sometime around 1936 when Roosevelt's Rural Electrification Act made life easier for farmers, Grandpa purchased a Maytag washing machine. We were thrilled to have it. Of course, we still washed all of the clothes in a single tub of water, but the chore of push-pull, push-pull was eliminated. That square, brushed alu-minum Maytag did duty in our family for over twenty years (though for the last half dozen it was used only to wash dog beds).

Once the clothes were clean, using a wooden wash stick—best described as an unpainted broomstick—we lifted them out of the steaming water and put them through the hard rubber rollers of the hand-turned wringer, from whence they fell into a tub of cool rinse water. After being rinsed, they had to be wrung out again.

Rinsing and wringing was a two-person activity. One person turned the handle of the wringer, while another rinsed the clothes by hand and fed them through the rubber rollers which ejected them into the wicker wash basket below.

Then the whole process started over again with the next load of clothes, which was placed in that same wash water, followed by the third, fourth, and fifth loads, until all were washed, rinsed, and wrung out.

A much-admired accomplishment in those days was the ability to make smooth starch. Here is how you made and used it. First of all, you prepared a paste by adding cold water to the dry, powdery starch and stirred it until it had the consistency of thin toothpaste. Then you stirred this mixture constantly while you poured boiling water into it. If you stopped stirring or pouring, even briefly, you created a lumpy, unusable mess. For the final step, after pouring this starchy liquid into a dishpan half filled with cool water, you dipped the freshly washed shirt fronts, collars and cuffs, aprons, blouses, dresses, and tablecloths into it and hung them out to dry.

We considered it a badge of honor to get all the wash on the line by ten o'clock in the morning, and to hang the clothes according to the strict method dictated by the housewives of the community. Sheets and pillowcases, handkerchiefs and towels had to be hung just so, the edges pulled taut between thumbs and forefingers. We called this procedure pressing by hand, for if done properly, it saved a lot of ironing later. We turned all the colored clothes inside out to discourage fading. We hung shirts, blouses, and undershirts by the tails; we hung pants and shorts from the belt line; we pinned all socks in pairs by the toes; and we hung all like items together.

Is there any sense in trying to make the modern-day reader

understand the immense satisfaction we experienced in viewing our bright, clean wash arranged in such a meticulous fashion on the clothesline? Heaven knows we had more than enough to do without this added display of superhousewifery. But the whole ritual was a matter of pride.

There was a rumor in Garrison that a wily housewife, whose husband drove a long-haul semitruck, resulting in frequent and erratic absences, chose the clothesline method for signaling her handsome, blond lover. When her husband was in residence, she pinned the belt of his pants to the line; when he was absent, she pinned the legs of the pants to the line so they hung upside down. I never knew whether this was true or not, but it did make for good gossip.

There were a few years when the women in Garrison hung their panties and bras inside a pillowcase to conceal them from the eyes of any lascivious males who happened to pass by while these unmentionables were drying. But people made fun of the practice and it was soon abandoned. I don't recall that we ever engaged in that bit of silly primness on the farm.

In the summertime the clothes would sometimes dry so fast that by the time we got the second basket out to the line, the first batch was already dry. We removed the clothes from the line as soon as they dried, being careful not to wrinkle the sweet-smelling, deliciously warm, sun-dried garments. We, meaning Grandma, Mama, my little sister, and I, would immediately put the sheets and pillowcases back on the beds, looking forward to the time when we could lie down on them. To crawl between crisp sheets, warm and fresh from the sun and air, at the end of a bone-wearying day, is one of the true soul-restoring luxuries of life, which hardly anyone of the current generation will ever know.

If the weather presented us with a quick drying day, we did the ironing as soon as we brought the clothes indoors, using the three heavy flatirons that had been heating on the back of the stove. Otherwise, we dipped a small vegetable brush in water, sprinkled the clothes to be ironed, rolled them tightly, placed them in the wash basket, and ironed them on Tuesday.

In the winter, to limit our exposure to the freezing weather, we carefully folded the wet sheets, pillowcases, and towels, shook the wrinkles out of the shirts and blouses, and warmed the clothespins in the oven before dashing outdoors to hang the clothes on the line. Sometimes the clothes would freeze stiff before we ever got the clothespins on them. However, we pinned them on the line anyway, for the wind usually evaporated the ice and they would flap fairly dry before too long. If they didn't dry, however, the great heater that served the living and dining rooms had to be stoked with chunks of oak, and then we had to remove the frozen items from the line and dry them on long wooden sticks placed on the backs of wooden chairs. These two-by-two-inch sticks were twelve feet long and did double duty as frames for quilting at another time. Sometimes it would take two days to get the whole wash dry.

At the end of wash day we had to drain and clean the washing machine and move it back to its proper place. But if it was summer, we emptied the wash water into buckets and took them out to the outhouse where we used the dirty but soap-laden water to scrub down the oak seats and the floor. Remember: Waste not; want not.

16

Outhouses

The little house out back—the privy, the biffy, the backhouse, the toilet, the can (considered coarse)—no discussion of life in Iowa during the thirties is complete without noting the outhouse.

Even in Garrison very few houses, maybe four, had indoor bathrooms. The rest of us used outhouses. Nearly every family made an attempt to camouflage the privy with a growth of trumpet vine. Sometimes we would be rewarded with the sight of a ruby-throated hummingbird dipping into the depths of the harsh orange blossoms.

Generally, in both town and country, the outhouse was constructed of wide pine boards; if cracks or splits developed along the wall, they were not repaired. Welcome streams of fresh air entered through these splits. Unfortunately, hornets and yellow jackets also entered in the summer and frosty snow dusted the seats in the winter. Near the top of one wall was an opening in the shape of a quarter moon, exactly the way you've always seen them in cartoons.

The door always swung inward so the occupant could leave it open to enjoy the fresh air but could easily slam it shut should anyone approach. This was important for obvious reasons. The seat was usually a heavy slab of splinter-resistant hickory or oak, worn smooth from the many fannies that polished it, day in, day out, year in, year out.

The inside configuration varied little. Ours was arranged so that there were two holes for big folks and a low-down one for little tykes. Not infrequently, two people of the same age and sex would visit the outhouse together; my sister and I would do that, and my brothers would do the same. Adults would usually go separately.

There were minimal amenities in the outhouse—the Sears Roebuck and Montgomery Ward catalogues, possibly some corn-cobs, and a large covered pail of lime. One of the more sagacious tricks we learned from our elders was to select a Bible-paper-thin page from the back of one of the catalogues, and scrunch and crumple it over and over again until it became as soft as tissue paper. This was its last and most important service.

In some farm families, as hardy as they were frugal, the men used corncobs instead of paper. Indeed there was a crude joke around Garrison that a respected member of the community was so stingy that he kept a basket of red corncobs in his outhouse and a large white one tied to a long string beside the seat. The white one was to insure the red one had done the job efficiently.

Before leaving the outhouse, the user would toss a small scoopful of lime down the hole. I am fascinated to learn that lime has been used for this purpose much longer than one would think, according to a report in the May–June 1991 *Biblical Archaeology Review*. In the city of David in the oldest inhabited part of Jerusalem, archaeologists have found two ancient toilet seats in their original positions with cesspits beneath them. Scientific analysis of the cesspit soils reveals that the 2,600-year-old remains of fecal matter are mixed with calcareous ash. The researcher speculates that "the calcareous ash appears to have been introduced as a liming agent to sanitize the contents of the latrine by reducing bacterial and fungal activity."

Men working in the field simply took care of their needs by going wherever they happened to be on the farm. Of course, even us Little Kids, both male and female, learned how to go behind a tree, under a bush, or on the far side of a shock of oats. We were ever-respectful and would turn our attention discreetly away from the person who was seeking a bit of privacy. It was Mama who instructed my sister and me how to tidy up a soiled bottom by using a smooth stick that had all of the bark removed. She also taught us to identify poison ivy, nettles, and especially smartweed, so that we could make sure to avoid them before pulling down our bloomers and baring our butts to the elements. The common name for smartweed is "arsemart" because "if it touch the taile or other bare skinne, it maketh it smart" according to John Minsheu's 1626 *Guide into Tongues*. A member of the buckwheat family, smartweed was ubiquitous along roadsides and fences. Since chickens, pheasants, and quail loved to eat its nutritious seeds, we let it grow freely.

We were expected to be in complete control of our bladder and our bowels at all times. We visited the outhouse in the morning, maybe again at noon, and ritually before we went to bed. We tried not to go at night because we didn't want to stumble outside half asleep, especially not in cold weather. Of course, there was a heavy ceramic chamber pot in the oak chest at the head of the stairs. The older folks called it the "white owl"; the men referred to it as the "thunder mug"; and, out of hearing of the adults, we Little Kids, following the lead of the Big Kids, called it the "piss pot." It was to be used only in emergencies, and the person who used it had to empty and scrub it clean the next day.

On the infrequent occasions when bowels went into business for themselves, we got no sympathy from the family: "Serves you right. Next time don't make such a pig of yourself!" "Your eyes were bigger than your stomach. You know you shouldn't eat three pieces of raisin pie." "It's good enough for you. You were told eating so many wild plums would give you the carbolly-marbolly shoot-the-shoots."

Around Halloween the youths in both town and country could be expected to engage in mischief that would not be permitted or even contemplated at any other time. The inventive pranks varied from year to year, but one activity was regularly repeated: upsetting outhouses. Generally, outhouses on farms were left alone; only those in town were tipped over. "It gets dumped in; it gets dumped over!" quipped easygoing Ide Davis. (Ide Davis and his wife, Ida, lived a block from Grandpa's house in Garrison.)

Not everyone was so philosophical about this prank, however. One year, Old Man Mealhouse decided he didn't want the aggravation of a tipped-over outhouse. He announced his sentiments at Sant Gulick's pool hall and let it be known that he was going to sit in the outhouse with his .410 shotgun all night if necessary. Well, that should have scared the young men into staying off his property. In Garrison, in those times, when a man said he would shoot you, you took that threat seriously.

What the pranksters did was to quietly slip up behind the outhouse and, with one gigantic shove, tip it over with the door to the ground, imprisoning Old Man Mealhouse and his .410 shotgun for the rest of the night. He was teased about that down at the pool hall for days. Even Little Kids on the street taunted him from a safe distance. So the local youths won round one. But wait.

The next year the old geezer announced that he would occupy his outhouse in the same manner as he had before, only this time he would be more alert. Not many folks thought the local youths would attempt anything in the face of the old man's anger, and worse, his .410 shotgun. They were wrong.

The pranksters waited until just after midnight. Stealthily, in total silence, they crept toward the outhouse and, at a pre-arranged signal from a flashlight, rushed forward to make a single concerted effort to upset the building with Old Man Mealhouse and his shotgun in it, in the same way that they had done the preceding Halloween.

How could they have known that the night before, the canny (pardon the pun) old guy had moved his outhouse three feet forward, so that when they rushed it, they would all drop into the smelly pit before they could accomplish their dirty deed?

Sitting comfortably in the branches of a nearby Wealthy apple tree with his trusty weapon and a flashlight, Old Man Mealhouse rejoiced and jeered as he watched the youths mushing around in the stinking stuff, unable to escape until they were covered up to their shirt pockets.

You can believe that his sublime victory was noised about down at the pool hall as well as at every gathering in Garrison. Teasing the young men provided thoroughly satisfying entertainment for days.

PART THREE

Fall/Winter

One-room country schoolhouse

17

Country School: Monroe Number 6

JAKE BARNES IS A DAMN FOOL. There was no explanation, no elaboration, no qualification. Just a succinct statement in four-inch-high block letters that someone had used a ten-penny nail to score deep into the siding of the Monroe Number 6 schoolhouse. Though it had been painted over many times, it could still be clearly read. The economy of the assertion was singularly appropriate to the times and to the building itself.

As I have already noted, we attended school in town from January until the middle of May, and in the country from September until Christmas. Monroe Number 6 was the basic one-room country schoolhouse you've seen in countless pictures of rural life in the early twentieth century. It was completely typical of its kind except that it had no bell tower. The teacher summoned us to classes by ringing a small, handheld brass bell with a black wooden handle. We entered the white clapboard building through a narrow hall and hung our coats on wooden pegs attached to the wall. Three windows on each of the long sides of the room provided the light on most days. Glass kerosene lamps squatting in ornate iron scroll holders attached to the walls provided additional light on cloudy days.

To the back and in opposite corners of the ample playground were the typical wooden outhouses: one for the girls and one for the boys. The playground was empty; there were no slides, swings, or carousels. The school provided the bare necessities, with but few amenities.

The single classroom, which housed all eight grades, contained about fifteen ink-stained wooden desks of varying sizes, each with a hole in the upper right-hand corner to hold a bottle of ink. A long bench and the teacher's desk—with the appropriate modesty shield—occupied the middle of a platform about eight inches high. An upright piano, a small Victrola, and a large American flag tacked to a wooden pole graced the left end of the stage. (From time to time, while standing with our right hands over our hearts, we pledged allegiance "to the flag and to the republic for Richard Stands, one nation and a dirigible, with liberty and justice for all.") A portrait of George Washington hung in solitary splendor above the large blackboard on the wall behind the teacher's desk. A potbellied stove stood smack in the middle of the room.

At the back of this room, on one side of the door, was a small gray painted bench on which a gray graniteware pail, dipper, and washbasin were placed. The pail supplied us with drinking water, which we sipped from the tin cups hanging from the hooks above the water pail. Each family supplied its own cup, and in our family all four of the kids used that one tin cup. Across from the bench, on the opposite side of the door, was—wonder of wonders—a shallow, sturdy box on wooden legs, about five feet long, three feet wide, and eight inches deep, filled with clean, fine sand. When you had successfully finished your spelling and your arithmetic lessons you were rewarded with some stand-up time to play in the sand. How good could life get?

Country school started right after Labor Day. My siblings and I attended Monroe Number 6, where our mother had once been a teacher, and since our cousins lived on the opposite side of the road, they went to Monroe Number 7, where their mother had once been a teacher.

Needless to say, the family values of the home were reinforced at school. The same attitude toward industriousness and diligence that applied to our chores was applied to our schoolwork.

Nothing was more important than getting to school. No matter what the weather, we trudged off every morning with our dinner pails (half-gallon tin buckets that had originally held sorghum or molasses) filled with sandwiches of homemade bread and meat left over from the night before, often sliced pork tenderloin slathered with freshly made chili sauce. We would eagerly trade this hearty fare to anyone who had the good fortune to bring a peanut butter sandwich on two slices of Wonder Bread, soft, white, and tasteless as cotton. We wrapped our sandwiches in wax paper that had been salvaged from the occasional loaf of Wonder bread or from the inside of a box of Post Toasties, rare treats purchased from the Farmers Store in Garrison. After lunch at school, we smoothed and folded the treasured wax paper, returned it to our pails, and took it home to be used again and again and again.

We walked to school, one mile if we cut through the pasture and one and a half miles if we went along the road. We usually chose the pasture route, which took us out the door across the stockyard, the stubble field, and the slough, then through the hazel brush, and on to Old Man Shaefer's horse pasture. We hugged the fence as we walked through that pasture because four huge, powerful workhorses, with glistening chestnut haunches and feet the size of water pails, grazed there. Unusual for farm horses, they were temperamental, and we were afraid of them—not without reason, I might add, for on at least one occasion one of those horses charged me as I was crossing the field alone. Just as I was certain that I was to be trampled, he came to a thundering halt, reared abruptly, and galloped off to the right, snorting loudly. I was tingling with terror and my heart thumped so loudly I could hear it.

After we crossed this pasture we followed Platt Creek a short distance until we came to the main county dirt road. Monroe Number 6 was just a few hundred feet to the left.

The hours we spent walking to and from school with our friends were exquisitely free from adult supervision. We reveled in this unique time of total independence, in the warm interaction with each other, and in the assured confidence of our relationship with the group. This was our world.

It would be nice to report that on these treks to and from school we discussed what we learned in class, reviewed what the teacher told us, or discussed our homework, but in truth very little of our time was spent in such edifying pursuits. We were like ordinary, half-civilized kids everywhere and we delighted in reciting vulgar verses taught to us by the Big Kids, particularly those that focused on peeing and farting—always good for a laugh, then as now. We relished the opportunity for such free and uninhibited expression precisely because we knew that coarse language was forbidden at home. A session with a bar of Lifebuoy awaited us if our folks found out.

Besides being crude, we could also be mean. A city cousin from Detroit who was visiting saw the mean side one fall day when we were walking home from school with him. The cousin, Wilfred, was a spoiled, arrogant bully, an only child who was out of the city for the first time in his life. So out of his element was he that he refused to drink our milk because it didn't come out of a glass bottle. This meant that my uncle had to drive the three miles into Garrison to buy bottled milk. Besides being catered to in a manner that made us resentful, since none of us had ever been indulged, he was at an age—a little over eight years old— which meant that he fit into neither the Big Kid nor the Little Kid group. In just about all ways, he was an outsider.

As we walked along with our unwelcome visitor, we spotted a lone unhatched egg remaining in a wild duck's nest. It was heavy, and gruesomely colored a splotchy, rusty green. The egg was probably over two months old; we Little Kids and Big Kids alike knew that the gases stored in it made it the equivalent of a hand grenade—nature's most outrageous stink bomb. The Big Kids made over the egg, telling Wilfred that it had magic qualities and that if he just tapped it gently on a fence post he could make a wish and it would come true. Here I have to admit that we Little Kids enthusiastically egged them on (couldn't resist the pun) and urged Wilfred to accept the invitation. At the very first tap, the gaseous egg exploded all over him—hair, face, neck, ears, shirt, arms, and chest. Wilfred was drenched with the most suffocating, disgusting, putrid, nauseating, foul liquid that carried the most offensive stench anyone could ever imagine. From the point of view of us kids, it was an altogether satisfying prank. Mama and Aunt Hazel, who had to bathe and shampoo Wilfred several times before they eliminated the odor, didn't see it that way. The Big Kids were sent to bed right after supper without their dessert as punishment. We Little Kids were roundly scolded.

This incident is a children's version of the age-old rivalry between the country bumpkin and the city slicker. Perhaps that's why the Big Kids received such a relatively mild punishment.

Country teachers were selfless and saintly. Many times in

those awful, below-freezing days, when we would arrive at school almost frozen, Miss Zimmer would wrap two or three of the coldest children (and I was always one of them) in her good fur coat, place them in the huge captain's chair, and allow them to warm up close by the potbellied stove.

Probably the kindest thing Miss Zimmer ever did for me was when she took me home with her the night before a social or a program and cut, washed, and set my hair with a gelatinous blue mixture. That kind of beauty parlor treatment was so far out of the normal realm of possibility for me that I viewed her as my fairy godmother and myself as the princess she had transformed by her magic.

If you have any doubt concerning the heroism and dedication of the small-town and rural school teachers of that day, note the following clauses from a typical contract, which happens to be the one I myself was given to sign in LaMoille, Iowa, when it became my turn to teach, in 1942.

> *The teacher agrees to well and faithfully perform the duties of teacher; She is . . . to teach and assist in the supervision of the children on the playground as well as in the buildings and assist in any other work that may be required of her.*
>
> *The school board reserves the right to take what vacations they deem necessary.*
>
> *She shall agree not to keep late hours as to interfere with her schoolwork, and if she should marry during the life of this contract, such act shall terminate this contract.*

Please note the pronoun "she." It was assumed that the teacher would be both unmarried and female. If you read those sentences carefully you will see that they make a virtual slave of her. The stipulation that "the school board reserves the right to take whatever vacations they deem necessary," for example, meant that the board could require the teacher to stick around to aid in Easter and Christmas programs before she went to her own home for the holidays. And do not fail to note the broad implications of "...to assist in any other work that may be required of her."

Typical country school teacher's contract

You may think these demands sound unbelievable, but teachers signed such contracts all the time. Is it any wonder that in those days the goal of almost all young women was to get married?

Country teachers were expected to arrive at eight o'clock in the morning to build and light the fire in the stove so the room would be warm when students showed up an hour later. They swept the wooden floors and carried out the waste and the ashes.

Country teachers were miracle workers for, with only the barest necessities and very little money, they taught all eight grades, with students of widely varying ages and talents (though I must point out that only rarely did a rural school have students in all eight grades, or more than sixteen students at most). One of the strategies they used to make this feat possible was to assign the older or the higher-achieving students as aides to the younger and less talented ones. For instance, eighth graders who had finished their work might be assigned to give spelling or reading lessons to the third graders, while the teacher instructed the fourth graders in long division on the blackboard behind her desk. Even sixth graders could teach third graders multiplication and addition using flash cards. We high-achievers were proud to be selected for such tasks, and though we didn't recognize it at the time, the teaching served to reinforce our own learning experience. Besides instructing us in American history, arithmetic, English, civics, geography, reading, spelling, and writing, our teachers also introduced us to the satisfying pleasures of singing and memorizing poetry. Imagine, if you will, a teacher working under these circumstances from eight in the morning until four in the afternoon, and then having to grade papers and prepare lessons for the following day.

To get our cooperation in washing the desks and blackboard and cleaning the erasers, they used the Tom Sawyer fence-painting ploy; thus, we considered it a privilege and an honor to be chosen for these tasks. We especially loved to clap the felt erasers together to clean them of chalk dust, because it meant that we could go outside.

Another highly sought-after honor, and an incentive to get schoolwork done promptly and correctly, was the hope that you, along with a classmate, would be chosen to walk to the Moore farm a little less than a quarter of a mile down the dirt road to fetch drinking water from their windmill. We kids carried the full pail of water between us, with a sturdy stick under the bail. Water is extremely heavy, and we had to stop often to rest and change hands in order to complete our task. But we didn't mind, especially in the heavenly fall weather, when song sparrows and meadowlarks, as well as the dozens of goldfinches clustered on milkweed pods and thistle plants, gracing our idyllic trek.

The routine that marked the orderly closure of the country school day remains with me after all these years. It was an unvarying procedure. At precisely ten minutes before four o'clock our teacher would say, "Put your work away and stand beside your desks." Then, after blowing C on her brass pitch pipe, she would lead us in her thin, milky soprano as we sang.

> "Work, for the night is coming,/Work through the
>   morning hours;
> Work while the dew is sparkling,/Work 'mid
>   springing flowers;
> Work when the day grows brighter,/Work in the
>   glowing sun;
> Work, for the night is coming,/When man's work is done."

"Good. Now the second verse." C on the pitch pipe again.

"Work, for the night is coming,/Work through the
sunny noon;
Fill brightest hours with labor,/Rest comes sure and soon.
Give every flying minute,/Something to keep in store;
Work, for the night is coming,/When man works no more.

Work, for the night is coming,/Under the sunset skies;
While their bright tints are glowing,/Work, for
daylight flies.
Work till the last beam fadeth,/Fadeth to shine no more;
Work, while the night is darkening,/When man's work
is o'er."

Note that last chilling line.

After these inspirational verses we would sing "Now the Day Is Over," and I think we all felt a little comforted that it was just the shadows of the evening that were stealing across the sky. Did the adults know the effect that these words had on us kids? I know I took them seriously, and I think other kids did, too.

18

Box Social

Among their many other responsibilities, teachers were expected to develop programs for Halloween, Thanksgiving, Christmas, and Easter. In the country, these celebrations usually took the form of box socials and involved the entire rural community. Need I report that we always had a packed house at these events? Everybody attended.

There must be more than a few people who do not know what a box social is, so it merits a description. Whatever else was planned, it always involved auctioning off homemade meals prepared by the women in the community and packed in containers they decorated lavishly with ribbons, lace, and flowers.

Housewives used boxes that were large enough for food for the entire family—typically fried chicken, dill pickles, homemade sweet rolls, oatmeal cookies, angel food cake, and devil's food cake. A single woman with a sweetheart would choose a box that held just enough supper for two. Great care was supposedly taken to keep the decorations secret, but in reality, the women always told their husbands and boyfriends how to identify their creations so they could bid on the right box when the auction began.

The evening of the event everyone gathered at the schoolhouse.

After we kids presented a program of poems, songs, dances, and skits, the gaily decorated boxes, piled high on the teacher's desk, were auctioned off. Only males were allowed to bid.

Much jocularity accompanied the spirited bidding, and sometimes a mischievous neighbor would drive the price way up before allowing the husband to buy his own wife's sumptuous supper. It was a pleasant way to raise money for the rural school; the proceeds were used to pay the piano tuner and to purchase crayons, construction paper, kerosene for the lamps, and brooms.

One year, before I was even dimly aware of the boy-girl thing, Miss Sturtz, my first rural schoolteacher, offered to create a beautiful box especially for me if I were to agree not to tell a soul. She even offered to fill it. I was thrilled, and immediately agreed to her proposition. Now in second grade, I had adored her since the first grade the year before. Had I been less trusting I would have been suspicious of this plan, since no children ever brought boxes.

The evening of the social, taking me aside, she pointed out a container decorated with two tiers of ruffled Denison crepe paper. The upper tier was a heavenly blue, the lower one a rosy pink. A neat pink bow covered the lid. This work of art was the most lavishly decorated offering, far and away, and I was filled with pride.

When the bidding began, the auctioneer held this box up for all to see; his comments made it clear to the several young men of marriageable age who were vying for the favors of the pretty young schoolteacher that this treasure could belong to none other than the lissome Miss Sturtz. He set it aside to be sold last. When it was finally time to auction off this lovely creation, the spirited bidding went all the way up to four dollars, top dollar for a supper for two. Slats Bowman placed the winning bid. And then the box was opened, only to reveal my name on top. The whole assembly in the crowded schoolroom exploded into derisive laughter.

You see, the tradition was that you sat, ate, and enjoyed the evening with the owner of the box.

For the rest of the evening, with raucous guffawing and kidding all around us, the deeply chagrined Slats shared a double desk with me, a not very pretty, plumpish second grader with two missing front teeth. He sat sideways at the desk, his back to me, while I serenely gobbled the delicious supper.

Mercifully, my naiveté, which resulted in a near-total lack of awareness of what had just occurred, was my shield that night. I was further protected by my absolute faith that a teacher could do no wrong. Certainly Miss Sturtz could do no wrong. I learned extra verses for her; I did extra homework for her; I drew and colored pretty pictures for her. I adored her. In my nightly prayers, I asked God to bless her.

But the merriment of the farmers, the gangly youths, and even the wives, roiled my memory and disturbed my delight in the lovely pink and blue box packed with mouthwatering goodies. Vaguely uneasy and agitated, I mentally reviewed the scene for years. When my terrible epiphany finally came, I was struck by the monumental cruelty of that mischievous but callous deception. Cruel to the excessively thin, love-struck youth who exposed himself so trustingly to ridicule, and cruel to me, a totally innocent and equally trusting second grader. I'm glad I didn't comprehend that scene then; I don't think I would ever have recovered.

19

Gathering Nuts

Once every spring and fall during the early thirties it was the custom for our immediate family—Grandma, Grandpa, their four daughters and husbands, and all of the grandchildren—to skip church and meet up on Sunday morning in Yankee Grove, picnic baskets in hand. In October, the get-together was for three purposes: To clean up the family cemetery, to gather the black walnuts, hickory nuts, and butternuts that were now ready to be harvested, and to have a picnic.

Grandpa and Grandma Urmy in Yankee Grove

We began with the cleanup. Sometime before 1850, Grandpa's grandfather's family had donated land for a cemetery, now called the Urmy Cemetery and sometimes, by locals, Yankee Grove Cemetery. (It shows up on Google Earth as Urmy Cemetery.) The Urmys magnanimously permitted nonfamily neighbors to bury their dead there when the deaths occurred in the winter, with the agreement that on the arrival of spring, the bodies would be disinterred and reburied somewhere else. Of course, this preposterous promise was never honored, which accounts for there being quite a number of unmarked graves as well as stones bearing the names of persons who did not belong to the Urmy family.

To find the Urmy Cemetery, you have to approach Yankee Grove from the east and follow the road until you spot a barbed-wire gate on the left. Unlock the gate and follow the path along the fence and up through the enclosed cornfield. At the end of the path, on the left, you'll see a grove of gigantic oak and hickory trees. Once you're about forty feet into the grove, you will see the cemetery.

An imposing, shoulder-high, oblong stone with gleaming, smooth sides marks the graves of Grandpa's father and mother, Jonathan and Harriet. This shining granite stands in sharp contrast to the moss-and-lichen-covered unfinished sandstone slab markers of Grandpa's grandparents, Susannah, who died in 1857 in her ninety-seventh year, and Jacob, who died in 1864, age unknown because the writing on his stone is no longer legible. (It was this couple who contributed the land for the cemetery.)

The next largest marker is a tall, four-sided pillar of gray granite that is crowned with a peak. Each of the four faces of the stone notes the name and death of an Urmy infant: two boys and two girls. These babies were my mother's brothers and sisters. Half of Grandma and Grandpa's children died before the age of two:

They succumbed to diphtheria, pneumonia, croup, and whooping cough. Family members have observed that a kind of natural selection seemed to be in operation here, in that all the survivors were so hardy that they lived well into their nineties. The last of them, Mama's youngest sister, Aunt Wilma, died on July 21, 2005, ten days after her hundredth birthday.

Urmy tombstone in Yankee Grove Cemetery

My mother's siblings were not the only ones whose tombstones tell of early deaths. If you rub a handful of cornstarch onto the face of the markers, you may still be able to read the nearly obliterated names and dates. Your heart will break when you note how many died in infancy or early childhood. Some parents found the loss so wrenching that they noted the days as well as the months and years they were privileged to share with their precious children: *Here lies Jacob Franklin Cross, 11 months, 12 days. "Sleep on, sweet babe, and take thy rest. God called thee home. He thought it best."* Baby Jacob, who was named after his mother's grandfather, Jacob Urmy, died in 1854, ten years before the death of his namesake.

There are more graves of infants and children: *Margaret Anne Urmy—1 year, 3 days; Amanda Volgmore—2 years, 10 months, 11 days; George Mosher—7 years, 6 months, 3 days; Florence Young— 11 years, 2 months, 26 days.* Grief for Florence who died in 1870, is commemorated in one poignantly economical line: *"It was an angel that visited the green earth and took the flower away."*

The cemetery area is small, perhaps one hundred feet square, and is fenced in rather carelessly. I should use the past tense here, for in 2000, friends and relatives sought and received government help in renovating it, since two Civil War veterans, both Urmys, are buried here. I am told that the cemetery is now quite well maintained.

But in my childhood the graveyard was sadly unkempt. So the first priority of the Sunday morning mission was to tidy up the cemetery. This meant pulling ragweed and daylilies, cutting the grass with a hand scythe, resetting some of the smaller crude sandstone markers, tightening the barbed wire fence, and straightening the fence posts. The men sometimes used an ax to split the closely packed bulbs of the daylilies that bloomed over the graves. There was something obscene about their profusion and vigor; we were all perfectly aware of where their nourishment came from!

We children worked right along with the adults, careful where we stepped, for to walk on a grave was to show extreme disrespect. We listened intently to the invariable arguments about who was laid next to whom in the sunken, unmarked grave sites. I learned something new about the relatives on every cleanup occasion.

With all twenty-one of us working, it didn't take long to do the modest tidying up of the graves. Then it was time for our picnic. We knew we could expect to pig out on fried chicken, thick slices of crunchy-crusted homemade bread and butter, potato salad, cabbage salad, scalloped corn, chocolate cake, ground-cherry and apple pies, and huge pots of delicious hot coffee laced with heavy cream, while lolling on the astonishingly thick green grass that carpets the woods in Iowa.

After our feast, we turned to the main reward of the day: gathering nuts. Gunnysacks and galvanized water buckets were hauled out of the cars, and we kids divided up into groups determined mainly by age and sex. My cousin Vera and I, being the same age, were a twosome. Carrying the pail between us, we headed into Yankee Grove. The high blue sky, the brilliant leaves, the toasty warm earth beneath our bare feet, and the incredibly sweet air, cool and fresh, made these outings sheer bliss. A poem we learned in country school described our feelings exactly:

> O suns and skies and clouds of June,
> And flowers of June together,
> Ye cannot rival for one hour
> October's bright blue weather.

The walnut trees grew along the edge of the grove; the hickories clustered near the cemetery; and the butternut trees, only three in number, were found in Indian Hollow, deep in Yankee Grove. This little valley was named for the Tama Indians who used to winter there in Grandpa's youth, lured there by the isolation, the protection from the icy winds, and the dependable, sweet water flowing from the spring in the side of the hill.

I haven't met anyone in recent years who knows what a butternut is. While the tree itself is almost identical to the black walnut, the nut is quite different. An elongated ellipse in shape, the butternut is thinly covered with a sticky chartreuse hull which overlays the extremely hard, raggedy-jaggedy, coarse shell. As with black walnuts, it is necessary to hold the nut against a stone or an iron bar and give it a smart whack with a steel hammer in order to get at the two-lobed goody within. No other nut begins to compare in flavor with the butternut; they were a delicacy in our house during the thirties, second only to morel mushrooms, and were hoarded for special occasions like Thanksgiving, Christmas, and Easter.

We would go off into the woods, fill our pails, return to the cars, dump the nuts into gunnysacks, then return to gather more. At four o'clock we divided the bounty among the four families, packed everything into the bulging cars, and headed for home. Next came the job of hulling and storing our harvest.

Since the butternuts were so few and the hickory nuts were so easy to handle—their hulls divided cleanly and evenly into four parts, and could be knocked off the smooth, clean nut with little effort—it was the black walnuts that commanded most of our attention. About the size of tennis balls, they had to be set aside for a few days after harvesting to allow their hard, greenish, acrid-smelling hulls to soften and blacken. Once they were ready we kids knew that for days to come, after walking home from school, after feeding and watering the chickens, after gathering the eggs, after getting the cows up from pasture, after slopping the pigs and feeding the calves, we would have the added burdensome chore of hulling those horrid walnuts—a job we all hated.

We experimented with various inventive techniques to simplify the onerous task. Once or twice we fed the nuts into a hand-turned corn sheller. This seemed like a dandy idea at the time, but left the machine so badly stained that we could barely get it clean enough to shell corn, so that experiment was not repeated.

Sometimes we placed the nuts on a discarded barn door for a few days until they softened and blackened; then, donning our four-button overshoes, we stomped until the hulls came off. Our best idea involved boring holes in the barn door and placing it on bricks to raise it about half a foot off the ground. If we trampled and scuffed on the nuts long enough, they eventually fell through the holes, leaving the soft, black, outer hulls above. Years later, as a grown-up, I gloried shamelessly in my own resourcefulness when I placed the blackened walnuts in single layers inside sturdy, plastic garbage bags that lay on the apron of the driveway and gleefully ran my Cadillac over them a few times. The hulls were squashed right off, but the nuts were still intact. This was a most satisfying solution.

Perhaps the worst part of the hulling was that even with gloves on, our fingers suffered an almost indelible chartreuse stain that could be successfully removed only by soaking each hand inside of a large green tomato for about an hour. But the hulling was just one step in caring for walnuts. Next, they had to be dried in a single layer for at least a month or two, for newly harvested nuts are green and bitter to the taste. We dried them in the attic where they shared floor space with the supers of honey, the ripening pears, and the ground-cherries, still in their little baglike coverings.

Once, when the attic would not hold the last bushel of freshly hulled walnuts, we placed the basket on the porch to await proper disposition for drying and went to church. We came home to find that the red timber squirrels had scampered off with all but a few dozen of our treasure. Thus it was that we learned another bitter lesson in not putting off until tomorrow what we could do today.

There was one gigantic walnut tree that stood in lonesome grandeur by the side of the road between the two farms. Unlike the high-branching stalwarts that clustered in Yankee Grove, this one branched out starting about ten feet from the ground and spread lushly over an area of fifty feet. Since it produced the largest and tastiest nuts in the whole of Monroe Township, we kept its harvest separate from the others. It had been on the property when my great-grandparents had bought the farm, and each generation had transferred to the next the tradition of harvesting these special walnuts.

One year there was a bumper crop, and we were engaged in the annual collection along with three boys from neighboring farms who were around the same age as my brothers—part of the group we identified as the Big Kids. One of the Big Kids started zinging walnuts at people's rumps whenever they bent over. Taunts began: "You couldn't hit the broad side of a barn!"

The response was another hurled walnut and an incremental escalation of the insult: "You couldn't hit the broad side of a barn if you were on the inside!" This challenge was met with more flying walnuts and another increment: "You couldn't hit the broad side of a barn if you were inside and had all the doors and windows shut!"

Soon walnuts were whizzing through the air with dizzying speed; we Little Kids jumped for safety, belly down, into the ditch. Then a walnut thrown with particular ferocity hit my brother John, tearing open his whole left cheek. His face was instantly flooded with blood.

My uncle, who was the boss of all of us kids, didn't swear often, but he swore when he was angry. And now he was roaring mad. To the visiting Big Kids he shouted, "You get the hell home. If you come near here again I'll kick your asses up between your shoulders." He followed this wonderous threat with, "If I ever catch you on this property, I'll kick your asses up so high you'll have to take your hats off to shit!" We Little Kids tucked our faces down so he wouldn't see our secret delight in this forbidden profanity. John, who had gone into the house to take care of his wound, carried the scar for the rest of his life.

Some years later, again while we were at church, thieves sawed down the walnut tree and carted it off. A short stump, the smallest branches, and lots of sawdust were all that remained of that gracious tree. It was surely sold for a small fortune to some furniture maker. We all mourned its loss; my aunt and uncle cried.

However, we still have the hickories, walnuts, and butternuts in Yankee Grove, and more important, we still have our memories, lasting and sweet, of the three generations of the living who gathered under those stately trees to reaffirm their kinship with three generations of the dead. The wonder for me is that I feel the same kinship with those magnificent trees as I do for those relatives in the cemetery.

I now realize that during the days we spent tending their graves and feasting nearby, we were gathering something far more valuable than nuts.

20

Gathering Wood

In late October or early November I was allowed to accompany Grandpa, Grandma, and my two brothers, Jack and John, on the long trek to Yankee Grove to gather wood to use as fuel for the kitchen range and the living room heater of the house in Garrison. When the time came for this venture, we picked up the horses and wagon (the kind whose wheels had wooden spokes banded by steel rims) from my aunt and uncle's farm and then traveled the two and a half miles to the grove. We took along a hearty lunch of fried chicken, buttered homemade bread, and coffee with lots of pure cream, though I was far too young to drink the coffee.

It took about an hour to get there from the farm. On some days it was so cold we jumped out of the wagon and ran alongside of the horses to increase our circulation and get warmed up. On those really frigid days, Grandpa wore an elegant black bison coat that was so thick and heavy it would stand up all by itself. On his hands he wore fur mittens to his elbows. It was such a grand outfit that it warmed us kids just to look at him.

Since newly felled wood is much easier to split than dried wood, we looked for trees that we could cut down. We preferred dead hickories about two feet in diameter and about fifty feet tall. Cutting down trees is not for the unwary, but Grandpa was the soul of caution, and as he worked he taught us all how to do it. The first thing he would do after selecting a likely candidate for felling was to walk around the tree looking up for a "widow-maker"—a branch high up in the tree that had rotted almost through and was just about to drop, or had already dropped and was caught in the upper reaches of the tree. The careless woods-man striking the trunk with his ax might dislodge the precarious branch, and send it thundering down onto himself or someone nearby.

Sometimes Grandpa had to deal with a "fool-killer." This occurred when he chopped down a dead tree that fell onto a smaller, live tree and got tangled in its branches. The weight of the bigger tree bent but didn't break the other one, it would hang there, suspended above the earth. To the novice woodsman the way out of that dilemma looks easy: Just chop down the smaller tree so that both will fall to the ground. But one whack of the ax on its bowed trunk meant that the sudden release of tension could split it lengthwise, sending a spear of wood straight back into the unwary woodsman, and possibly even disemboweling him. Grandpa showed us the proper angle at which to stand before striking the trunk of the bowed tree, until both trees came crashing to the ground.

After Grandpa felled the trees, he and the Big Kids sawed the trunk and bigger branches into six-foot lengths, while Grandma and I trimmed the smaller branches with bow saws and nippers. Next, using a sledgehammer and three wedges, Grandpa showed us how to split the lengths into logs that two or four people could handle. We quickly learned the wisdom of the three-wedge sys-tem. *Whack!* Drive in one wedge. *Whack!* Drive in a second. The wood firmly clamps onto two wedges. Trying to knock one or the other out is no use. Drive in a third wedge and you can open a crack until one of the first two wedges falls out. Insert that one in the narrow end of the crack and continue until the log is split. It is a very successful and efficient procedure. Once we'd split a sufficient number of logs, we loaded them onto the wagon and headed back to Garrison, unloaded them alongside the grapevine at the house, and then took the team and wagon back to the farm—a long, long haul.

Millie at her wood pile, 2002

The logs we brought home still needed to be sawed and split, a process that occupied my brothers and me for many a Saturday. I was thrilled when I was considered old enough (probably at eight or nine years of age) to take my turn at the crosscut saw, and felt especially honored that the Big Kids would let me split wood. We used the crosscut saw to cut the wood into two-foot chunks, and a sledgehammer and the wedges to split the chunks lengthwise into stove-sized pieces. We made a game of seeing who could send a wedge ringing straight down through the chunk with one stroke of the sledgehammer. To this day I continue to derive great satisfaction from splitting wood, and I still think that newly cut wood produces one of the great fragrances of the world.

On one of those wood-collecting trips to Yankee Grove, Jack and John had a swell idea involving the blasting powder that Grandpa sometimes had to use to split some of the bigger trees. This substance consisted of tiny, black, square pellets of explosive. They were dense in weight and smooth to the touch.

Grandpa understood boys and he understood the danger of mixing boys and blasting powder, so he kept a careful watch on his supply. But my brothers, who positively itched to get their hands on some of it, were able to filch tiny amounts, probably no more than a sixteenth of a cup at a time, making their move whenever Grandpa's attention was distracted. They slipped the pellets to me and I stored them inside my thigh-high lisle stockings, scrunching around with them in my shoes all day. I have no idea how much of the explosive they ultimately accumulated. They also managed to swipe about six inches of the bright orange fuse that was required to set the blast. What did they want it for?

They let me in on the secret. They were going to celebrate the Fourth of July right. Here it was only October. Talk about planning ahead.

Months later when the Grand and Glorious Fourth (my mother actually used that term) came around, the cousins came over and the Big Kids drove an eighteen-inch lead pipe into the ground just behind the house. Since I was not in on the plans, I'm not sure of the exact details, but all apparently went well; the boys poured the blasting powder in the lead pipe, inserted the fuse, and lighted it. We kids scurried to the front of the house to await the blast.

It turned out that we showed remarkable foresight. The explosion split the pipe, blew fragments of it all over, and cracked the windows in the back of the house. A neighbor from half a mile away drove down to see what caused the noise.

The boys got the daylights whaled out of them and were confined to the farm for the rest of that glorious day. Of course we were all lucky; we could have been maimed or killed.

21

Winter Is Icumen In,
Lhude Sing Goddamm!

Parodying an anonymous verse written several hundred years ago, Ezra Pound expresses my sentiments exactly. My recollection of the horrors of the weather that we endured in Iowa is probably exaggerated, but to this day, I am sometimes tempted to cover keyholes in the front door with earmuffs, and my idea of winter sports is to sit around shivering violently. I can't even go to the beach in the middle of the summer unless I stash in the trunk of the car a few warm hooded sweatshirts and lots of extra-heavy beach towels.

However distorted my memory may be, it is a fact that the severe cold weather of the thirties was record-breaking, and we had little natural protection from it. If you look at a map of the Midwest you will note that no barrier exists to keep the icy Arctic wind, snow, and sleet from barreling into the area unimpeded. That's why nearly every Iowa farm family planted a small two-to-five-acre grove of trees directly north of the house to provide a windbreak from the brutal winter storms.

I do not know the exact year, but I definitely recall a winter when the temperature hovered around twenty degrees below zero for about a month. And I remember many times when the whole area was encased in ice and the Big Kids could sled all of the way from Grandpa's house to the Farmers Store—a distance of five blocks—without stopping.

But winter games were not for me. I was short and probably had some abnormal physical sensitivity in my extremities. For whatever reason, it seemed that no amount of clothing could keep me warm enough. Hearing of my plight, a dear, elderly friend of my grandmother's kindly contributed a skunk fur collar-scarf for me to wear when I was six years old. It had been designed for an adult and was far too large for a Little Kid. The ample collar came to the top of my ears, almost covering my head. Six—yes, six—thick, furry tails tipped with white were attached to the front, covering my chest. I was a ridiculous sight to behold and my classmates made fun of me. An even more serious problem was that because the fur was skunk, and because the tanner had not properly treated the skin, the collar and I both reeked. The choice was mine: Don't wear the skunk skin and freeze, or wear the scarf and be warm but smelly. Remember, we kids had been having our characters built from the day of our birth. I chose the skunky scarf.

Usually the worst blizzards occurred after Christmas, but during the years 1932 to 1935, we experienced some extremely cold weather and horrendous snowstorms during late November and early December, before we made our annual move back to Garrison. We had to walk one and a half miles to country school, facing into the north wind, which is no doubt why those winters are so indelibly imprinted on me. I recall one memorable day when the father of one of the students appeared at the schoolhouse door about three o'clock. Though the temperature had begun to drop, it wasn't terribly cold. But the sky was ominous, the sun appearing as a mere white spot, barely visible behind the leaden clouds. The memory of this sky came to me years later when I read Thomas Hardy's line, "The sun was white as though chidden of God," and again when I found Emily Dickinson's poem, "This Is the Hour of Lead."

The whole atmosphere was charged with foreboding. Mr. Moore conferred with Miss Axtle briefly, and we were told that school was to be dismissed immediately. We didn't even sing our two songs, "Now the Day Is Over" and "Work for the Night Is Coming." We were simply sent on our way home.

We were jubilant. We four, along with a neighbor boy who lived just beyond our farm, set out together. Snow began falling in huge, wet flakes before we were out of sight of the schoolhouse. Then the wind began to pick up and the snow turned to a fine meal. We decided to walk on the frozen creek where the high banks afforded us warm protection. Naturally we started sliding on the ice. Great fun. Soon we were all skidding and sliding on the ice-covered creek, merrily racing in the opposite direction of our houses.

The whiteness of the snow kept us from noticing that daylight was fading. By the time someone thought to wonder how late it was, the wind had risen to almost blizzard proportions. Suddenly we became aware that darkness was falling. We were freezing, and we knew only vaguely how far we had gone in the wrong direction. We headed back toward home, choosing to take the road rather than the pasture route, and that was a lucky decision. A county road maintainer who was heading to Highway 218 to keep that main thoroughfare open came into view. Unlike us, he must have realized the danger we were facing. He piled us all on to his maintainer—in those days we referred to both the man and his machine as "maintainer"—and drove us the mile and a half home.

We walked in the door, all maddeningly cheerful and idioti-
cally happy, only to find that everyone, including some of the
neighbors, had been searching for us on foot and on horseback,
half mad with worry. Once our parents determined that we were
all right, just slightly frozen, they set about heating up our back-
sides with the trusty buggy whip.

We were quite certain that we had been badly abused; it wasn't
until I was on the parent end of a few such episodes that I understood the reason for the severity with which we had been beaten.

As the cold weather approached in the fall of the early thirties,
Grandpa ever reminded us of Aesop's edifying tale of the feckless
grasshopper and the forethoughty ant. But even without such
prompts, experience would soon have taught us the wisdom of
the adage "plan ahead."

To compensate for the lack of insulation, every October we
made a family project of piling gleaming fresh straw between the
four-foot-high oak posts that were installed at six-foot intervals
around the back and sides of the house. Then when the first snow
fell, we shoveled snow on top of the straw, thus providing a surprisingly effective barrier to the cold weather we knew would
come soon.

Besides protecting the house from the outside, we made sure
to have plenty of fuel to warm the inside. We split and stacked
cords of wood, and piled more logs close by so that when the split
wood ran out we had an ample supply at hand ready to be sawed
and split.

On bitterly cold nights, and on nights when we expected a
blizzard, we all went over to my aunt and uncle's farm across the
road to help care for the livestock. From the youngest to the oldest, everyone in both households participated. We allowed the
milk cows to remain at their stanchions in the cow barn; we

rounded up the calves and consigned them to their own pen at the far end of the cow barn; and we left the herd of nonmilking cows in the stockyard where they could seek the shelter of the straw and haystacks. We tethered the horses two to a stall in their warm horse barn and saw to it that there was plenty of sweet hay for them to munch on; we closed the pigs in the cozy hog house; and we counted on the natural tendency of the sheep to cluster together in the protected shelter of the three-sided sheep shed, where their wool and their proximity to one another would keep them warm.

The Little Kids and the Big Kids usually cared for the chickens, providing them with ample fresh water and cracked corn. If we expected the thermometer to drop much below freezing, we protected the henhouse occupants by lighting a kerosene heater before we closed the door for the night.

All ten members of our two households were involved in these preparations. When we had finished taking care of the barnyard animals, the families separated and prepared their own homes against the weather, bringing in corncobs, wood, and water.

Since the upstairs of our farmhouse had no heat save for that created by the stove pipe that ran from the first floor through to the roof on the second floor, we had to go to great lengths to keep warm. Early in the evening we placed stones or clean bricks in the oven of the kitchen stove so that at bedtime, after they had become thoroughly heated, we could wrap them in newspapers and a pillowcase and put them under the covers at the foot of our beds.

Here's how we made our bed for the coldest weather, a complicated procedure that usually required the efforts of two people and was set into motion at the first sign of winter's freezing temperatures: We went to the linen cupboard where the wool quilts and featherbeds that we had all worked on during the summer (sometimes reluctantly) were waiting, ready for use. After placing a ten-inch thick featherbed on the mattress, we covered it with a heavy flannel double-length blanket, which we tucked in at the foot of the bed, creating a snug sack that kept our feet from sticking out in the cold. On top of the blanket, we placed another featherbed and a wool quilt.

My sister and I had a regular bedtime routine in winter. After donning our heavy flannel nighties, we hopped into bed and pulled the blankets and quilts completely over our heads, then snuggled together like two spoons. We were permitted one or two kittens, which would find us on their own and snuggle at our feet near the warm stones. Not infrequently we awakened in the morning to find the inside of the windows so thickly covered with ice from the moisture of our breath that we couldn't see outside.

My two brothers also shared a bed, and if the temperature was predicted to plunge toward zero, they declared it a one-dog night and were permitted to sleep with a dog; if the thermometer dropped below zero, then they declared it a two-dog night and enjoyed the pleasure of both Beans and Toby.

No matter how carefully one plans, it is not always possible to foresee all problems, and there is nothing like a tangle with the weather to make that evident. I remember one early December snowstorm that had set us all to taking the usual precautions. Settled in for the night, we were smugly looking forward to a happy snowbound day or two ahead, and when we woke we felt the usual excitement and lightheartedness in anticipation of those cozy days at home. All ordinary routines were stopped so that we could attend to the immediate needs of fetching water and wood, keeping the fire burning in the woodstove, and shoveling paths to the farm buildings. We could get to the woodpile just outside our door, but we couldn't get to the windmill for water so we had to melt snow in a kettle on the stove. We considered it all a joyous adventure.

This time, however, it snowed and snowed and kept snowing until we could not see out of the windows. We were completely cut off from the world. After four days we ran out of kerosene, the oil that we used in our lamps. Then we ran out of white flour, a staple we used in our bread. We all knew that it could be days before the three miles of dirt road to Garrison, now piled high with snow, would be opened.

It turned out that we had no reason for worry. Undaunted, Mama created her own oil lamps in the following fashion. She poured melted bacon fat into six Mason jar lids, placed one-by-four-inch lengths of cotton flannel in the fat, and loosely placed another lid on top, leaving a tiny corner of the cloth sticking out. When the makeshift wicks were thoroughly soaked with the grease, she lit them with a match and placed them about the house, permeating the air with the wholesome fragrance of bacon. I've often thought how this action made real the figurative expression, "Better to light a candle than curse the darkness."

Mama solved the bread problem with equal ingenuity. She washed the pint-sized, hand-cranked coffee grinder and set us kids to grinding the field corn that had been saved in the buttery. I recall that, working in shifts, it took us an awfully long time to get it to the consistency of fine cornmeal. But I also recall that the corn bread she baked with that meal, using an iron skillet, was unusually tasty.

Mama's ability to meet challenges head-on and with a positive attitude created in us kids a sense of confidence that there was a way to solve every problem—just find it. Of course, she had developed that attitude through the examples set by her parents, Grandma and Grandpa.

Now I've learned to enjoy winter, but only in the abstract. That is why I prefer to sit by an open fire and listen to Bing Crosby and Frank Sinatra sing songs about the ice and the cold and the snow, rather than experiencing them firsthand.

22

Town School: Garrison

The red brick school in Garrison went from first through twelfth grade, with grades one through six in classrooms on the ground floor, and grades seven through twelve, along with the principal's office, on the second floor. For reasons of space, the first eight grades were paired, two to a room. The classroom decorations were minimal, consisting usually of portraits of Washington and Lincoln. So from first grade on we knew who our heroes were. Gazing down on us from the walls, Washington in the front of the classroom (just as he was in our country school) and Lincoln in the back, these two great presidents inspired us to make something sublime of our lives, to follow in the footprints they had left behind in the sands of time.

Our families were expected to pay for our texts, pencils, pens, lined tablets, and composition books and notebooks, but the school provided students with construction paper, thumbtacks, crayons, huge jars of white paste, and a hectograph. This last item was an indispensable machine that employed a glycerine-coated layer of gelatine to make copies of typed or written material. A single hectograph served the entire school.

The Garrison Independent School District was organized in

1880. The original wooden schoolhouse was replaced by a brick building in 1912. Until 1936, when the new gymnasium was built, there were no indoor toilet facilities. Generally, we tried to avoid going to the toilet at school by waiting until noon, when we ran three blocks home to eat dinner. Classes started at nine o'clock in the morning and ended at four o'clock in the afternoon, with an hour for lunch and two fifteen-minute recess periods, when we played outside, no matter what the weather.

We had only one piano for the whole school, which was located in the room shared by the first and second grades. Since the music teacher taught all grades, she had to launch us into our singing lessons with a pitch pipe, blowing on it with touching confidence. She also lugged a portable phonograph from room to room, treating us to music far beyond our level of sophistication: Madam Schumann-Heink singing "Lo, Here the Gentle Lark," and a milky-sounding violin rendition of "Humoresque." She promised us that, in time, we would be able to appreciate such music. I have yet to solve the mystery of how one could progress from this base to a fervent appreciation of Mozart and Wagner, but I did.

In 1936, a school bond offering raised enough money to build a new gymnasium-auditorium with a stage. Finally we had a proper place to put on our glee club performances, school plays, declamatory contests, band concerts, and graduation ceremonies, and the school bought another piano to provide accompaniment for all these events. We also used the auditorium for the big productions that we put on for Thanksgiving, Christmas, and Easter, three holidays that were celebrated by public schools throughout the area. There was no consideration given to anyone who wasn't of the Christian faith. Not that it mattered, since almost everyone *was* Christian, and virtually everyone—except for two Catholic families—was Protestant.

Millie, first row, far right

The school employed one janitor, Mr. Irwin, a widower, who was the sole custodian of the entire property, including the furnace room. We all knew him and he knew all of us by name. He had as much authority as the principal when it came to enforcing discipline. Principals came and went but Mr. Irwin endured forever; he was there when I entered first grade and he was there when I graduated from high school.

The students had a love-hate relationship with all of the principals, for they could and did administer strict discipline. One principal in particular, Mr. Woehlk, who came to Garrison in the early thirties, became a godlike presence to the student body. We admired him, we respected him, and we feared him. He greeted every child every day by name at the entrance and we considered his greeting a blessing. We cared what he thought of us. Once, when I was in sixth grade, a friend gave me a copy of *True Story,* a magazine considered unfit for young people. Mr. Woehlk saw me reading it, but instead of bawling me out, he changed my behavior by simultaneously shaming and flattering me. "I had more faith in your taste, Mildred. Would you want your little sister or your friends to know you were reading this trash?" In tears, I promised him I would never read "trash" again.

Mr. Woehlk's influence on me went far beyond that. An exchange between us when I was in eighth grade could be said to have changed the course of my life. "What are you going to make of yourself?" he asked me one day, sitting down in the middle of the stairs to have a quiet chat.

All of us youngsters knew that we could expect to hear some variation of that formulated phrase at least a few times a week, and when we did, we felt exactly the pinned-and-wriggling-on-the-wall sensation it was meant to induce. But on this occasion I didn't feel that I'd been asked a rote question, designed simply to put me on the spot; I felt Mr. Woehlk had a genuine interest in me.

"I've always wanted to be a teacher."

"Good! You'll have to go to a university, you know. You can do anything you make up your mind to."

I was thrilled by this remark. If he said I could, I could!

I thanked him, feeling especially honored at having been granted this private consultation, and then mentioned the obvious obstacle to this glorious future he was envisioning for me. "But I don't have any money."

"I have every faith in you, Mildred. You'll find a way."

With that, he stood, and bounced up the stairs two at a time, keys and coins jingling in his pockets. Only a brief moment out of his life, but it made an enormous difference in mine, for from that moment on, deep in my being, I knew that, someday, somehow, I would end up going to college.

Our teachers, too, were kind and caring souls. To my mind our teachers in Garrison were just as saintly as the ones at Monroe 6, and I adored every one of them. Their many acts of kindness have stayed with me throughout my life. One year, in fourth grade, my sister developed a raging fever. Her teacher, Miss Lorber, after asking the principal to watch her classroom, picked my sister up in her arms and carried her all the way home to our house.

Parents stood foursquare behind the teachers in all matters. "You get a lickin' at school; you get another one when you get home." Everyone accepted this and knew it to be a fact.

Because of the closeness of the community, there wasn't much of a discipline problem. We all knew one another well; we knew each other's families, too—brothers, sisters, fathers, mothers, cousins, aunts, uncles, and grandparents. There was no way that anyone could misbehave without everyone knowing about it. You couldn't even play hooky and leave the school ground at the fifteen-minute recess period to sneak down to the Farmers Store to buy a Baby Ruth because Jim and Mabel Crossley, who ran the store, would have sent you right back to the schoolhouse where you belonged.

The school curriculum emphasized reading and ciphering, which we did every day. At various times during the week we had classes in English, spelling, arithmetic, geography, history, art, civics, and music, and once a week, on Fridays, the Palmer handwriting method. I remember one year when I was in fourth grade, our art lessons were combined with health lessons. This happened because the Ipana toothpaste company, as part of a promotional venture, supplied us with free samples of toothpaste as well as coloring book–style pictures of bathrooms we could fill in with our crayons. Never mind that not one of us kids had ever seen the inside of a real bathroom! The pages we colored instructed us in the art of brushing our teeth and massaging our "gooms," and told us to be on the lookout for "pink toothbrush." For some reason I missed the crucial information that this warning referred to blood on the brush end, not the color of the handle, so for years I diligently avoided buying a pink-handled toothbrush.

School took on an importance beyond its strictly educational role. During the fall, winter, and spring months it provided the main social connection in our otherwise isolated lives—and not just for the children, but for their parents and extended families. The extracurricular activities were the main draw. Glee club, regular and marching bands, baseball, softball, and basketball— these activities in particular knit us together as a community, because everyone came out to attend the concerts and the sports events. Basketball, both boys' and girls', was especially popular. Nothing quite united and focused the attention of Iowans the way basketball did, whether at the county, district, or state level.

I loved school and desired nothing more than the opportunity

Garrison Public School, circa 1912, before the gymnasium addition

to go there every day. However, I was subject to severe chest colds and often "barked" all night, disturbing the sleep of everyone in the family. After one of those wakeful nights, my main concern was that I would be kept home from school to convalesce. Being a conscientious student who got good grades and would do anything to gain my teachers' favor, I was often granted special privileges and praised in front of my classmates. This was quite a contrast to my home environment where the adults were constantly critical of me. At home I couldn't do anything right; at school I seemed to do everything right. So, school is where I wanted to be.

PART FOUR

Spring/Summer

Yankee Grove

23

Leisure Time

With all of the demands on us kids, you might have thought that we wouldn't have had time for games, reading, or any other kind of diversions, but one of the reasons I wanted to document our lives was to describe how we invested our free time in the days before it was swallowed up by radio, television, movies, music, the mall, and the Internet.

Actually, we did have a grand, fancy Philco radio that occupied the corner of the living room in Garrison, but our listening was mostly limited to the news in the middle of the day, and to *The Lone Ranger, Jack Armstrong,* and *One Man's Family* in the early evening hours. Of course, Mama and Grandma listened to *Easy Aces* and *Ma Perkins* while we children were at school. Now and then, on Saturday nights when our cousins came in from the farm, we were permitted to listen to *The Grand Ole Opry.* There were other occasions, too, when we were allowed to enjoy this wonder: when Joe Louis fought and when Franklin Roosevelt had a Fireside Chat. But no way were we allowed to listen to *True Story.*

In the early years, our social life centered entirely on family get-togethers, school, and Sunday school. Our folks would have been appalled to the point of apoplexy if we had asked to engage in what is now called "hanging out." We never slept over at anyone's house and no one ever slept over at our house. But we did spend a lot of time with one another and with our cousins. When we lived in town, we also spent many of our evenings with neighboring children.

Early spring was a truly joyous time to be in Garrison. After supper dishes were washed and put away and after we finished our homework, we were allowed to play outside until it got dark. I remember the air having a balmy freshness and the sky looking soft and lovely. And I remember the feeling of running barefoot on that indescribably green, tender grass.

Because our house was the last one on a street that was on the edge of town, where there was lots of room to play, the neighborhood kids gathered at our place. Since Grandpa and Grandma wanted to know where we were at all times and they preferred that we remain at home under their watchful eyes, that suited them fine. Our friends were always welcome there.

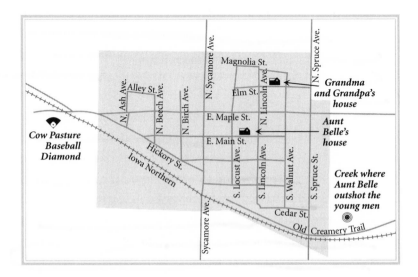

One thing we children all understood: The adults were the ones who made the decisions and the generation gap was not to be breached. Childhood and early adolescence were looked on as a kind of unmentionable affliction, somewhat like the huge goiter that tilted Great-Aunt Maggie's chin way up in the air; it was there for all to see, but no one ever commented on it. The desired condition was to be an adult. We also understood that we couldn't do or have anything that cost money. Nor could we ever suggest to the old folks that we were bored or didn't have anything to occupy ourselves, for in no time they would have had us restacking the woodpile, scrubbing the porches, or picking up fallen apples. Even before the saying was coined, we knew that adults were in some ways the natural enemies of kids.

We were, therefore, remarkably creative—especially on the farm. There, one summer, we created a golf course on the lawn in front of our house by sinking empty coffee cans in the ground where the grass was kept short by the sheep that grazed there. (One-pound coffee cans were squat in shape in those days.) We owned two well-used golf balls by courtesy of the local veterinarian who lived in Garrison. We thoroughly searched the hazel brush for sticks that had naturally curved ends, and made them into dandy clubs after we smoothed the roughness with a Boy Scout knife and sandpaper.

We also developed an exciting pole-vaulting competition. We would search out a sapling of just the right height and diameter to suit each individual. It was important that the wood be green, for the supple quality of young wood was crucial to the vaulting. Actually, the word "vault" was not in our vocabulary and we called our creations "jumping poles." We prized our personally selected poles and carved our initials into the bark. When we weren't using them for practice or competition, we hid them.

Why hide them? A splendidly satisfying way to get even with someone was to chop up his special jumping pole and use it for firewood.

One spring we made our own stilts from two-by-fours. Then we had contests to see who could stay on the stilts the longest time, walk the longest distance, or run the fastest. At some point, the Big Kids instituted jousting matches. Of course these got mighty rough for us Little Kids and we wisely refused to join in their fun.

Gymnastics contests caught our interest for a time. A low branch of the Greening apple tree was just the right diameter and height from the ground to use for chin-ups and skin-the-cat and to hook our feet on so that we could hang from it upside down. We little girls participated in these unladylike activities with our modesty protected by bloomers banded just above the knee. We were better at gymnastics than any of the boys. I marvel that not one of us was ever seriously injured: no broken bones, no broken necks. Not one.

For several summers we enjoyed a dandy though dangerous swing made from a gunnysack partially filled with straw and suspended from the branch of a tall maple tree by a long rope. We placed a twelve-foot wooden ladder at an angle against another maple tree about fifteen feet away from the sack swing. To get a thrilling ride required that we take the sack by its "ear" and climb up the ladder as far as we could go, holding on to the rungs with one hand and the sack swing with the other. Then, in a split second, we would release our hold on the ladder, grab the rope above the sack with both hands and simultaneously leap, clasping the sack tightly between our legs. Swoosh! Awa-ay we'd fly! However, if our coordination was off and our legs failed to get a good grip on the sack, we would plummet to the ground and our bare feet, knees, and legs would be badly scraped and bruised. On the farm, cuts and abrasions came with the fun.

I remember one period when we seemed to have more free time than usual and all seven of us—Big Kids as well as Little Kids—decided that if we worked diligently, we could dig a hole to China. We calculated that China was on an axis on the other side of the world, directly opposite our farm. We gathered spades, hoes, a pickax, and a galvanized bucket, found a clear space in the woods behind our house, and started to dig. For some reason the Big Kids were more accepting than usual of us Little Kids. They didn't tease or make fun of us; they told jokes, gave orders in a kind way, and treated us as if they thought we were their equals. It was a merry occasion. Whenever we had even a few minutes of free time we would meet in the woods to dig. We fell to our digging with a right goodwill, and after a few days our efforts yielded a hole about eight feet in diameter and six or seven feet deep. It was so deep that we Little Kids couldn't help with the digging but were assigned to bring the Big Kids fresh drinking water and apples and to carry away the soil in buckets.

Now, you have to understand that farm people know their surroundings in a unique way. Before the advent of Roosevelt's Rural Electrification, most farmers did a lot of their chores in half darkness. The consequence of this was that we carried around with us a cognitive map of every building, every plot of land, and every tree in the vicinity. Young and old alike would remember the location of a depression in the field, a gap in a fence you could crawl through, a tree branch that had fallen, a rut, a gopher or groundhog hole, a stone partially submerged on a path, even a nail protruding from a board in the cow barn. Farmers who have lived in one place for a long time literally know the place as well as they know the backs of their hands. And so it was that my uncle, confident that he knew every inch of the woods, tore out after a pig that had escaped the pen. The night was falling very fast; it was almost dark, and he could hear the pig but he couldn't see it.

He also could not see our pit to China and plunged headlong into it. He erupted with such sublime profanity as to delight our souls. Well, the Big Kids got a thrashing with the slender buggy whip, while Sis and I got a scolding. The next day we were all set to the task of filling in the hole.

When our work in the fields was suspended because of rain, if the downfall was light enough, we took advantage of this respite to play, of all things, baseball. Our cousins would come across the road to our house because our front yard was bigger than theirs. I have no idea how the Big Kids managed to get a real baseball, but they did. We treasured that ball, repairing it again and again with a curved needle threaded with heavy linen cord that had been thoroughly waxed with beeswax by Grandpa. When, eventually, despite our care, the whole outer shell disintegrated, we salvaged the inner core, which looked like a tightly wrapped ball of rubber bands, wrapped black tape around it, and made it do duty as a golf ball (in another of our rainy-day activities).

Our bat was a horrendously heavy weapon, having been carved out of a solid piece of oak by Grandpa. (We took this mighty bat to Garrison when we left the farm every December and used it there for baseball and, also, as a goal when we got together spring nights to play throw-the-goal.) A solid connection with that bat could belt the ball over the fence and into the oat field. Since our ages ranged from six to thirteen, we Little Kids enforced a rule on the Big Kids: Over the fence counts as an out.

I was a fairly decent pitcher and batter, but I couldn't run very fast. Still, since there were so few of us, I was needed on the team.

Once, when pitching, I didn't duck a fastball slammed out by Jack, the hardest hitter; I was struck right between the eyes and knocked unconscious. The Big Kids brought me to with a splash of cool water from the windmill and we went on with the game.

Occasionally, when we had gathered for one of our frequent family Sunday dinners, the uncles joined us and our cousins and we played ball together; we Little Kids loved that.

Now and then the Big Kids would disappear, and I never knew what they were up to except for once when I caught them outside of the cow barn smoking corn silk cigarettes. They had collected the brownest silk from the end of a mature ear of field corn, rolled it in Bible-paper-thin squares torn from the Sears Roebuck catalogue, and were lighting their creations with matches pilfered from the Mason jar in the kitchen.

"If you don't let me try it, I'll tell on you," I threatened.

"All right, tattletale. Here. Have a puff."

I took a few deep puffs and started to gag. Within a few minutes my throat was stinging, my head was whirling, and I thought I would vomit. Jeering at me, the boys forced me to retreat to the orchard where I struggled to regain my breath and my equilibrium. I owe my brothers a big one for this experience. I never smoked again in my life.

One summer we made wooden guns cut from the ends of peach and apple boxes that were given to us by the owner of the Farmers Store. We cut the thicker end board into a piece about three inches by twelve inches; this served as the gun barrel. Then we fashioned a more slender piece about one inch by six inches to fit the end and fastened it to the "barrel" with a thick rubber band. For the trigger, we drove a nine-penny nail about three quarters of an inch into the underside of the barrel. By stretching one end of a rubber band cut from a discarded rubber inner tube around the tip of the barrel and inserting the other downward and between the slender piece and the butt end, we had a gun loaded and ready for action. The tension on the rubber band could be controlled by the depth that it was inserted. We played cops and robbers with these weapons and soon discovered that the rubber bands could deliver a really smart sting when they hit bare skin.

I don't know who got the idea, but one of the Big Kids developed a repeater by carving a gunlike replica out of a board two feet long. In the top he carved six notches about half an inch deep every two inches, starting at about ten inches from the pointy end. Along the top of the gun, he nailed a one-inch strip of canvas long enough so that the strip could be inserted into every notch. On the butt end, he devised a wire that could turn and tighten the strip. Utilizing the inner tube, he cut rubber bands and inserted them into each strip-covered notch, beginning with the notch that was nearest the pointy end of the gun. When he turned the wire handle, the canvas strip would be pulled taut, releasing the rubber bands, one right after the other. It made a dandy rapid-fire weapon. Soon we all had repeaters.

Naturally, we carried things too far. One late afternoon, having been sent to get the cattle and horses up from the hazel brush, we took our repeaters along and started shooting the rubber bands into the horses' flanks. The effect was electrifying. The animals went absolutely wild! Heads down, snorting, bucking, and farting, they charged this way and that. They galloped off across the slough, up the steep hill, thundered across the pasture and charged down the narrow lane at a breakneck speed toward the stockyard. A couple of them were going so fast that they didn't bother to go through the gate, but sailed in grand leaps right up and over the fence! On reaching the barnyard, they didn't head straight to the water tank, which was always their first stop; instead they raced madly from one end of the yard to the other, manes and tails flying, wheeling and stomping, scattering ducks, geese, chickens, sheep, and calves every which way. Soon the whole barnyard was in a chaotic uproar!

"Good Lord a' mercy! I wonder what's got into those horses? They're really tearin' up Ned tonight! It must be going to storm!" Aunt Hazel and Mama always read a portent into unusual animal and bird behavior.

We kids were well aware of two things. Horses could seriously injure themselves with such madcap cavorting, and if the old folks knew what we had done, we'd all get the daylights beaten out of us. We hid the guns and kept our mouths shut.

As must be clear to every reader by now, those guns were not benign toys. Not too long after that escapade, the Big Kids got into a fight with the Big Kids from a neighboring farm, significantly injuring some faces and necks. Our guns were confiscated forever, and not a moment too soon.

Mama taught us to love rainstorms so much that even the weather was an entertainment. When the thunderheads began to build up in the west, she would gather the four of us to admire the way they boiled and climbed higher and higher; we watched mesmerized as the black clouds advanced swiftly, turning darker and more threatening as they got closer, while thunder and lightning flashed from the topmost clouds to the very ground. Transfixed, we would watch the great wall of rain advance slowly across the oat field, eagerly awaiting that brief moment when raindrops the size of wild plums pelted us. And then came the deluge, engulfing us in a gigantic drapery of rain. We all reveled in such an event. Some years later when I read Mark Twain's description of a Midwest thunderstorm, I had what E. B. White called a

222 Mildred Armstrong Kalish

"spirit laid against spirit" reaction. I knew exactly what Twain was writing about. If we were in the fields or the garden when a storm threatened, we would wait for a signal from Mama or Grandpa; it was their contention that we had ten minutes from the time the wind "freshened" (the word used to describe a sudden noticeable increase in the strength of the blow) until the rain began. So at a freshening, Grandpa would yell, "Pull for the house."

Need I report that we got soaked more times than not?

One warm day when it was raining torrents without any wind, we begged to be allowed to run around and enjoy the downpour. Mama had us put on worn-out duds and turned us loose. In the driving rain we ran barefoot down the lane to the small creek, now swollen way up over its banks and flowing fiercely. We jumped into it, allowing the swift current to just carry us along. We were in seventh heaven. When the sight of a small bridge over a dirt road let us know that we were over a mile from the farm, we got out of the creek and started to walk home, happy as could be with our adventure, until we looked at each other.

"Holy cow! You're covered with blood!" "You're bleeding!" "I'm bleeding!"

We were all bleeding. We were covered in blood from our shoulders to our toes and continued to bleed as we walked.

We couldn't understand why we were bleeding, and the odd thing was that we didn't feel any pain. However, by the time we got home and entered the kitchen, we were certainly a shock to behold: four children in blood-soaked clothes, blood running down our arms and legs, hands and feet. Of course, the rain mixing with our blood made our wounds appear to be far worse than they really were. My aunt and Mama nearly fainted. The next morning we were hurting so much we could barely move. What had happened was that the sawgrass that grew on the banks alongside the swollen creek had superficially lacerated our chests, arms, and legs as the swift current carried us merrily along. We were so sore that we couldn't bend our wrists, elbows, or knees. Though it was several days before we could maneuver normally again, I still recall with true pleasure the glorious fun of careening down the flooded waters of that creek.

24

Gardening

Once they had retired from the farm, my grandparents kept a large produce garden, the equivalent in size of a quarter of a town block, at the back of their house in Garrison. Weather permitting, gardening season in both town and country officially began on Saint Patrick's Day, though it was usually too cold to plant anything but potatoes. As the dawn rose on March 17, we knew that out on the farm, Uncle Ernest would be plowing our garden with Jude and Ginger, the retired sorrels in their late twenties who were used only for light work. Here in town, we knew that Will Bustler and his team of horses would soon be arriving to plow and harrow Grandma and Grandpa's garden.

A tall, pleasant, elderly bachelor, Will lived a simple life in a stark clapboard house on the outskirts of Garrison, which he shared with his ancient mother. We kids referred to him as Wordless Will, for he seldom spoke more than five words at a time. He was famous in our area for his ability to find subterranean water by dowsing, and that is the way he earned most of his money. In fact, it was Will who found the site of the well that supplied the drinking water for Grandpa's house. He arrived carrying his own carefully selected divining rods: a single willow wand about two feet long and a forked willow branch no more than three feet long. He tested with the single wand first, holding it in one hand parallel to the ground. He allowed us Little Kids to tag along behind him as he silently, methodically plodded all over the property east of the house. It took some time, but suddenly the tip of the wand dipped toward the earth. In silent amazement, we watched the stick being pulled down with such force that he could not keep it parallel. And it was in a perfect place, right next to the summer kitchen. But this find had to be double-checked. Grasping the forked stick in both hands with his palms pointing upward, his thumbs pointing outward, and elbows close to his body, he held this divining rod with the pointy end aimed at the sky. Again we retraced the same area; sure enough, at the previously located site, the invisible force relentlessly pulled the tip of the forked stick from the skyward position down toward the ground. Despite his obvious struggle to maintain his grip, Will was unable to do so. We kids watched with respect and admiration. Equally pleased, Wordless Will turned to Grandpa and said, "Arthur, dig here." That well produced tasty, fresh, hard (drinking) water for our family for years and years.

Every Saint Patrick's Day when we came home from school we greeted the sight of Wordless Will's newly plowed earth with a special lightheartedness, for we knew that we would soon be planting potatoes, which meant that we would be allowed to go barefoot for the first time in the spring season. Shedding our shoes and wriggling our toes in the cool, black, mealy soil was such a joy that we were willing to overlook the fact that potato planting also meant that we were in for many hours of back-breaking labor, for which Mama, Grandma, and Grandpa were even now making preparations. Seated on her favorite round-backed chair, wearing her oldest apron—the faded, voluminous one with tiny brown and white checks—our small, fat grandma would be cutting the eyes out of the potatoes with a paring knife when we walked into the kitchen. "Always cut a big enough chunk of potato with the eye so the vine will have a chance to grow," she would tell us. And then she'd show us the several galvanized buckets that she, Grandpa, and Mama had been working on all day, filled with chunks of potato eyes the size of golf balls.

Oh, and we had met these fellows a few times before. We had dug them up the previous fall; we had piled them into a wheelbarrow and rolled them to the basement; and we had spent at least one long weekend in February knocking the unwanted sprouts from the eyes when they had volunteered to grow too soon. For the winter desprouting, all four of us kids were ordered to the dark, dank, cheerless, and cold basement where we sat on chunks of wood and snapped off the sprouts, one by one. Sometimes the cellar was so cold that we had to put on gloves and overshoes. We hated this job but it had to be done, because if the sprouts were allowed to remain, the potatoes would be wilted and spent by planting time in March.

Our work began as soon as we changed from our school clothes into our everyday togs, and it would continue through the weekend. Grandpa was obsessive when it came to planting potatoes. Working ahead of us, he dug holes about a foot deep. We followed along behind, placing four pieces into each hole, then reaching down and arranging each chunk so the eye was facing up. Grandpa insisted that this careful placement would permit the sprout to come up faster; he was scornful of the sluggards who just tossed the chunks into the hole paying no attention to whether the eyes were facing up, down, or sideways. He was right, of course. After he had checked each hole to verify that we had done our job properly, he filled in the holes, piling the soil into a small hill over each one.

Once the plants took root and grew, we had to perform the repulsive task of searching the vast potato patch for bugs. No one except the littlest of the Little Kids was exempt. There are several kinds of potato bugs; we were honored by the round, black and yellow striped Colorado beetle. Each person was supplied with a tin can with about a quarter of a cup of kerosene in it. We turned the leaves, and flipped the bug into the kerosene. As we hunted the bugs we also instituted a search-and-destroy campaign for their orangish egg clusters; these we rendered harmless by squishing them between our thumbs and forefingers. Memories of unpleasant activities such as these are probably the reason that I no longer grow vegetables.

After we finished planting the garden in town, we hied out to the farm to do the same thing there. In both places during the March–May period, we planted onion sets, peas, yellow wax beans, radishes, sweet corn, plus several kinds of lettuces, and we set out tomato, cabbage, and pepper plants. Females and children did most of the gardening maintenance. We would usually get to work early in the morning before the sun got too hot. Grandma, Mama, and I wore sunbonnets; not those tiny, decorative affairs you see on ladies in frontier movies, but the old-fashioned, no-nonsense bonnets with shades so deep that we could hardly see daylight. Grandma made them. As I have reported elsewhere, we also protected our arms by donning a pair of worn-out mercerized cotton stockings fastened at the shoulders with three-inch safety pins.

Every few days, as we weeded by hand and hoe, we would take note of which wax beans, which peas, which beans, which tomatoes, and which potatoes were ready to be gathered for the next meal.

Since I've invested a lot of time in reporting on how hard and sometimes distasteful the work of growing potatoes was, I think it appropriate that I also mention how much joy we took in the harvesting. The appearance of the first new potatoes was an event. Along about the middle of June we would pull up a plant and discover five or six golf-ball-sized potatoes clinging to the roots. Great! They're ready. Using a potato fork, we would dig up several of the hillocks until we had about five potatoes for each person. Wash these potatoes and boil for about fifteen minutes, place in a bowl, add pure farm cream and maybe a little butter, salt, and black pepper—and dig in. Now that's a treat worth working for.

We ate tomatoes all day long when they were in season. Our garden on the farm was located right next to the stockyard, where there was a huge block of snow-white iodized salt propped onto a stake for the sheep, cattle, and horses. We thought nothing of striking off a small chip from the salt lick so we could jump the fence to the garden and use it to season the radishes and tomatoes we harvested and ate on the spot. (As I remarked earlier, we didn't worry much about germs in those days.) Taking a lick of the tangy salt, we would then bite into one of those perfectly ripe tomatoes and have a little feast.

Grandpa was particular about his tomato plants. He preferred the Abraham Lincoln, and every fall he mashed a carefully selected specimen onto a newspaper. As the mess dried in the sun, the seeds would stick as if glued to the newspaper, which Grandpa folded up and placed in a brown paper bag. There the newspaper remained until spring rolled around and it was time to plant the seeds. In our family, the Abraham Lincoln remains the taste criterion for tomatoes to this day. I'm pleased to report that it can still be purchased from plant preservation companies dedicated to keeping these heirloom varieties alive.

Blue sweet corn was another of Grandpa's special crops. He said his father had gotten the first blue ears from the Indians. Every year Grandpa selected the best blue ears to save for seed for the next planting season. But eventually he forgot to save the seed ears—I don't know why—and so we lost that exceedingly tasty corn. We preferred the blue corn to the yellow by far. Does anyone ever eat blue corn on the cob these days, or is it all used to make blue taco chips?

Strawberries were to us what ambrosia was to the pagan gods. The modern berry—developed to withstand picking, packaging, and transporting—bears faint resemblance to the fruit we ate. Our berries were spectacular, huge, deep red, and full of flavor. There was good reason for this. We fertilized them with cured cow manure; we mulched them with sweet, clean straw, which kept the ground moist and the berries clean; and most important of all, we ensured that the patch remained continuously young and productive by moving it, one row at a time, into fresh soil each year. We did this by extending the runners of the newest plants, at the front edge of the patch, onto uncultivated ground, where we anchored them with two-pronged hairpins, and digging up the oldest, most spent plants at the opposite edge.

That strawberry patch yielded dishpan after dishpan of luscious fruit. We ate strawberries from the vine; we made strawberry pie; we made strawberry jam and we made strawberry sauce. One of our favorite concoctions was old-fashioned strawberry shortcake piled high with whipped cream.

The current practice of using a sponge cake to masquerade as shortcake simply will not do. Here is Grandma's shortcake recipe:

First, pick, wash, and hull two quarts of dead-ripe strawberries.

Sprinkle half a cup of sugar over the berries and set them aside while you make the dough.

In a bowl place two cups of flour, two tablespoons of sugar, one teaspoon of salt, and one tablespoon of baking powder. (Grandma swore by Calumet!)

Cut in half a cup of white lard, butter, or Crisco. Use that gadget that looks a bit like a stirrup made of wires; it was designed for cutting shortening into flour. The mixture should look like very coarse cornmeal.

Add one beaten egg to two thirds cup of whole milk. Now add this to the flour in the bowl all at once and stir with a fork until the mixture is just barely moistened. This is the crucial instruction for flaky shortcake. You will ruin the whole thing if you mix thoroughly.

Using a fork, gently spread this dough into a greased eight-by-eight-inch pan. Bake for sixteen minutes in a 450° oven until nicely browned. Remove from the oven, cool in the pan for about ten minutes and, with a fork, carefully split the shortcake horizontally.

Divide the strawberries between the layer and over the top. Slosh with great gobs of not-too-stiffly-beaten whipped cream and enjoy.

During the hot, dry days of summer when the scallion, lettuce, and radish beds, along with the cabbage, pepper, and tomato plants, had to be hand-watered, the whole family would sometimes join in to help. Gardening was hard work, but at the same time it served to draw us together, since even the smallest of the

Little Kids (my four-year-old sister, Avis, and our two-year-old cousin, Harold, Aunt Hazel's latest contribution to the family), could participate, if only in the watering process. The Big Kids, who were all boys, carried the heavy galvanized buckets of water, two at a time, from the windmill to the garden. The Little Kids dipped a tin can into the buckets and poured water to the base of each and every plant.

The adults usually sprung the gladsome news of this task after we had already finished our other chores and washed the supper dishes. I recall that there were times when we grumbled mightily, but it didn't really make sense to water until after the sun had set. So that's when we did it, no matter how tired we were.

Both the farm and town gardens were central to our households. They were the main supply stores for our table beginning in the spring, and as far into the fall as we could find anything to harvest. Long after most other people had abandoned their gardens, Mama led all four of us kids there for a final foraging. This pleasant event usually occurred on a warm Saturday in October, during which we engaged in a lively competition to see who could spy and harvest the most vegetables. We gleaned the last few red and yellow onions, the three remaining turnips, the last four hills of potatoes, and the four or five gnarled red and green peppers that had earlier been rejected because they were small, misshapen, and not good enough for the table. Mama directed us to pull every last carrot, no matter how small. She peeled the unappetizing, wilted outer leaves from a cabbage to reveal a perfectly sound and edible head beneath. She tugged the massive dying vines to reveal a dozen or so tomatoes hidden under the plant. We picked the ripe ones, then took the entire vine with the green ones still clinging to it into the barn, where one of the Big

Kids hung it on a high hook and covered it with a horse blanket to protect it from the frost. Over the next few weeks tomatoes would ripen, providing us with one last taste of summer on a cold fall day.

Our fall harvest was yet another example of the "Waste not, want not" ethos by which we lived. Do you need to be told, that with the addition of a marrow bone, Mama produced a magnificent soup from this final gleaning? Need I add that I adopted this final gathering routine right down to making a great soup in my own gardening days?

25

Spring in Yankee Grove

Yankee Grove held other fascinations besides nuts, a cemetery, and firewood. In the spring, often as early as mid-March, we would go there to ferret out the tiny Easter lilies snuggled in the warmth of the dead leaves, blooming under the melting snow.

Aunt Belle always accompanied us on these jaunts; it was she who taught us where to look. Indeed, it was Aunt Belle who taught us to identify most of the plants and wild flowers in Yankee Grove. In April she would take us to gather spring beauties with their delicate, pinkish blossoms and dainty leaves. Soon after they bloomed we would be rewarded with hosts of Dutchman's-breeches, bloodroot, and bluebells, which we took home in great bouquets. Aunt Belle showed us where to find the spectacular lady's slippers, both pink and yellow, but she forbade us to pick even one. Nor would she allow us to pick the jack-in-the-pulpits, but she did point them out to us and urge us to return in September to note their transformation into the short wand of spectacular scarlet berries known as lords-and-ladies.

One edible plant Aunt Belle introduced to us was the may-apple, a delicious yellow fruit the size of a small lemon that emerged from between two umbrella-like leaves. She warned us not to eat the mayapple until it reached its wrinkled, overripe stage. But when I discovered years later that the leaves, the stem, and the root of this plant are poisonous, even though the pulp of the fruit is not, I could not understand how we were able to consume all those mayapples without any problems, given how little care we took in handling them. I wouldn't eat one now on a bet.

There was another even more delicious—and less dangerous— spring treat to be harvested in Yankee Grove. In mid-May, a hot humid day following a warm rain was the signal for us to put on with speed our woodland dress, grab a brown paper bag, and go out in search of the most delectable of all mushrooms—the morel. We always parked the car in the same spot near the cemetery, and then we would fan out into the grove, looking for the places we remembered finding morels the year before, because if they'd been growing near an old rotting log or under an elm or apple tree one year, they were likely to be at the same location the next.

Morels bear no resemblance in either taste or appearance to the common commercial button-shaped mushroom that most people are familiar with. Shaped like spongy little Christmas trees on a short stalk, they are usually two to four inches high, though my brother John once found a gigantic one eight inches high. He wouldn't pick it until we had all gathered around to "ooh" and "ah" over it. Say "morel" to a knowing Iowan and you can expect a beatific smile to appear beneath eyes cast heavenward in blissful memory of a gustatory delight unlike any other. It is with more than a little happy anticipation that I greet the report that some professors at Michigan State University have finally solved the mystery of how to grow morels commercially. This scientific advance will bring untold pleasure to those who have never eaten morels, and quite a thrill to the rest of us.

I have seen various recipes for morels: Some suggest that they be used as a garnish with filet mignon; some suggest they be mixed with capers and truffles and served as an appetizer; some say they should be mixed with scrambled eggs.

The true-blue morel lover expects to pig out on this delicacy and this delicacy alone. Here is how to prepare and serve morels:

> First acquire about ten morels for each diner. Gently brush the debris and dirt from the stem end. If there is dirt on the heads, give a fast dunk in water but do it as briefly as possible because mushrooms, being spongy, absorb liquids, which will affect both texture and taste. Next place the largest cast-iron skillet you can find over a medium burner and place two to four tablespoons of salted butter in it. Split the mushrooms so they will lie flat, dust them lightly with ordinary white flour, and when the butter is sizzling, put the morels in a single layer into the skillet. Sauté them until they are just slightly browned. Now you have come to a choice point. You can serve them as is, or you can add half a cup of heavy cream and continue sautéing for about two to five minutes before serving. Either way, serve with nothing else but homemade bread and some salad.

Don't let anyone talk you into varying this recipe. Morel connoisseurs tend to be opinionated.

Once in a while when we were working in the grove Grandpa would spot a honeybee; if it kept coming back he would eventually "line" it. He must have had telescopic vision, for he could lock his eyes onto a bee and follow it far into the woods. He knew every tree in Yankee Grove and could pretty much tell which hollow the bees were headed for by the direction of their flight.

After lining several bees he would say, "Well, I think they're in that old hickory beside Indian Hollow. Next week we'll have a look." Some days later he would prepare to rob the nest of its honey. This was a delightful adventure for us all. It required tying black mosquito netting over wide-brimmed hats, buttoning long-sleeved shirts all the way up to the chin, donning heavy cotton work gloves, and closing off pant legs with rubber bands cut from old inner tubes. My sister and I wore heavy ribbed cotton stockings.

Grandpa led the assault, carrying a contrivance that looked something like a copper teapot with a small hand-held bellows attached to it. He built a smoldering fire of green hickory in the can and, by pressing the bellows occasionally, used it to belch smoke at the bees when they went on the attack.

Grandpa would usually be the one to climb the tree, since even the Big Kids were considered too young to be trusted with this job. Our task was to stand under the tree, throw a rope over a branch, and hoist the one-gallon pail that was tied to the rope up to the bee nest where Grandpa was waiting. I don't remember Grandpa's ever harvesting more than a half gallon of honey, and he was always careful not to take the beebread, the brownish honey that the bees would need to survive the winter.

Unlike hornets and bumblebees, which can sting again and again, the honeybee can sting only once, because when it stings, the stinger stays in your flesh along with about half of the bee's insides, and the bee dies. Despite our precautions, we always got stung several times. The accepted remedy for honeybee stings was to pull the stinger out immediately to prevent it from continuing to pump venom into the flesh, and to cover the area with a dab of mud or ear wax. Grandpa always got stung more than anyone, which he insisted was the reason he never got rheumatism.

One May we were in Yankee Grove cleaning up the cemetery and picking bloodroot, bluebells, and Dutchman's-breeches, when I slipped away from the family to attend a call of nature. As I dropped to the ground to slither under a barbed-wire fence, I heard a distinct buzzing sound. I looked up. There, hanging from a branch, not five feet from the ground, directly over my head, was a huge clot of bees—enough to fill a five-gallon cream can. A great dollop they were, hanging down in a buzzing, quaking, nervous clump. Forgetting the urgency of my original mission, I ran back and reported my find, because I knew that if Grandpa found a "good" swarm in the wild, he would hive it and take it back to Garrison to add to the hives he kept under the plum trees in his backyard. The value of these swarms was summed up in a ditty he used to recite: "A swarm of bees in May is worth a load of hay. A swarm of bees in June is worth a silver spoon. A swarm of bees in July isn't worth a fly."

One look told Grandpa that this was a "good" swarm. Clearly, the bees were surrounding their queen and were on their way to a new tree somewhere in the woods. A wild swarm has to be captured immediately or it will just take off and disappear. We had brought no equipment for hiving bees on this foray, but Grandpa ran back to the parking area where he found a wooden box that had held our picnic goodies. With his knife and hand ax, he fashioned a five-by-one-half-inch entry into the box and we watched, enchanted, as he got down on his knees and eased the box to within about six feet of the massive swarm.

What followed next we had never seen before. With a long stick, Grandpa gently brushed the bulk of the mass from the branch to the ground. Then he slowly edged the box closer and closer, tapping steadily and loudly on its sides with his hard hands. With the stick he directed the clumps of bees toward the newly fashioned slit in the box. No one talked, no one moved, as we watched this procedure with baited breath. Wonder of wonders, the bees began to pour through the slender opening, apparently in response to the tapping.

Grandpa continued the drumming, which had a Pied Piper effect on the swarm. The bees streamed into the box for over an hour. When he was satisfied that he had the queen along with most of the swarm, he stuffed the hole in the makeshift hive with a cotton work glove, tied the box onto the running board, and headed for Garrison. I don't know the year of the Buick, but it boasted isinglass curtain panels which, in cold weather, were clipped on with fancy wing nuts. This being a warm spring day, the isinglass panels were not in place. We knew that swarming bees aren't supposed to sting because they're too full, but everyone in the car got stung as some of the angry bees escaped the box. Everyone, that is, except Grandma, who always wore a long, cream-colored gossamer silk scarf that she wrapped over her hat and tied under her chin.

Once back in town, Grandpa transferred the bees to a regular hive out in the plum orchard. A few days later I witnessed the following scene between Grandpa and my brother John.

"Hey, Grandpa, Rich Bushnel is tellin' everyone down at the pool hall that those bees you got out at Yankee Grove belong to him."

Grandpa, standing perfectly still, kept his eyes on the end of his forefinger. A honeybee had tumbled into the shallow dish of water that had been set out for the bees to drink from, and Grandpa had rescued it. The trembling bee pivoted around the

*Grandpa
holding great-
granddaughter
Sherry,
whose father,
cousin Dean,
a fighter pilot
on the U.S.S.
Enterprise, was
killed a few days
before she
was born*

end of his finger, buzzing audibly as the sun dried its soggy wings. Grandpa was like that, gentle and considerate with all living things. If the bees were working the dandelions on the lawn, he would delay mowing until they had taken their business elsewhere. When he was in his eighties, he placed beebread on a precious, antique blue plate out near the hives. He liked the look of the honey on the plate. Every time my husband and I came from Iowa City to visit him, I would substitute a cheaper plate for the valuable antique, and every time I came back, he would be using it again. I finally stole the blue plate to preserve it.

"Well, they were on my property, but if he can prove they are his, he can come and get them."

Smiling triumphantly, he held his hand aloft; the bee, now

fully dry, took off. That hive turned out to be especially productive, in the first year producing two supers for us as well as ample beebread for the bees.

There were a lot of bumblebees on the farm doing service to the sweet red and white clovers as well as the alfalfa. One year the Big Kids discovered a bumblebee nest between two doors lying on the floor of an abandoned farmhouse. In an expansive moment, they permitted us Little Kids to join them, and with great excitement all seven of us trekked down the dirt lane, across the creek, and up to the dilapidated house, armed with half-gallon tin pails and brown gallon jugs. The Big Kids were in possession of the latest information on how to collect honey from bumblebees: Fill gallon jugs with about two inches of water from the creek, set them near the nest, and then, with large sticks, disturb the area surrounding the nest. We made our preparations with intense glee and also with great caution, for we all knew that bumblebees can sting many times and that their stings hurt like crazy.

Setting the jugs close by, we jostled the doors with our sticks. The bees roused to their own defense while we lay on our stomachs, out of reach and not moving. Sure enough, the bees were doing exactly as we had been told they would. They flew to the jugs, hovered, buzzed angrily over the mouth, then dropped straight down where they were trapped in the water. We were overjoyed. This was the moment to grab the honey: translucent, marble-sized balls of liquid succulence. I had never seen nor tasted bumblebee honey before.

What we hadn't counted on was the immense number of bees. Not all of them had been attracted to the jugs, and the survivors started to attack us. They were furious. And they were relentless.

They kept coming and coming. We were stung over and over again.

We stuffed our sweet harvest into the pails and ran to the creek to immerse ourselves in the water where the bees couldn't get us. Then we went home to share our treasure. Oddly enough, only one of us suffered severely from those stings. My brother Jack's eyes were swollen shut like two huge, hot, pink biscuits. He lay in bed with a high fever for several days, his whole face covered with a cool poultice of wet baking soda, until the swelling subsided and he could see again.

We returned the next evening (without Jack) to retrieve the jugs, pouring the water and the dead bees onto the ground. We were totally unaware that we had perpetrated a tragedy. For less than a pound of honey, we had devastated a nest of bumblebees. But I don't think there was much awareness at the time of the intricacy of the web that binds plants, animals, and humans together. My farming relatives almost certainly did not understand how crucial a role the bumblebee played in pollinating red clover, a hay they depended on to feed their livestock, summer and winter; otherwise, they would have told us it was unforgivable to destroy bumblebees. I learned years later that only the bumblebee with its long proboscis is able to pollinate red clover, for other bees cannot reach the nectar. But even though this was news to us, such knowledge had been around for a long time. In fact, Darwin had used it to plead for allowing cats to roam the countryside without restriction. He argued that since the bumblebees were necessary to pollinate red clover, and since mice and voles were the great destroyers of bumblebees' nests, it was necessary to allow cats to range freely so that they could eat the mice and the voles.

I have never met another person who has robbed a bumblebee's nest, nor have I ever met a person who knows what wild bumblebee honey looks or tastes like. As children we swooned over the crystal clear globes of heavenly sweetness, and I wouldn't have missed this excursion. As an educated adult, I am happy to report that we never robbed another nest of bumblebees.

26

May Baskets

When I was growing up we had an endearing tradition of hanging May baskets on the first of May. Starting around the middle of April, after our homework and household chores were done, we girls devoted much of our free time to making these baskets. There were many sizes and shapes, but by far the most popular one was made from an eight-inch square of paper folded into a basket that looked like two ice cream cones with a handle long and sturdy enough to hang over a doorknob.

The girl who managed to cajole an outdated book of wallpaper samples from the hardware store was the envy of all, for her May baskets would be particularly beautiful. A few girls had parents who went as far as Vinton, the county seat and a big town of at least 1,700 people, to get one of these sample wallpaper books. My cousin Maxine earned our undying envy when she brought home a special selection all the way from Waterloo. We were already jealous of Maxine for a number of reasons: She was a blue-eyed blonde, she was tall, she had curly hair because her mother gave her a permanent every three months, and she was smart. There was more: Every week her mother drove her the thirty miles to Waterloo for private tap-dancing lessons. Home to the John

Deere Farm Implement Factory ("We stand behind all of our farm implements except the manure spreader") and the Rath Packing Company ("We use everything from the pig except the squeal"), Waterloo seemed a grand metropolis to us. The fact that Maxine had real talent and performed in store-bought costumes made us even more jealous. Our envy did not, however, prevent us from fawning all over her for a chance at the few pages that were left over after she had taken all she wanted from her treasure.

As May first approached we made lists of the people to whom we would be giving the May baskets we had crafted from Maxine's leftovers, planned what we would use to fill our baskets, and prayed for a balmy evening. Now it was my turn to be courted, because everyone knew that Grandpa's Yankee Grove was the best source of the bluebells, bloodroot, and Dutchman's-breeches that we liked to put on top of our baskets.

We all hoped we would be on Virginia Bowman's list, because her father owned one of the two grocery stores in Garrison. A basket from her meant that you would receive store-bought stuff: yellow and orange candy corn; small spicy lime, lemon, and strawberry jelly drops; tiny cinnamon and clove-flavored candies covered with what looked like red enamel; and orange jelly slices rolled in coarse sugar. We courted her without shame.

On the afternoon of May first, we ran straight home from school, filled our May baskets with the chocolate fudge, penuche, and popcorn that we had made the night before, topped them with the wildflowers we had gathered, and set out at dusk on our distribution rounds. We went from door to door, hanging our baskets on doorknobs, knocking and running like the devil before the recipient got to the door. If it was a girlfriend who received the basket and she caught you, there was a cheery exchange of greetings and thank-yous; but if it was a boy, when he chased and caught you, he got to kiss you. You know—a little smack on the cheek.

It wasn't until I was in sixth grade that I realized that the edible goodies weren't the main point of the May baskets tradition. I was only beginning to be aware of the boy-girl thing. But that year a shy boy, Tim, caught my fancy, and I knew he liked me, too. One afternoon when Miss Buffington left the room for a brief moment, he had belted me an awful whack right between the shoulders with his geography book. Updegraf never sent a clearer message. Furthermore, Tim couldn't talk to me without a burning red blush suffusing his transparent skin right up to and including his outrageously large ears and the scalp beneath his pale blond hair. So I planned to hang my prettiest goody-filled basket on Tim's doorknob.

What I failed to anticipate was that he would be lying in wait for me. No sooner had I positioned my knuckles on the door, when he bounded out like a shot. He caught me by the lilac bush at the corner of the house and gave me a kiss full on the mouth. I was so startled I protested, "Hey! What are you doing?"

Holding me by my upper arms, shy Tim said, "I caught you, now you gotta kiss me."

So I gave him a peck on the cheek.

"No," said shy Tim. "You gotta give me a real kiss." And he proceeded to give me my first real kiss. Wow! How come nobody had told me about this? And that was how and when I discovered what hanging May baskets was really all about.

Did this custom stop suddenly or did it just ebb away when no one was paying attention? Does anyone, anywhere, hang May baskets anymore?

27

Birds

Not until many years after I left Benton County did I become aware of what a rich store of knowledge about birds, plants, trees, flowers, and animals had been bestowed on us by life on that simple farm. We were saturated with information that is now hard to come by. I know of no comparable body of knowledge that young people today possess.

There didn't seem to be any active effort on the part of the old folks to teach us, nor do I recall any real effort on our part to learn. Observing the abundance of life around us was just so naturally a part of our days on the farm that it became a habit. Of course, we were fortunate in having such knowledgeable adults to learn from.

Take birds, for instance. As a matter of course, Grandpa and Mama almost always identified the birds they mentioned in conversation. "Hey, listen! The blue jays are back!" "Listen to that robin singing for rain." "Hear the screech owl calling to his mate." "Listen to the wren, happy she's found a nesting box." "Sometimes the chickadee sounds exactly like a bluebird." "Those crows must be tormenting an owl. Just listen to the ruckus they're kicking up." "Something must have scared that cock pheasant by the sound of his cackling." "By the sound of that rain-crow and the mourning doves it must be going to rain." "The Baltimore orioles are up in the top of that maple tree. They're repairing the same nest they used last year. They must have gotten back last night."

The adults took such delight in sharing these observations that, without even thinking about it, we kids looked, listened, and learned. And there was so much to see and hear. Crows yacked up a storm in the dead branches of the ancient cotton-wood tree. Robins, meadowlarks, vesper and field sparrows sang as we walked by. Bluebirds perching on the hand-hewn cedar fence posts in which they'd built their nests whistled "bluebird" in the pure silvery tones of a tiny bell. Meadowlarks turned their backs to us to hide their lemon yellow breasts before sounding their calls. Chicken hawks soared overhead searching for the fat field mouse and the witless striped squirrel resting outside of its tidy hole in the ground. Pheasants, quail, and killdeer patrolled the long grasses.

But much as we enjoyed the presence of all these creatures— we were just as gladdened by the return of the red-winged black-bird as the adults were and we looked forward to the golden warble of the Baltimore oriole—I'm afraid we took the riches of our Iowa meadows for granted. Certainly we took notice of all the animals and the birds, for we could identify them and their calls, but not once do I recall our expressing any appreciation for how they enriched our lives. Still, there were moments when we felt it, even if we didn't articulate it.

One year a quail built a nest in the far corner of the strawberry patch. It was hidden in the tall grass and protected by an angled pole bracing a corner post. She allowed us to work quite close to her as long as we ignored her. When, infrequently, we would dis-cover that she had left the nest, we had a chance to take a good look. We found that she had laid exactly one dozen smallish, cream-colored eggs splotched with tan. I have no idea how pheasants, domestic hens, and quail know when they have produced twelve eggs, or what it is that gives them the notion that twelve eggs are sufficient for them to start to brood. But they do.

I was quietly determined to see the hatchlings, and one morning I noticed that two eggs had the outlines of a perfect circle chipped on their ends. I waited awhile, but I spied the mother quail nearby and decided not to keep her from her nest. I left the garden and returned about an hour later expecting to find at least a few chicks.

How was I to know that quails are going propositions at birth? There was nothing in the nest but twelve empty shells, each with the ends neatly chipped out. I couldn't believe it!

A few days later I did see the clutch along the hedgerow by the currant bushes. A sharp whistle from the two adult quails signaled the chicks to freeze while they themselves took wing in a low, whirring arc and landed a short distance away. Those chicks had been ordered to freeze and freeze they did. Becoming all but invisible in their total stillness, looking more like wood chips or clods of dirt than living things, they simply disappeared from my sight. I had to blink to keep my eyes focused on the tiny earth-colored blobs. Not wanting to keep the family separated any longer, within a few minutes I retreated a distance. After I quietly backed away, I realized that I was holding my breath. I was quite aware that I had witnessed something very special.

Even though it certainly added to my knowledge of birds, I cringe to mention one pastime that I engaged in with great industry. Between the ages of eight and ten, I collected birds' eggs. Since teachers and parents encouraged me in this endeavor, and brothers, cousins, friends, and classmates envied my collection, I had neither the wit nor the wisdom to stop.

Here is how I built my collection. Generally, I would spot a bird, say a wren or a ground sparrow, building a nest. I watched and waited until I had the chance to steal one or two eggs. Gently, with a needle, I punched a hole in each end of the egg and blew the contents out. Then I washed the shell with cool water and placed it on a bed of cotton in a flat box.

I collected the blue-green egg of the robin, the tan speckled egg of the wren, the thrush, the brown thrasher, and the blue jay. I thoughtlessly stole the eggs of the goldfinch, the cardinal, and the oriole. Into my collection went the eggs of countless downy and hairy woodpeckers, yellowhammers, redheaded woodpeckers, crows, owls, pheasant, quail, and sparrows of many varieties.

I invested a lot of time in this and received a real education. I know how, where, and out of what materials many birds build their nests; I know the various songs and calls these birds make; I know what their habits are and what they eat. For a peek into another dimension, just watch a redheaded woodpecker, with its long, hairy, wormlike tongue, slurping insects out from under the bark of a half dead cottonwood tree! I'm talking about a real redheaded woodpecker with its scarlet head, blue-black wings, and white underbelly! Of course, seventy years later, I recognize that I bear some guilt for the fact that I haven't seen this handsome fellow in a long, long time!

Bird watching has remained a hobby throughout my life, but my innocent marauding (isn't that an oxymoron?) of so many nests will ever make me uneasy!

28

Animal Tales

We lived in intimate contact with the animals on our farm. Interacting with them was second nature to us. The list was long and varied: cows, calves, sheep, lambs, horses, colts, pigs, hens, chicks, ducks, geese, cats, kittens, dogs, puppies. We fed them, watered them, played with them, petted them, loved the way they felt to the touch and even the way they smelled. Clasping an animal in our arms, we would bury our noses in its breast or under the chin and breathe deeply. To inhale the sweet fragrance emanating from the clean body of a colt, calf, lamb, puppy, or kitten that had been sleeping on the grass and warmed by the sun was one of those pagan pleasures that could be counted on to elicit a "little heathen" comment from Grandma.

The domestic animals were almost like people to us, and we treated them with respect. Their welfare was always our prime concern. If there was a blizzard or a thunderstorm brewing, or if there was a heat wave about to envelop the county, which often happened during those hot, dry summers of the thirties, we saw to the needs of the animals first. At times this concern was carried to extremes as far as Grandma was concerned, especially on those cruelly cold nights when Grandpa would stuff large gunnysacks in the oven of the kitchen range to take out to the henhouse to warm the feet of the biddy hens.

Grandpa used to entertain us with stories of his pet civet and the crows that he had tamed when he was a newly married young man. We loved hearing how his pet crow would find a mud hole in the stockyard, dip his feet into it, fly to the freshly laundered bedsheets drying on the clothesline, and walk along the line, all the while looking behind him and commenting admiringly on the muddy tracks he left on the sheets. He would do this again and again until my exasperated grandmother would lock him up in his cage.

Grandpa's example gave us all the encouragement we needed to indulge the idiosyncrasies of both beast and bird. We would toss a few fresh apples to a colt, throw a pail of cool water on an old sow baking in the hot sun, sneak a handful of cracked corn to the handsome Rhode Island Red rooster before we fed the rest of the flock, and we never separated Jude from Ginger if we harnessed a team for a special job, because we knew those old horses liked to work together.

One summer much of our spare time was taken up with two two-year-old colts, Ted and Dick, beautiful chestnuts with luxuriant, long black tails sweeping almost to the ground. Since training is not begun until colts are four years old, they had been given free run of the yard and grove along with the sheep and left pretty much to the pleasure of their own company, until we got interested in them.

I don't know who started it, but we kids began sneaking handfuls of sugar to lure Ted and Dick to us. Soon we discovered they liked fresh eggs (stolen from the henhouse) broken into their daily pan of oats. Who would have thought that horses liked eggs? Though we knew that they provided our family with precious dollars when sold to the Farmers Store on Saturday night,

I don't recall that we had the slightest compunction about feeding the colts those freshest of eggs.

It's a wonderful feeling to gain the confidence of a horse, or any animal for that matter. The poet James Wright describes it as an almost transcendent experience: "Suddenly I realize/That if I stepped out of my body I would break/Into blossom." The colts would canoodle their velvety muzzles in our hands and necks. We were ecstatic. Soon we were spending every minute we could with them.

Since we knew that what we were doing was forbidden, because of the very real danger to us from these untamed beasts, we offered the oat-egg pies to Ted and Dick from the safety of a slant-roofed henhouse, which also had the advantage of concealing us from the adults up at the house. Every day we fed them from that roof, where we were at a height level with their backs and heads, and every day they became a little less agitated when they were in our presence. We calmed their frenetic dancing and capers by caressing and cooing to them in soothing voices. One day we took a gunnysack up on the roof with us, and I climbed onto the low-hanging branch of a maple tree that was suspended right over Ted's back.

"Dare ya' to get on him," said John.

"Double dare?" I countered.

"Double dare!" exclaimed both boys together.

"Just watch!"

Gently, slowly, I dropped the sack on the colt's back; he reared and snorted but not as much as we had expected he would. We coaxed him back under the branch and then, without breathing—none of us was breathing—I placed one bare foot on him. Still sitting on the branch I placed my other foot next to the first one. A quaking tremble rippled the length and breadth of Ted's skin.

I had the good sense not to try anything further that time, but we experienced a sense of exhilaration at this breakthrough. The next day and the day after that we followed the same procedure until one day I slid off the branch and onto Ted's shiny, smooth back. I was shaking. He walked around sneezing, snuzzling, and prancing, flicking his long tail. After a bit I slid down onto the ground. Then the boys took a turn, though my sister refused. After that we all took turns taking short rides on both of the colts' backs; many oat-pies later they would tolerate two of us kids at a time on each back.

It wasn't long before we were nudging the colts toward the narrow lane that led to the grazing pasture and the hazel brush. We were cautious about urging them to gallop, which is the most pleasant gait for a rider. Though the colts wore halters, we really had only minimal control over them, and cocky kids that we were, even we knew that they would never put up with wearing a bridle. It should be noted that from the time we learned to walk, by word and example, we were instructed to be calm, cautious, considerate, and consistent when we were around the so-called domestic animals on the farm—especially the larger ones, like hogs, cattle, and, particularly, horses. A bite from an angry hog could maim, a butt from a recalcitrant cow could injure, and a kick from a startled horse could cripple or kill.

All that summer we secretly rode Ted and Dick until they became so tame that they would be waiting for us in the hazel brush when we came home from school and would come when we whistled. The way to whistle for a horse is to purse your lips together loosely, blow moderately hard and sing "Whee-oo! Whee-oo! Whee-oo!" in a high-pitched voice. Try it. You can do it.

Breaking is a term applied to taming or training a horse so that it will accept a bridle and harness and obey half a dozen commands: Giddyap! Giddyup! Whoa! Back! Gee! (turn right) and Haw! (turn left). When it came time to break Dick and Ted, Uncle Ernest, who was known all over the county as being the best at this task, marveled to his beer drinking pals at Sant Gulick's pool hall about how he'd never encountered two such mild-mannered, intelligent, fast-learning colts. This got back to us kids, and, as usual, we kept our mouths shut. We didn't disclose our secret until Uncle Ernest was ninety-one years old. All that time he'd thought that it was his special skill and patience that had accomplished such an easy breaking.

Mating was a common scene on the farm: I saw bulls mount cows, rams mount ewes, and roosters chase and tackle hens. I watched with fascination the failure of the bumbling billy goat who always mounted the female sideways, tracing unseen patterns with his pink, slender, pointy male organ on her coarse, hairy flanks in his fruitless search for an entry. Having been taught at church about the separate creation of man and beasts, I was a believer in this fable for a long time. I was slow to acknowledge that if animals did it, then people probably did also. Further, I knew by the adult silence on the matter not to call attention to such goings-on and, of course, not to ask questions.

Once, we children watched our mare, Nellie, being serviced by the stud that had been trucked in from the Boyd farm an hour away. To make sure that we youngsters couldn't observe this event, the adults consigned us to the far side of the house. But they hadn't counted on our climbing the good old box elder tree with the giant limbs and luxuriant foliage that extended beyond the periphery of the porch. Hiding among the leaves, we were fascinated and vaguely ill at ease with what we could see of the awkward proceedings.

Births, too, were regular—but still memorable—events. I well remember a spring day when I was gathering kindling in the woods behind the house, and I happened upon a fat ewe squatting to give birth to a lamb. Fascinated, I watched breathlessly as the slender package of purplish-red flesh slipped from its secret place and plopped steamily to the ground. The ewe kept looking back, bleating softly. At the moment before she expelled the entire mass, she uttered a soft cry that was almost human. Bloody strings still hanging from her rear end, she quickly turned, and, starting from the nose of the lamb, licked away the covering from its little body. It wasn't until many years later that I learned that if the ewe didn't start cleaning the lamb immediately, beginning with the nose, it would suffocate. Within moments, still warmly damp, the lamb staggered to its feet, wobbled, shook its long woolly tail, searched for and found the bag, and began nursing with surprising vigor. It was one of the most profoundly exhilarating moments of my life! I was sure that I was the only person in the whole world who knew where little lambs came from. I swelled with pride over my secret, but I couldn't share it with anyone because the lamb had come from the mother's private parts, so I had no words to describe what I had seen. But I did somehow know that the ram topping the ewe and this event were connected.

Ever so gradually, enlightenment about the facts of life came to me, although, as so often happens for children in communities that don't speak openly of such matters, it came in bits and pieces replete with distortions and inaccuracies. A few years later, I caught fragments of forbidden conversation among the Big Kids as we walked to country school. With a mixture of awe, jocularity, and disbelief, they were discussing the coupling of men and boys with calves and sheep. A note of seriousness came into their voices when the topic of the bizarre offspring of such activity was considered. "Aw! That could never happen!" "Yes, it can! Walt says his uncle saw it! Half sheep! Half man!" Then the voices got lower. "Well, you know a thing like that can't live. It's in a jar in a doctor's office in Iowa City." "Oh yeah? Well, I don't believe it!" "No, I don't believe it, either!" Then we all walked on in total silence, consumed with our own thoughts for, in our heart of hearts, we did believe it more than just a little bit.

Every once in a while one of our pets met with one of those accidents that are endemic to farm life, as occurred one day on my aunt and uncle's farm, during an episode which to this day I have never been able to discuss with another living soul.

Our two families were devoted to animals and we shared just about everything, especially the pets. Beans, a small energetic rat terrier, had satiny-smooth white hair speckled with black spots the size and shape of navy beans, hence his name. Technically he belonged to my eight-year-old cousin Robert, though all of us kids considered him to be our best friend. One late afternoon my Uncle Ernest was mowing in the hay field near the house. Beans liked to accompany him, for the noisy mower would flush the resident wildlife from the field and provide him with a merry chase. Apparently, he was walking ahead of the machine when he paused, his attention possibly diverted by a rabbit. Uncle could not stop the steady forward movement of the horse-drawn mower and, in an instant, the scissorslike, razor-sharp blades did their dirty work.

Aunt Hazel, Mama, and I were on the kitchen porch shelling peas. His overalls covered with blood, my uncle suddenly appeared before us cradling Beans in his arms. Our little dog's two back feet were not there—just bloody, bony sticks. One of the front paws dangled from a sliver of skin; the other was untouched. The mangled creature's soft brown eyes went from face to face, searching for help. Though he was quivering, he emitted not a sound. No one spoke. As Uncle Ernest gently placed Beans on the green grass, Aunt Hazel put her peas aside, ran into the kitchen, grabbed the gun from behind the door, and handed it to Uncle, who fired a single bullet into the brain of our precious pet. The rightness of this shocking act was reinforced by the equally selfless and decisive manner in which Mama had dealt with her wounded bird a few years later. I was profoundly moved by both events.

A special situation occurred late one summer when an old Barred Rock hen surprised us with an even dozen of newly hatched chicks. She had done her brooding in a nest hidden out in the raspberry patch. The end of August is not a good time to start raising chicks because freezing weather will arrive before they have a chance to feather out and grow large enough to survive the harsh winter.

We kept a casual eye on Old Biddy and her brood, saw to it that they got mash and water, and generally permitted them the free run of the orchard, away from the rest of the flock. The expected happened. Drenching rains drowned a few chicks; weasels, sparrow hawks, and other predators snatched a few more; and finally there remained just one lone survivor.

Chickens were banned from the house yard because no one could stand the smell and the mess of the droppings. But Old Biddy's pitiful plight and her lone chick aroused our sympathy. The two of them were allowed to take up residence in the front yard, and they slept at night under the front porch, Old Biddy standing up while the chick tucked its head under her wing. After a few months, it was clear that the lone survivor was a rooster. We called him Buddy; Biddy and Buddy. They made us laugh.

Biddy would find seeds, crumbs, angleworms, bugs, and

tender grass shoots, and before she would devour any of the goodies she always clucked an invitation to Buddy. In response, he would gallumph awkwardly and noisily to her side and gobble up her find. He was not a sharer. He was also not very smart. If it rained she would run under the porch for shelter and cluck frantically for him to join her. Fat chance! He would stand in the downpour, head held high, tail drooping low, until she came out and herded him to the dryness under the porch.

We loved looking under the porch at night, or under the lilac bush in the afternoon when they had siesta. There the two of them would be: Biddy standing up; Buddy with his head under her wing. Under Biddy's excessive care, Buddy developed into a huge and handsome fellow with soft and bounteous black and white barred feathers and an enormous bright red comb. Only he had grown so large that his head under her wing lifted her foot way off the ground and she would be balancing precariously on one leg. It was a ludicrous sight—a clear case of arrested development on his part and overprotective mothering on hers.

I never knew exactly what happened to Biddy and Buddy, but they probably ended up in a tasty chicken and dumpling stew served to the Methodist minister one happy Sunday.

29

Raccoons and Other Critters

We didn't confine ourselves just to domestic animals on the farm. We made pets of field mice, red timber squirrels, striped or ground squirrels, and raccoons. Once we even ventured to befriend an opossum. One fall day while we were restacking a pile of logs that had been selected for fence posts, we disturbed an opossum den. All but a few of the eight or ten babies that we had accidentally uncovered clambered onto the mother's back at lightning speed and were ferried away in the blink of an eye. That opossums could move that fast was a revelation to us. Later, we caught one of the young opossums and tried to make a pet of it; but he was a disappointment. He was strictly an opossum with opossum inclinations. The moment we tried to entertain him or interact in any way, he would simply play dead. Lying limp on his side, he would close his eyes, open his mouth slightly, allow saliva to drip out, and reveal an incredible number of jagged teeth. We would pick him up, carry him, jostle him; he still played dead.

The opossum's lassitude was in marked contrast to the liveliness of our raccoon pets. Several times in the evening when we were playing with the raccoons on the Greening apple tree, we hooked the tail of the opossum around a small limb while he insisted on playing dead. The alert raccoons took this opportunity to entertain themselves by using him as a kind of soft punching bag, batting him back and forth as he swung from his tail. They took turns at this, and there was no doubt that they enjoyed the fun.

One evening when the opossum was playing dead, we forgot about him; when we looked for him, he had vanished. We were not grieved by his disappearance.

Of all our wildlife pets, the raccoons were the most exciting and the most satisfying. Sometimes we caught a baby that had left the protective hollow of a tree. Other times one of the Big Kids would return from the cornfield holding a snarling four- to six-week-old coon by the scruff of the neck, having found it while plowing the field. For several years, we managed to capture two or three in this fashion. After confining them to a pen of rough boards we built in the grove behind the house, we would set about the taming process. Wearing heavy work gloves, we visited the pen often, talking to them in soothing voices and offering bits of fried chicken and milk-soaked bread.

During the first few days of their capture, they would refuse the food, snort and growl ferociously, and bite our extended hands. We cleverly allowed the frightened animals to clamp their jaws on one gloved hand and chew away while we gently petted the head, ears, and neck with the other. All of us kids carried permanent scars on our knuckles where those teeth penetrated the thick gloves. Though their bites brought blood, they were always superficial. Not one of us ever developed an infection from these bites and why we didn't, I'll never know. The standard treatment was to pour a small amount of peroxide on the wounds. I shudder when I remember that we had neither rabies nor tetanus shots at that time.

After a few days, hunger would force the raccoons to accept the milk-soaked bread from our hands and we would pet and coo softly to them all the while they were eating. It wouldn't be too long before we could handle them without gloves and release them from the enclosure.

The raccoons became attached to us in the same way the dogs and cats did. Indeed, they became special friends with the cats, being about the same size. We enjoyed watching the spirited, playful wrestling matches and games of chase that they engaged in. Alas, one kitten who engaged in a wrestling match was inadvertently strangled by a coon. It was then that we realized that the wild animals had considerably more strength in their front legs than the domestic cats had, and we watched them more closely after that.

For a few summers these raccoons were almost the complete focus of our leisure time. We invented ways for them to entertain us. One never-ending source of fun was to place a dishpan of water on the ground, call the raccoons, and offer them sugar cubes, which they loved. They would drop the sugar cubes into the pan of water and start to wash them, because raccoons in the Midwest always washed their food if water was available. Within seconds, the cubes would dissolve. Chirruping all the while, keeping their eyes fixed on our mischievous faces, the coons proceeded to try to solve this puzzle. Placing one front paw on the edge of the pan, they would use the other to search all over the bottom for the lost goodies. Sometimes, to add to the fun, we would add some glass marbles to further confound them. To make amends, we would eventually reward them with some dry sugar cubes or a cookie. Many years later at our home on Long Island, I discovered that the local raccoons almost never washed their food no matter how convenient the water supply was. I do not know how to account for this discrepancy in behavior.

There was one raccoon who was bigger, less dependable, and more cantankerous than the others. His fur was longer, grayer, more yellow on the ends, and of a rougher quality. We speculated that he might be part wolverine or badger. He wasn't, of course, but we were trying to account for his unique appearance and for his lack of patience with our attempts to tame him. He would snap and snarl at us for no apparent reason; once he flew at me in a rage and bit me severely on the inside of my knee. I bear the scar to this day.

But we admired him and we kept him because he was the smartest animal we had ever captured; he could open a jar with a screw top lid; he could pry the lid off a gallon tin of sorghum; and he could eat an ice-cream cone sitting on his haunches. The men and the Big Kids took him into Garrison to Sant Gulick's pool hall, and reported that there he impressed the constituency by drinking beer and a cherry Coke out of a bottle. I never saw him do that since that establishment was out of bounds for girls, but it certainly seemed on a par with the rest of his accomplishments.

We couldn't trust him not to run away, so we chained him to a huge soft maple tree in the barnyard near the henhouse. Every night after supper someone would set a pan of food at the base of the large tree and leave it for him to eat. Fine.

But one night when we watched him, it suddenly became all too clear that this was no ordinary coon who could be satisfied with ordinary leftovers. He ignored the full plate left at the base of the tree, and climbed up to his favorite resting place in the lower branches. Then he did something that is quite hard to believe.

He pulled his chain up alongside the tree trunk where it would be hard to see, and waited quietly out of view among the leaves. Shortly, his patience and ingenuity were rewarded. Unwary chickens, attracted to the goodies on the plate, came in for a feast. In a flash, Mr. Raccoon was down the tree, and had snatched a chicken and carried it back up to the lower branches for his own feast.

We allowed him to get away with this for a few days as we all stood around admiring his ingenuity. Then Uncle Ernest took him over to Yankee Grove and returned him to the wild.

During the period when we had the baby raccoons, Old Puss, queen of the farm for years, felt slighted. She was accustomed to enjoying a special status with everyone, including the outsized Kinardly, Toby. (A dog is called a Kinardly when it is a mixture of so many breeds you can hardly tell what it is.) Toby was very protective of Old Puss and would place himself between her and the feet of the cows when she came to the barn at milking time. They frequently slept cuddled up together on the wooden cellar door where the sun struck first thing in the morning, and greeted each other on awakening. Though he was many times her size, Toby knew who was boss. When these two were eating out of the same dish, if Toby gobbled the food with a bit more enthusiasm than Old Puss thought proper—which happened frequently, since dogs typically wolf their food while cats take dainty nibbles—she would slow him down or stop him altogether by placing one paw on the tip of his nose, with her claws ever so slightly extended, and holding it there until she had eaten her fill.

She wasn't afraid of anything, kept the rat and mouse population under control in the barnyard, and did her share in eliminating gophers, ground squirrels, and even very large snakes. The value of snakes to the farm was not appreciated at that time, so we praised her whenever she arrived from the stubble field with a black snake or a blue racer dangling from her mouth.

Because we admired and respected her, we gave her a lot of loving attention. When she had a new litter of kittens, which was at least once a year, she would allow us to pet them for a few days. Then, one by one, she would drag them to a hiding place that was inaccessible to us. Frequently she would burrow way back in the haymow and leave them there until their eyes opened. We were sure that she did this because we handled them too much and gave them infections. Before she started hiding her kittens, they always got sore, runny eyes because of our carelessness. That meant that we had to wash their eyes with a boric acid solution twice a day.

But when Old Puss thought she was being ignored because we were so occupied with our newly acquired baby raccoons, she wasn't above using her kittens to get our attention. We woke up one morning to find her whole litter on the front porch. She had arranged them in an irresistible platter of six soft, adorable balls of fur atop a basket of clean corncobs waiting to be taken into the kitchen. While we admired her pretty babies, she purred up a storm, all the while making figure eights around our ankles. It was a clear case of jealousy and we knew she must have been feeling neglected, so we all set about letting her know we were right proud of her pride of pussycats. She allowed us to shower the kittens with attention all day and then, satisfied that she had reestablished herself in her rightful position as queen of the farm, she quietly took them, one by one by the nape of the neck, back to the haymow and stashed them out of our reach.

One summer we and our raccoon pets nearly drove Mama out

of her mind. She was incredibly accepting of the animals we brought in, but she did not like to have them in the house when we were eating or sleeping. However, raccoons are so adept (and children so sneaky) that even she couldn't keep them at bay. When we were eating the noon meal, dinner, she would shut the screen door tightly; our wily pets simply inserted their claws into the screen, opened the door, and slipped into the house.

Well, Mama decided to fix their wagon. She nailed very thin boards across the lower part of the door. Undaunted, the chief raccoon managed to find a slight crevice, inserted his claws in it, opened the door, and was in the kitchen in a trice, soon to be followed by the others, who quickly learned to perform this trick themselves.

Once in the house, they were so exceedingly quiet that Mama wouldn't notice that they were there. They would climb up on the round braces under our chairs and wait silently for handouts. None of us kids thought anything of taking a bite of buttered bread, then lowering it so a raccoon could have a bite. Share and share alike was our motto. It is nothing short of miraculous that none of us ever picked up some strange and loathsome disease.

The fall that followed that summer was particularly mild and dry, and several of the raccoons stayed around a lot longer than usual. This was before rural electrification, and our only light source was a gigantic kerosene lamp with a beaded glass chimney which Mama and one of the Big Kids lighted every evening. After supper we four kids did our homework gathered around the large oak dining table. The raccoons would go from one to the other, perching on our shoulders, lying across the backs of our necks, playing with our hair, or chewing gently on our ears. This scene of complete contentment is one of my most cherished childhood memories.

Though they were extremely active in early evening, several of our generally nocturnal captives would not be able to stay up past our bedtime. Of course we put them out of the house before we went to bed, but they quickly learned that they could climb the wooden post supporting the porch roof just under our windows and crawl right into our upstairs bedrooms. One of the smallest raccoons chose to sleep curled up under my chin and another, along with a kitten, shared a space down by my feet. Years later Mama described what she saw when she checked on us before retiring for the night.

"I'd stand on the first landing on the stairs and look toward your bed; first two eyes would glow in the dark, then two more would appear, then two more. If I went beyond the first landing, the raccoons would skedaddle out the window and onto the roof of the porch. Most of the time I just went back down the stairs to bed."

Since we always moved back to Garrison in late December, we never had to face the inevitability of parting with our pets. We left them in the care of our cousins, who reported that all of the raccoons drifted back to the wild to join their kin, and the kittens were given to farmers in the township. That's what we were told, though I'm not sure if it was true. I do know that Old Puss enjoyed a very long life for a farm cat. She passed away when she was around twenty years old.

Interacting so closely with the wildlife, along with the domestic farm animals, was not a trivial aspect of our young lives. I have come to believe that this close relationship not only immensely enriched our growing-up experience, it made us kinder, more empathic, more understanding human beings. In addition, it clarified and defined our responsibility to these creatures and the entire natural community.

Epilogue

Millie at twenty

30

Me

Retrospection can be illuminating, it can be numbing, it can be sobering; it can be fruitful, it can gladden my heart, and it can drown me in despair. But looking back on my early days on our farm in Iowa, I find that I take enormous satisfaction in my memories of the past, and my reflections on how that time, so rich, so satisfying, so fulfilling, yet so undeniably challenging, affected me.

I've only recently become aware of my good fortune in having grown up in an environment where everyone knew everyone else. In our community no one was a stranger. If we met an unfamiliar face on the way to the Farmers Store, we offered a greeting because we knew that person had to be a guest in the house of someone we knew. We were privileged to live with the comforting conviction that we had absolutely nothing to fear from people. Of course, we were quite aware that there were dangerous forces and conditions over which we had no control, but we were confident that no person was out to do us injury. This atmosphere created in us a sense of security, a sense of belonging in the world. Is there a more valuable gift than that?

All that security notwithstanding, I did have some personal insecurities that marked me for years. I was quite sure that I was not pretty, and certain events confirmed my self-assessment. I couldn't have been more than eight years old when Grandma's sister, Aunt Grace, arrived for a visit. I had met her once before when she had come for a visit four years earlier. Aunt Grace was considered very important company, for she had been to university and she and her minister husband had been missionaries in China. Anything that came out of her mouth therefore carried a lot of weight.

"And you remember Merle's girl, Mildred," Grandma said.

"Ah, yes, Mildred. But isn't there also a pretty one?" Aunt Grace cooed.

She was, of course, referring to my sister. And she was right. Avis was the pretty one, petite, with fine features properly arranged and hair that was lush, rich brown, and curly. Because she had been a tiny baby, she was coddled and treated with special care during her early years. I recall Mama and Grandma feeding her rich food like mashed bananas. No one in our family ever got to eat bananas—store-bought, you know—unless they were sick. To assuage the pain of teething and help her gain weight, she had been encouraged to suck on raisin tits, which were made by tying about five raisins in a square of white cotton. To make her strong she had been fed beef tea, a teaspoonful at a time, which Grandma prepared by heating lean, ground beef in a double boiler, and then putting the beef through a metal potato ricer to extract its juice. Before she grew up to look like a beautiful movie star, Avis was bony, skinny, birdlike, and downright puny. How I ached to be that thin.

As for me, I was fat and had curly, unruly brown hair that

never looked combed. My face was asymmetrical, with an off-center nose and a crooked mouth, and I just plain looked odd. I knew I wasn't pretty because everyone said so—in an oblique way (most of the time), of course.

"What nice eyes Mildred has." "What soft hair Mildred has." "What a nice smile Mildred has." Then, my canine teeth erupted high in my gums; it would be years before I heard that last compliment again. The teeth were the final straw. I thought I couldn't bear the disgrace. One Saturday when I was about twelve years old and was supposed to be cleaning house for Grace, the lady who ran the dry goods department at the Farmers Store, I hitchhiked to Vinton to see a dentist. There I whined, pleaded, and cried, "Please, please pull these two teeth that make me look so hideously ugly and are absolutely ruining my life!" Wise man that he was, the dentist refused and explained to me that eventually the lower teeth would fall out and the upper teeth would ease into place if I massaged them downward constantly. The dentist was right, of course, but I was miserable for years.

It was a little later when the boys at school made fun of my hair, which I could never get to stay in place. "Hey, Mil! Did you comb your hair with an eggbeater this morning?" "Hey, Mil! What did you use to cut your hair—a knife and fork?" That was about seventy years ago and I still remember. Not only do I remember those cruel taunts, I remember the names of the boys who uttered them. The result of these assaults on my ego was a severe lack of confidence, which lasted until I became more self-sufficient and gained acceptance in the adult world.

My interest in boys, and theirs in me, was slow to develop, perhaps in part because of my homeliness, which I gradually grew out of in my teens, and in part because life was just different then. My girlfriends and I existed in a state of innocence—and ignorance—that would be scarcely credible to today's worldly, sophisticated children. Which isn't to say that young people of the time were immune to the hormonal storms of adolescence.

I vividly remember an incident when I was six or seven years old and we had all gathered for Sunday dinner at Aunt Hazel and Uncle Ernest's farm just across the road. After dinner we had separated into our various groups—the women and girls gathering in the kitchen to wash and dry dishes, exchange recipes, and trade gossip, the men going out to look at the crops, the boys taking off to play baseball or go swimming. But I wandered away by myself and went down toward the cow barn. I was attracted to the area because I recognized the riding horses of our neighbor Donald. I then caught a glimpse of the neighbor himself, a handsome lad about sixteen years old, and with him was his fabulously gorgeous cousin, Roberta, whom I knew to be from a far off, exotic town, La Porte City. To get to La Porte, you had to leave Benton county and travel almost eighteen miles up Highway 218 on the way to Waterloo. At that time, I had never been farther than Garrison, three miles away.

I knew about Roberta; she was one of the Big Kids. She had visited us before. A self-assured beauty of about fifteen going on twenty-five, she was already in full bloom. She was slim, long of limb, and had a head of luxurious, curly brown hair.

As I neared the barn, I saw that Roberta and Donald were climbing up the ladder to the haymow, where several of the Big Kids were waiting for them. A few minutes later I quietly climbed the ladder after them, knowing full well that I was not welcome among these Bid Kids but too curious about what was going on to be deterred. Lying close to each other on the hay, the boys and Roberta were laughing and bantering with each other, until they saw me watching them. I wasn't really listening to what they were saying until one of the boys told me to go to the house and get a soft blanket—a good one, he said. "Sneak it out of the house!" someone called to me as I descended the ladder.

Wow! They didn't holler at me. They didn't insult me. They sent me on an errand. To me this was tantamount to being accepted into the group of the Big Kids! Full of self-importance, I dutifully trotted up to the house. As I was reaching into the linen closet, Aunt Hazel spied me. "What are you doing?" she asked.

"Getting a blanket," I reported with all candor and innocence.

"What for?"

"The boys and Roberta sent me to get it for the haymow. They want to lay on it!"

For a moment Aunt Hazel froze. Then her eyes opened wide. She turned briskly and marched toward the barn, her sturdy hips vibrating back and forth—*boom! boom! boom! boom!*—with me tagging after. Maybe you've heard the expression "You could see the steam a-comin' outen her boot heel"? Well, that accurately describes her trip across the barnyard. She tore open the lower barn door, strode to the vertical ladder, and fairly skimmed up to the haymow where the boys and Roberta were reclining in the hay. The next thing I knew, Donald and Roberta had dashed onto their mounts and galloped out of the barnyard as if the very devil was after them.

Once out of the hearing of my aunt, my brothers and cousins turned all of their fury on me. "You dumb shit!" "You pissant!" "You shit-ass!" "How could you be such a dumbbell?" I had no idea what all the furor was about.

However, I'm glad they called me those bad names, for the epiphany I eventually had about this event didn't occur until many years later, and if I hadn't felt so mystified by the question of what I had done to merit such abuse I might have completely forgotten my part in interrupting this tumble in the hay.

One thing I did know for sure, even then. I couldn't ask any adult to explain what had just occurred. There were certain mysteries that no one was going to enlighten us about. These included anything having to do with sexuality and reproduction, of course.

My girlfriends and I did not talk about our bodies with one another, nor did any of our parents tell us anything. I got my first period in the spring just weeks after I turned eleven years old. My breasts had begun to bud; but this was not happening to any of my friends. When I remember how we averted our eyes when we changed our clothes after gym class, I can hardly believe our modesty. However, I peeked a bit, and I did observe that I seemed to be the only one who was getting breasts. Then, in late March, after a few friends and I had been wading in the creek, I found a small, wine-dark spot about an inch long in my bloomers. I was terrified. I was pretty certain that my budding breasts and the blood in my bloomers meant that I was going to have a baby. I worried myself sick about this for some time.

Finally I got up enough courage to tell Mama about it. It was Saturday. Mama, my sister, and I bathed in the kitchen wearing our voluminous nightgowns. Since early childhood we had been taught to be ashamed of our bodies, so we never looked at each other. After we had bathed and were getting into our clean clothes I blurted out, "I think I'm going to have a baby!" Mama whirled around on her toe and clutched me by my shoulders, digging her nails into my flesh. Bringing her face close to mine, she hissed: "What did you say?"

"I'm going to have a baby. See?" I lowered the top of my

princess-style cotton petticoat from my shoulders, disclosing my developing breasts. "And I had some blood down there."

Visible relief flooded her face and she almost fell to the floor with the sudden release of tension. "Oh, no. You're not going to have a baby!" Nowadays, with all of the openness and communication between mothers and daughters, this scene would be followed by Mama taking me in her arms and telling me the facts of life. But I was not to be part of such a tender scene. In those days, we were supposed to get such information from the gutter. Alas! I was deprived of the gutter, too.

Instead of a loving, understanding discussion in the quiet of the kitchen, Mama abruptly marched me upstairs to her bedroom, pulled out a long pad made from strips of old cotton blankets from the lower drawer of her bureau, handed me two large safety pins, and said, "The next time you see blood in your bloomers, pin this inside. When you take it off, drop it in the pail of water there by the dresser." No more explanation than that. From then on she referred to that makeshift pad as a "granny rag." (Later, one of the unsung pleasures of earning my own money would be the luxury of buying real sanitary napkins.)

Eavesdropping on the Bethany Circle meeting later that month as my mother recounted this story, I couldn't understand the rollicking fun the ladies got out of my misunderstanding. Of course, many of those ladies were themselves rather unsophisticated about such matters. Women in our small town and the surrounding farm community were captives of their fertility; it was always the woman who was held responsible for getting in the family way—which seemed universally acknowledged as some kind of failure on her part. At least so it seemed to me in my very limited view. Indeed, it was my firm conviction that, generally speaking, babies were unwanted. What else could be made of the song trilled by a popular radio singer of the time: "The rich get rich and the poor get children"—followed as it was by hearty laughter? My habit of sitting as quietly as I could to listen in on the conversations of women in the various do-gooders groups, like the Ladies' Aid and the Women's Auxiliary to the American Legion, reinforced me in this belief. The women always used a euphemism to indicate a pregnancy. "Gladys has to leave her job because she's in the family way." "Mary Beth got caught this month!" "How old is their last baby?" (This said with a very disapproving cluck of the tongue.) "It looks as if Louise swallowed another watermelon seed." "Mercy! That'll be their seventh kid!" "I saw Charlotte Henry at the post office yesterday and she's beginning to look as if she's eaten a bag of dried apples." These mischievous comments were freely offered until someone happened to glance in my direction and whispered to the others: "Little pitchers have big ears!"

The message was clear: Babies were a bit of a plague, and no one seemed to know how to prevent them. This message appeared in print, too.

Among Grandpa's books were several novels by Harold Bell Wright. I read one part of *The Shepherd of the Hills* over and over because I didn't understand what Howard's transgression was. Appropriate for the time, Wright's allusion to the seduction Howard had perpetrated was so obscure, so veiled that I was left to wrestle with my ignorance. The author wrote something like, "He's gone and left the trouble with us." Trouble? What trouble? Then with no further explanation, "She died when Pete was born." And so I read and reread the wrenching and puzzling scene when Howard's father walks the floor at night soliloquizing. "Howard! Howard! That I should live to be glad that you are dead!" I simply did not understand the father's dreadful agony.

✳

While I have largely confined this tale to my early childhood, I think it might be informative to briefly outline my work experiences, which bear further witness to the work ethic that had been imprinted on all of us during our years with Grandma and Grandpa. Except for the pittance I was paid for picking green beans for the canning factory and pulling morning glories out of cornfields, I never earned any money for my work until I was in sixth grade and the lady who ran the dry goods department of the Farmers Store hired me to clean her big house for her. Grace was the widowed mother of three girls. Her husband, a cattle buyer, had been killed when an electrical storm caught him out in the open field. (His death was rather callously described by some of the more insensitive louts in the area as due to "a shock in the jock"—a gallows humor reference to the fact that he was wearing a steel truss when the lightning struck him.)

For seventy-five cents an hour I did the washing and ironing, vacuumed, and cleaned the floors, bathroom, and refrigerator. This was a job that carried some prestige, for Grace was highly regarded as a pillar of the community, and her house was one of the few in Garrison that boasted an indoor bathroom. After her daughters left home, Grace paid me an extra dollar to stay in the lonely house with her all night on the weekends.

The summer after I graduated from seventh grade, I became the live-in caretaker and companion of an elderly, arthritic, cranky, devout, retired Methodist missionary. When I wasn't in school, we prayed together every morning at ten o'clock. Here, in addition to helping her with dressing, bathing, and toileting, I did all of the washing, the marketing, the cooking, the baking, and the cleaning. The discipline of my early years in building fires in the kitchen stove, planning and cooking meals, cleaning house, washing, and ironing were paying off. I knew how to run a household. I must add that the missionary's home was two blocks from Grandpa Urmy's house in Garrison, so that any time I needed advice I could skip over and consult Mama and Grandma.

Though I had no leisure time to speak of, I was finally acquiring what I craved most: the approval of the adult community and a modicum of independence. I was thrilled to be earning four dollars a week. I now had my own money to buy such luxuries as Tangee Lipstick, hair set gel, an extra pair of shoes—and Kotex sanitary napkins. In those days one could buy a very nice sweater for seventy-five cents. I even bought a Hawaiian guitar and took lessons, for which I paid one dollar. The sheet music also cost a dollar, but here is another of those situations where the habit of thrift and discipline that I learned on the farm really paid off. I found that by concentrating, I could memorize the piece in the hour-long session and not have to buy the sheet music. So that is what I did.

With the money I earned that year, I was well-nigh self-supporting. My sense of my own worth soared right along with my finances.

The summer after I graduated from eighth grade I left the missionary and was delighted to go to work as a hired girl on a large farm south of Garrison. The family consisted of Cecil, Anna, and their two girls and four boys, ranging in age from one and a half to eleven. Cecil hired one or two extra men in the summer. That meant that Anna and I cooked, set the table, and did the dishes for at least ten people, three times a day.

Anna paid me four dollars a week for my work on the farm, and I was especially proud of that for my closest girlfriend and all of my other friends were being paid only three and a half dollars. Of course, we all received room and board, too.

Here I should report that we were also accepted as full-fledged members of the family, for hired girls were not treated as maids. In fact, I was the only one in this family who had a private room. Located at the top of the crooked stairs, it was about five feet wide by ten feet long, and it had a window overlooking the huge vegetable garden. To me it was a palace.

During those summer months we rose at five-thirty A.M., unless it was haying or threshing time on the farm; then we got up at four-thirty. Anna and I timed it so that we got up just after the men, who immediately disappeared to the barns to do the morning chores. Anna built a fire in the iron kitchen range, while I put the copper teakettle on along with the gray, graniteware coffee boiler and got the bacon started. As the kitchen filled with the delicious fragrance of the bacon crisping and browning, I carried jam, a whole pound of butter, sliced bread, a large pitcher of milk, and a smaller pitcher of heavy cream to the table, which was already set for ten people. Then I carefully broke twenty eggs into a mixing bowl and waited for one of the boys to report that the men were ready for breakfast. At that point I poured the bowl of eggs into the gigantic iron skillet and fried them to perfection in bacon fat, sunny-side up.

If there was a delay, or if the men had an especially busy day before them, I might make an applesauce cake—the very one I described in an earlier chapter. Here again, the family training in thinking ahead and always doing more than was required stood me in good stead. I could whip up that cake in just a few minutes since I kept a ready supply of homemade applesauce in the pantry; it would bake while we were eating breakfast and would be ready to eat with our second cups of coffee.

I could handle almost every task in Anna's household; I could even make gravy without lumps, for heaven's sake. There was always something to do on that farm: cakes, cookies, and pies to bake; potatoes, radishes, beets, carrots, peas, lettuce, tomatoes, and beans to pick, wash, clean, and peel; chickens to kill, scald, pluck, singe, draw, and disjoint; dishes to wash and dry; clothing to wash; laundry to be hung on the line, then taken down from the line, folded, and ironed. And every day, we made beds for ten people. Everything I had learned in my early years I put to use as a hired girl for this family.

The children all helped in as many ways as they could. They would make their own beds, wash vegetables, carry wood and water, set the table, dry dishes, and gather eggs and apples. Like the children I grew up with, they understood that they played a part in making the family work.

We had fun with one another. There was a lot of joking, laughing, and good-natured teasing. And often in the evening, on those occasions when we had somehow managed to finish our chores as well as our supper before dark, the kids would help me with the dishes if I would agree to come outside afterward and play with them. We played hide-and-go-seek, touched-you-last, and may-I. Some evenings we would have water fights, tossing pails of water on one another. Or, we might just sit out on the front porch and sing.

It's hard to believe, but one day there was actually a lull in the daily work, so Anna loaned me to her sister-in-law, Molly, who was entertaining the Ladies' Auxiliary at an afternoon luncheon. I was to help prepare food, serve, and clean up after the gathering. Outrageous as this may sound, in those days this practice was not in the least unusual. Far from resenting it, I rather looked forward to the change of pace it brought. I loved preparing for parties since I had a knack for cooking, baking, and preparing fancy dishes, and parties were few and far between. I also loved meeting new people. Remember, I was a hired girl, and not a maid, and was treated as an equal at such events. Need I add that I did not expect nor get any additional pay for this venture?

After the ladies had departed, Molly, Anna, and I were cleaning up. While drying dishes I twisted the fragile stem of a Heisey water glass from its bowl. Heisey was the prestigious glass in Iowa in the thirties, something on the order that Fostoria became later.

Molly's response was crisp, clipped, critical, and accusative. "That's a Heisey glass. It was a wedding present. I think you owe me four dollars." The following Saturday, at the time when Anna usually handed me four one-dollar bills for my pay, she casually informed me that she had given the money to Molly in payment for the broken water glass.

I did not protest. I thought it just and right that I pay for my careless destruction of the precious Heisey glass.

It was on Anna's farm that I furthered my understanding of the mechanics of reproduction. By this time, an orphaned classmate and I had become inseparable friends (and have remained friends to this day). Margaret had passed on the basically accurate if scant information about reproduction that she had learned from her married sister, with whom she made her home. But I still had a lot to learn.

The breakthrough in my sex education occurred one midsummer afternoon when our day was interrupted by the all-purpose, busybody practical nurse who had moved to Garrison from rural Missouri. It was highly unusual for us to have an unexpected visitor on a weekday. But on this afternoon, Matt McBain appeared with no advance warning and announced that she wished to speak with Anna. We went into the living room where Anna was darning socks; I poured coffee for the three of us, and Matt abruptly pulled a small item from her purse. To me, it looked like a packet of matches. Matt didn't beat about the bush. Ignoring me completely, she started lecturing Anna on her lack of foresight in producing six children one right after another, asserting that this was irresponsible behavior, ought not to be continued, and could be controlled. Her face completely impassive, Anna dropped her head to attend more closely to her darning; I listened and watched in total fascination. Matt unwrapped what looked like a deflated, elongated, ivory-colored balloon, slipped it over her left middle finger, and proceeded to describe how Cecil should use it. It was never given a name. I was all eyes and ears; Anna remained mute, her face expressionless and her lips tightly closed, and continued to give her darning her total attention.

Matt's visit was brief; she placed two small packets on the arm of Anna's rocking chair, tossed back the last drops of coffee, and left. Now Anna spoke.

"I think God takes care of those things."

I was dumbstruck and thrilled. I thought that I had acquired information that none of my friends had.

We never referred to the visit. And Anna and Cecil never had any more children.

The next two summers, I was a hired girl on a prosperous model farm owned by Anna's elderly father, her arthritic and asthmatic mother, and her bachelor brothers. Anna's mother, Liz, had lured me away from Anna by paying me four dollars and fifty cents a week. In addition, she gave me a huge corner room with bright oak floors and, wonder of wonders, access to an indoor bathroom. Electricity for the house and summer kitchen was produced by a Delco system—a huge bank of wet cells lodged in the corner of the basement. What a draw. Besides, this family had a very high social standing, for several reasons: Anna's younger brother, who ran the farm, owned a snazzy, light blue Lincoln Zephyr, and raised Black Angus cattle and duroc hogs. Not only that, the farm itself was so advanced that it provided the hogs with a clean concrete platform they could climb onto in order to press a lever which delivered a cooling shower whenever the sun got too hot. I swear, one could see the hogs smile when they did that.

Under the watchful eye of Liz, who was largely confined to her wicker rocker, I did the cooking for the family, plus two nephews and a hired man. Liz washed, peeled, and prepared all of the vegetables for me. As with many of the people of my grandparents' generation, Liz had little use for leisure. She thought people ought to be busy. This was especially true for paid help. If I had somehow caught up on household obligations, she would insist that I clean the aluminum kettles and pans with steel wool until they were bright as mirrors. I would do the scouring and she would do the drying immediately after, for water darkens aluminum. If their interiors were not up to her standards, she asked me to make tomato soup in them, because tomatoes brightened that metal.

Liz and I got along so well that I stayed with her family through the summers until I was a senior in high school. But the summer after I graduated from high school I had a kind of Saul-on-the-road-to-Damascus experience. No light from heaven surrounded me and I didn't fall to the earth blinded. Quite the opposite.

It was a cloudy, rainy Saturday; we were tootling along a dreary, rural road headed for dismal, cheerless Van Horn, a town even smaller than Garrison, to do the weekly marketing. Like Saul, I had no premonition, no warning of any kind that I was about to be enlightened. I suddenly sat bolt upright in the Lincoln Zephyr, suffused with a profound awareness that I had to make changes. I actually said to myself, "This is not going to be my life!" It was a pivotal moment for me.

Mildred Armstrong, class valedictorian, 1940

The adrenaline surge prompted me to hitchhike to Cedar Falls a few days later and enroll in the Teachers College for the fall quarter, though I had no idea how I was going to pay for the tuition. Then I quit my job on the farm, hitchhiked again, this time to Cedar Rapids, and found a position in the household of the most successful physician and surgeon in that thriving city.

A whole new way of life opened up to me that summer in Cedar Rapids. Here again my early training in accepting responsibilities, doing more than was expected, and making myself useful, all developed on our family farm, were invaluable assets. My job introduced me to a society that was more elegant than anything I had ever been exposed to. I helped in the preparations for glamorous weddings, elaborate dinners, formal teas, lively social gatherings, and theater parties, all of which spurred the development of my natural culinary interests. Perhaps most important of all, participating in this gala round of social events, rubbing shoulders with interesting people, and living on Country Club Boulevard defined for me what I now aspired to. This was the life for me!

Borrowing a little money from Grandpa, a little from Mama, and saving almost all the money I earned, I was able to pay my tuition in the fall. And working as a hired girl to a professor's family, I was able to earn my room and board. Just as Mr. Woehlk had predicted, I had found my way to college.

In June of 1942—six months after the Japanese bombed Pearl Harbor and I heard Franklin Roosevelt declare December 7 a Day of Infamy—I received my two-year Teacher's Certificate from Iowa State Teachers College in Cedar Falls, Iowa. Following graduation, I narrowly escaped the tyrannical demands of the Midwest school board. Remember the elementary teacher's contract I described when I reported on the country school? I came within a gnat's eyelash of signing that contract, but during a brief, serendipitous stint as an aide to the City Welcoming Agent of Waterloo, Iowa, I met Nanny, the visiting mother of a famous bandleader who had just lost his wife to brain cancer, leaving their two recently adopted youngsters motherless. Since my newly acquired teacher's license qualified me to become a governess for three-year-old Jimmy and five-year-old Ruth Ann, Nanny offered me the job.

And so it was that I moved to Yonkers, New York, and entered a world of heretofore unimaginable luxury and lavish living in a mansion high on the banks of the Hudson River. Nanny selected silk and sequined dresses, mink coats, and stoles from her dead daughter-in-law's closet and lent them to me; treated me to Broadway plays and dinners at nightclubs owned by friends of her son (the Gamecock and Jack Dempsey's were two of her favorites); she even chose a couple of boyfriends for me and acted as chaperone for us when we went out.

So why didn't the little match girl have a Merry Christmas after all? My joy in this exciting environment was short-lived. Nanny and her husband were newcomers to the area themselves, having been summoned by their son to become caretakers of the toddlers after the unexpected death of their daughter-in-law. Their son's duties as a bandleader meant that he could be home only occasionally, so they were on their own most of the time. Thus, though they were acquainted with many people, they had no close friends, and Nanny became very dependent on me for companionship.

Within a few months I knew I had to leave, for Nanny, although the sweetest and kindest of ladies, had taken complete control of my life. Not only was I a governess and caretaker for the children, but I had become her confidante and constant companion. Perhaps worst of all, she burdened me with family secrets that I was not ready to receive and that weighed on me most grievously.

While her generosity toward me knew no bounds, she would accept nothing from me. When my brother who was in the infantry sent two pairs of nylon stockings, a treasure during the war, she refused to accept one pair for herself. That refusal was a wake-up call for me.

I had to face the reality that Nanny was a smothering

emotional cannibal. But I couldn't simply leave, for that would have hurt her feelings, and besides that, I had no place to go.

Millie at radio school

World War II was now in full force; all of my brothers and cousins who were eligible had joined the armed services, and their enlistment pointed the way for me to make what I saw as the one acceptable escape. The United States Coast Guard—one of the five categories of National Defense, along with the Army, Navy, Air Force, and Marines—was recruiting women to serve in the war. On my twenty-first birthday, with Nanny proudly watching, I was sworn in to the United States Coast Guard Women's Reserve, where I was selected for radio training at Miami University in Oxford, Ohio. On completing radio training, I was dispatched to the headquarters of the Fifth Naval District in

Norfolk, Virginia. During wartime, the Coast Guard falls under the operation of the Navy. There I met Harry, a fellow radioman in the Coast Guard. We have been married since April 27, 1944.

Using the GI Bill, we received our advanced education after the war and I later taught at the University of Iowa at Iowa City, the University of Missouri in Columbia, Adelphi University in Garden City, Long Island, and Suffolk County Community College, also on Long Island. My husband taught, too, first at Duke University while I took time off to have children, later at the State University of New York at Stony Brook on Long Island where he built a first-rate psychology department and was heavily involved in the recruitment process that built that university from the ground up. Before we retired, we both became professors and accumulated eighty-four years of teaching between us.

Our two sons, Doug and Greg, the two women they married, Donna and Carol Ann, and the four much-loved grandchildren they produced are, of course, the greatest gifts of our lives. But my past, and the memories it has left me with, are also among my treasures.

I feel fortunate to have so many memories and such happy ones. They bring back a time that seems incredibly remote, so different is it from today's. Of course, it is well known that the identical circumstances can affect people quite differently. My sister, Avis, for example, fled the farm, Garrison, and Yankee Grove, seldom to return unless forced to. I could never draw her into a discussion of our lives during the thirties. For her, that subject was off limits. For my part, I wallow in reminiscing on that decade, though I am aware of the all-too-human tendency to gloss over the bad and glorify, or at least magnify, the good. While as a child I wanted to believe that I could pluck silver apples from the moon and golden apples from the sun, I now revel in memories of the sun-warmed silkiness of a horse's neck or the fragrance of long dappled grass—remembered pleasures that seem just as sublime to me as any of my earlier fantasies. Yet I have occasionally come face-to-face with the significant truth that, as one farm expatriate declared to me, I wouldn't say "Get up" to a horse again unless one were sitting on my lap.

Very little is left of the world I left behind. When last I visited the area, I was brokenhearted to learn that due to the shortsighted farm taxing policies, which tax land much higher if it has buildings on it, all the houses, corncribs, machine sheds, chicken houses, and barns on our family farms had been deliberately destroyed, along with the woods that protected the farmhouses. The nineteenth-century barn on our farm, though dilapidated and hopelessly out-of-date, was a magnificent creation, roughly constructed of hand-hewn, whole hickory logs fastened together with hand-tooled hickory pegs. The logs atop the mangers were as smooth as glass and had been burnished to a beautiful, satiny glow from the breasts of many horses and cattle.

Garrison, too, is a very different place. It now has public water and sewers, its streets have names, and its houses have numbers. The Garrison public school has been turned into a retirement residence and the children are bused to a megaschool in Vinton, while the rural schools have long been closed. The Methodist Church is still thriving, though it suffered major damage in the 1961 tornado that injured and killed several of its parishioners.

Of the people I knew in the thirties, only a few members of my generation are still living, and I am the sole survivor of my immediate family.

Now, how to conclude my story without making comments

that will probably seem sappy about the virtues of resourcefulness, dedication, hard work, discipline, creativity, and goodwill? Isn't it perfectly obvious to all that those early childhood experiences, under those special conditions with those particular relatives on that Iowa farm, prepared me for the modestly successful, hugely satisfying, truly blessed life that has been my lot? I shall always be grateful.

Acknowledgments

In the preparation of this manuscript my indebtedness is great to many.

To my cousin Joan Peters, writer, professor, wife, and mother, whose whole-hearted enthusiasm encouraged me to tell my story. Your cheery support helped me in ways you'll never know.

To my husband, Harry, who helped by being supportive in countless ways. Your infinite patience with refereeing the adversarial position between me and my word processor and arranging it so that I always won deserves special commendation. Further, for your constant belief that I could write a book of my early years that would be honest, informative, and above all, fun to read, I owe you big.

To Donna Bohling and Douglas Kalish, who for the last year made their many resources, tangible and intangible, available to me. Your unwavering commitment of time, energy, and patience has contributed immeasurably in bringing this book to completion. I truly could not have done it without both of you.

To Carol Ann and Gregory Kalish, who beamed your support and goodwill across the thousands of miles that separate us. Your excitement and good wishes energized me in accomplishing this task.

To my grandchildren Ana and Hector, Nathan, Meredith, and Benjamin, and to the great-grandchild on the way (thanks to Ana and Hector). You are the special people for whom this book was written.

To Barbara Cree, Myra Noe Klopping, Carol Miller, Sandy Wienken and Shirley Schlitter. You patiently searched your family albums and invested hours in searching the countryside to contribute pictures for this book. I do thank you.

To Virginia Norey. Your special understanding and insights as exhibited in your brilliant design of this book contributes mightily to its appeal. I am thrilled with your work.

To Beth Rashbaum, my editor, who unstintingly shared her notable talents and has earned my respect and admiration. From the very beginning you seemed to have an overall vision of the coherent structure for the tales I presented to you and proceeded to guide me accordingly, utilizing your instincts for logical organization, for appropriate content, and for clear expression. I am forever grateful to the good fortune that brought us to work together and let it be noted that I am fully aware of the time, energy, and patience you invested in developing this book. I thank you.